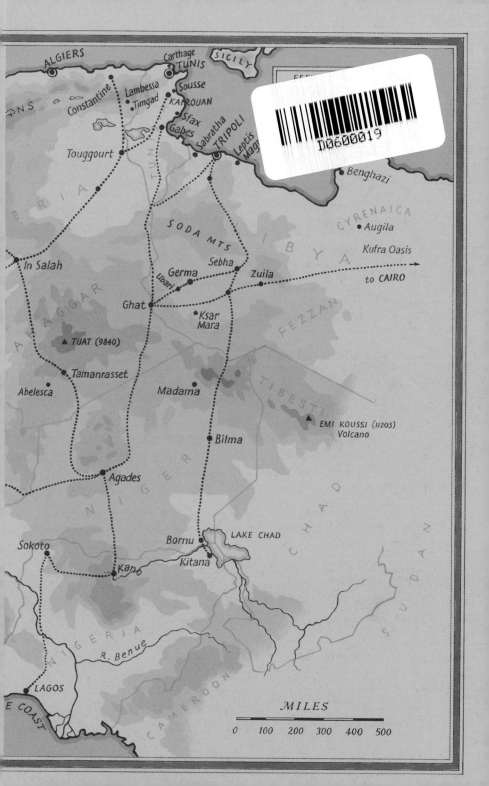

THE GREAT SAHARA

James Wellard
THE GREAT
SAHARA

E. P. DUTTON & CO., INC.

NEW YORK   1965

FIRST EDITION

CONTENTS

ILLUSTRATIONS

PREFACE

TO CROSS the Sahara Desert a hundred years ago was just as daring a feat as manned flights into outer space are today; the enterprise required the same attributes of courage and endurance then as now.

This much, then, is common to the two eras of exploration: the willingness of brave men to venture into the unknown. The significant difference between the early-nineteenth and late-twentieth-century exploration is in the character of the pioneers themselves. Very simply, the early explorers of the Sahara called themselves 'African travellers', implying by this modest title that they were private individuals, with an 'amateur' status, and not highly trained and conditioned professionals. These 'travellers' were, it is true, usually sponsored—albeit in a penny-pinching manner—by a learned society which was only interested at first in filling in the blank spaces on the map. In fact, the whole purpose of early Saharan exploration was scientific in the old sense of the word: that is, the search for, and dissemination of, knowledge which was thought to be the common property of all mankind, irrespective of nationality, strategic advantages, or considerations of prestige. Thus, Frederick Hornemann, one of the original 'African travellers', though a German engaged by a British learned society, was given aid and safe conduct by the Frenchman Bonaparte in the middle of his war with England. Nowadays, one assumes, Hornemann, the first European to reach the Niger River since Roman times, would be shot as a spy.

But a history of the Sahara must begin long before the initiation of exploration at the end of the eighteenth century. The entire desert, to all intents and purposes lost to Europe before that period, was inhabited and known for at least 7,000 years when our first records appear on the rocks. The Sahara of antiquity, moreover, is well worth study, for it once teemed with life in

9

whole vast regions where it is now lifeless. In view of our concern
with *Lebensraum*, this is surely worth thinking about.

The plan of this book, then, is to begin at the known beginning
—or partially known—and to proceed to our own period when
the desert can be crossed in a few hours, at night without ever
seeing it at all, if desired. Modern luxuries, including air-conditioning and ice-cold martinis, can now be found in the sand
seas where so many African travellers were murdered or died of
their 'fever'. The economy, and therefore the life, of the Sahara
is about to change. From what I have seen of it, it will be a long
time before it reaches the level of prosperity, law, and order that
it enjoyed 2,000 years ago, but the tide of history is running fairly
fast here, as everywhere else. Even so, for a little while longer
the traveller who cares to leave the tourist tracks can still see
what Major Gordon Laing saw in his journey to Timbuktu in
1826 and, for that matter, what Julius Caesar himself saw when
he landed on African soil at Thapsus in 46 B.C.

There are thousands of books dealing with North Africa and
the Sahara, beginning with the description of Herodotus, who
was there in the fifth century before Christ, and ending with this
year's travel book. A list of the more useful of these references
will be found in the Notes at the end of this volume. In general,
prehistoric and Roman Africa is the reserve of the classical historians and the archaeologists; Islamic Africa of the Arabic
writers; nineteenth-century exploration of the British and
German travellers; and the later nineteenth and early twentieth
century of the French. Most of these books have long been out
of print, and it was thanks to the facilities of the British Museum
Reading Room and the co-operation of the staff that I was able
to consult them.

Thanks and acknowledgements are also due to many people
who have helped and encouraged me: to the publishers of this
book; to the keepers of the museums I visited in Europe and
Africa; to the directors of the African Departments of Tourism;
and to the personnel of the oil companies who were generous
with their advice, knowledge, and facilities.

I also owe a special vote of thanks to Dr. M. S. Ayoub, Controller of Antiquities for the Fezzan, who enabled me to visit and work in one of the most interesting yet difficult regions of access in the Sahara.

Special thanks and acknowledgements are due to both the authors and publishers for permission to use quotations from the following books: Abbé Henri Breuil, *Les Roches Peintes du Tassili-N-Ajjer* (Éditions Arts et Métiers Graphiques, 1954); Maurice Magnus, *Memoirs of the Foreign Legion* (Martin Secker, 1924); Conrad Kilian, *Au Hoggar* (Éditions Maritimes et d'Outre-Mer, 1925); Jean Baradez, *Fossatum Africae* (Direction de l'Intérieur et des Beaux Arts, Service des Antiquités, Algiers, 1949); the Provincial Superior of the White Fathers, Bishop's Waltham, *The African Missions* (No. 3, November–December, 1927); Henri Lhote, *Le Sahara: Désert Mystérieux* (Librairie Armand Colin, 1937); Jean Larteguy, *Sahara: An I* (Éditions Gallimard, 1958); José Germain et Stéphane Faye, *Le Général Laperrine, Grand Saharien*. Appendix 1, 'Le Journal du commandant Vuillemin' (Librairie Plon, 1931); Georges-Marie Haardt and Louis Audouin-Dubreuil, *Across the Sahara by Motor Car* (T. Fisher Unwin, 1924); H. M. D. Parker, *The Roman Legions* (W. Heffer & Sons, 1958); Colin Legum (editor), *Africa, a Handbook to the Continent* (Blond, 1961); and Olumbe Bassir (editor), *Anthology of West African Verse* (Ibadan University Press, Nigeria, 1956).

The portraits of Dixon Denham, G. F. Lyon and Cardinal Lavigerie are reproduced by permission of the National Portrait Gallery; those of Hugh Clapperton, Major Gordon Laing and Miss Tinne by permission of the Royal Geographic Society. The Radio Times Hulton Picture Library provided the seventeenth-century map and the portrait of the Algerian Spahis. Mr. Abdelhamid Kahia of Tunis took the photograph of the Antonine Gate at Sbeitla (Sufetula) illustrated.

Unless otherwise credited, the remaining illustrations are from photographs taken by the author.

INTRODUCTION

To the desert . . .

I

I LEFT Murzuk, the old slave mart and capital of the Fezzan, to go down into the desert and stopped at the oasis of Tsaoua to pick up a Tuareg guide. In the old days a Tuareg escort was essential, and even then the chances of being murdered in this country were considerable, as the unmarked graves of so many of the first African travellers remind us. There is no danger of being murdered today, however, and the Tuareg headman of the palm-thatched village received me with great cordiality. We drank many small glasses of green tea in his hut, and he wrote his own and my name in *tifinagh*, the ancient writing of his people, and assigned me a veteran to take me to the place I was looking for.

Now the three of us—myself, the Libyan driver of the Land Rover, and the Tuareg guide—were going into the sand sea known as the Idehan Murzuk to find a fort called Ksar Mara, marked on the World Aeronautical Chart with a minute square and the word 'ruins' beside it. Ksar Mara, some archaeologists say, is derived from *castra Maria*, which would indicate that the site was a Roman fort. This was what I had come to see.

It soon became obvious that it was not an easy place to find, for the landmarks in this particular region of the desert are vague and confusing. Only a Tuareg who had lived here all his life could differentiate between one dune and another. In fact, we were sometimes boxed in, and then our guide would leave the car and run to the top of a sand-hill with that peculiar gliding motion of his race, so that within a few minutes he seemed to be a long way off, a small white-robed figure signalling from the top of a dune. He had found the best way out of the valley and we followed his directions.

After two hours of picking our way across the desert, always looking for the good sand by noting the colour and texture of the surface, we rounded an escarpment and were in a long valley which was absolutely barren and absolutely devoid of any form of life. The Tuareg pointed. He was pleased, as he had reason to be. For there, standing up quite alone in this wasteland, was the place I had come to see, Ksar Mara. We zig-zagged across the sand and stopped at what must have been, and certainly is today, one of the loneliest man-made habitations in the Sahara. The World Aeronautical Chart shows nothing within an area of some 25,000 square miles except uninhabited and waterless desert.

Ksar Mara is a 1,600-year-old fort built on a strong foundation of hewn stone, six courses of which are still visible above ground. Its superstructure is of mud bricks bound with pebbled cement. Its existing dimensions are thirty by thirty feet, and it still rises to a height of twenty-five feet. Immediately to the west are visible the foundations of two other structures; and, to the north, the vestiges of a wall forty yards in length. The place was therefore a stronghold on the northern edge of the Murzuk sand sea; and it must have been, to some extent, self-supporting. It seems inconceivable today: the Tuareg said there was not a drop of water in the area, no well, and certainly no rain. But there could have been water, he said, and 'the sand had swallowed it up'.

Was Ksar Mara a Roman fort, then? Was it conceivably built by a detachment of the Third Augusta Legion which built the great forts 500 miles to the north? Or was it an earlier or later site? We won't know until the site is excavated; and who, one wonders, will have the time, energy, and fortitude to undertake this task?

While I was making the best survey of Ksar Mara I could under the circumstances, the Tuareg had lit a small fire of dry camel-thorn and was squatting beside it juggling the two miniature teapots in which the desert people make the strong sweet tea they call 'whiskey Libya'. He had also laid out a piece of sacking on which were spread the dates, dried and seasoned by being buried in the sand. The flies had already arrived from nowhere to share the meal which was now ready. I was called over to drink the first glass of tea and sample a date well squeezed between dirt-encrusted fingers. Both tea and dates were delicious.

It was then, sitting there in the sand with two strangers with whom I could scarcely communicate, but conversing none the less with a few words in various languages, and with smiles and gestures, choosing a specially nice date for each other, drinking out of the same little glass (courteously washed between suppings), exchanging cigarettes or whatever we had brought with us—it was then that I suddenly realized what the real desert was like, and why those who had actually seen it, as apart from making a week-end trip to some tourist resort, could never quite forget it, and some could never leave it.

And here I want to make sure that I am not misunderstood. I am not intending to add to that vast literature of romantic rubbish about sheiks, palm trees waving their fronds in the breeze, desert sunsets or moons, or any of that entertaining nonsense which purports to give a picture of what this part of the world is like. The novelist, certainly, is heavily handicapped in writing about the desert, since the locale is both formless and timeless. It is really all hard geological fact, and there is no room for the refinements of European imagination. The same general criticism is valid, one feels, for those personalized descriptions of the desert written by enterprising travellers who take the north-south routes across the Sahara on their well-organized safaris, travelling from the Mediterranean ports to Central Africa by way of the Tanezrouft, Hoggar, or Tibesti tracks. These tourists do not lose touch with their European outlook, because the much-travelled roads are now part of an international highway network, with the welcome shingles of the petrol stations along the way, apart from certain stretches where proper precautions must be taken to keep the motor running. Given that, such journeys are no more sensational than a trans-European run from London to Rome down the Rhône Valley. They are merely more monotonous and less hazardous.

But the real desert is here at Ksar Mara, or the nearby 'lost city' of Sharaba where the Tuareg took us next, after much gliding up and down the sand-dunes to get his bearings. More mysterious and evocative ruins: this time of a large settlement with forts, houses, roads, and cemeteries, all being relentlessly swallowed up by the sand. Sharaba, like Ksar Mara, and a thousand abandoned forts, towns, and oases, all across and up and down the Sahara, is the real desert; and it is in these places, which no tourist could find alone, that one feels this curious quality of a world which has nothing in common with the Western concept or manner of life.

What, then, is the essence of this quality? Romantic, mystical, or purple passages won't convey it; and in an case there remain to remind us of the hard truth the dirt, disease, poverty, ignorance, cruelty, and downright ugliness of practically all the towns and oases through the length and breadth of the Sahara Desert. So we can't talk of beauty, or romance in the language of travel-agency brochures. Beauty! Romance! The lady tourists would take one look at the camel being butchered in the fly-blown sand and demand to take the first plane home.

But the quality, or aura, of the desert persists and becomes almost tangible in a place like Ksar Mara, far away from the nearest oasis where squalor reigns supreme. If one tries to capture it by a mental effort it tends to be completely elusive. All that one can intimate is an awareness of a silence such as is never *heard* outside the real desert, neither in the mountains nor on the sea; a sense of timelessness which transcends even the sense of mortality; and a glimpse into the mystery of life in its most primeval form. These are intuitive experiences which are seldom, if ever, vouchsafed the city-dweller, beset by his immediate problems and endless distractions, and obliged to spend a considerable part of his waking life pushing and shoving his way from place to place. In the true desert such intuitions suggest the kind of reality the early mystics (many of them desert-dwellers or hermits who deliberately created similar conditions) used to talk about and, evidently, in some cases, managed to identify with a comprehensible God. Today, in the modern metropolis, admittedly such theocentric speculations are absolutely beyond our ken; and the majority of urbanized people would reject them as an outdated occultism, along with the writings of the mystics themselves. Let us admit, though, that some such interpretation of the true reality is not so remote or bizarre in the middle of a Saharan sand sea.

Whether anyone wants to believe this or not, there is one impression conveyed by the desert which is inescapable, and that is the fact of both timelessness and continuing time: in other words, the certainty that men have lived in a region of the globe we in the West have come to regard as uninhabitable for thousands of uninterrupted years, so that there is a remarkable, and possibly unique, continuity of history in the Sahara. It is a desert which has never been deserted. In some respects it is at its lowest ebb of human activity today. It was certainly teeming with both animal and plant life 10,000 years ago; and each group of inhabitants has left unmistakable records of its occupation. You climb a mountain which is collapsing on all sides and find the rock engravings of men who hunted elephants and giraffes 7,000 years ago. On the sides of this same mountain you find the rock tombs of their successors—not a score or so of tombs but hundreds. In the clefts of the mountain you can see the patient and skilful work of later inhabitants who dammed the torrents, built rock barrages in the rain-courses, cemented the channels, and constructed hundreds of water-tunnels from the mountain across the desert to the palmeries. In the plains stand the abandoned towns, forts, and tombs of later nations—Garamantes, Romans, Byzantines, Arabs. An archaeologist in the Valley of Ajal in central Libya has only to put a spade into the earth to find the vestiges of some civilization he may never have known existed.

Parts of the Sahara, then, are perhaps the richest archaeological sites of the world—because of this continuity of history. And it is this timelessness and continuing time which one senses sitting in the sand at the foot of a forgotten monument like Ksar Mara, so that there awakens an awareness of some reality other than the price of this year's car. The handing of a glass of tea from one stranger to another, the Tuareg smiling through the slit in his veil, the silence, the immensity, even the desolation, entitle you to feel that you have had a glimpse of reality; or, to put it in prosaic terms, that you have seen the real desert.

II

Up to 150 years ago, no European could say that, because up to that time not one of them had seen it this far down. The first 'official' crossing of the Sahara was made by a British army officer, Major Alexander Gordon Laing, who left Tripoli in 1825, partly in the role of an investigator into the slave trade and partly as a contestant for the £3,000 prize money offered to the first European to reach Timbuktu by the British Association for Discovering the Interior of Africa, or the African Society, as it was later called.[1] Though Major Laing did arrive at his destination after indescribable hardships, he never returned to tell the tale. He was murdered in his tent by Tuaregs on the night of September 26th, 1826, after setting out on his return journey. His last letter, dated Timbuktu, September 21st, 1826, stated that his position was 'very unsafe'.

The second crossing of the desert was made two years later by the French traveller René Caillié, who reached the mysterious negro city in 1828 disguised as an Arab. Caillié managed to get safely back to civilization where his claim was promptly dismissed (by the English) as false and pretentious. The journey of 2,000 miles across a waterless desert and back was apparently considered impossible by a Frenchman.[2]

Such distrust of the first trans-Saharan travellers' tales was not surprising, for the Great Desert was *terra incognita* throughout the nineteenth century and well into the twentieth century. Much of it still is. Within living memory there were no accurate maps of

1. Perhaps one should say to reach it 'voluntarily'. There is some evidence that two shipwrecked sailors, one French, the other American, were taken there as slaves by the Moors: the Frenchman, Paul Imbert, in about 1630; the American, Robert Adams, in 1810. See Chapter Nine, III.

2. Comparably, the French tended to doubt the validity of Major Laing's journey. The process of annexing vast areas of Central Africa on the basis of 'explorations' was about to begin, so there were political reasons for casting aspersions.

these 3,000,000 square miles of the earth's surface, and the only information that European geographers had of the region was derived, almost without the addition of a single new fact, from the descriptions left us by the classical and Arab writers, beginning with the fifth-century B.C. historian Herodotus and ending with the fifteenth-century Spanish Moor, Leo Africanus. In fact, the Sahara Desert disappeared from the maps of the civilized world, except for an empty space marked with the traces of non-existent rivers and suggestions of misplaced mountain ranges. All the cartographers could do was to base their scrawls and cross-hatchings on the data available in *Geographia*, published around A.D. 150. At least Ptolemy gave some useful hints concerning the source and flow of the two greatest rivers in Africa, the Nile and the Niger. Up to 100 years or so ago, Europeans knew of the existence of these rivers, but had no idea of where they rose, or, in the case of the Niger, in which direction it flowed. The ancient travellers and geographers at least seemed to know this much, for some of them had seen evidence with their own eyes, and we might have had the necessary facts if Ptolemy had been more exact in his astronomical readings.

In short, the European exploration of North and Central Africa, for all practical purposes, stopped with the fall of the Roman Empire and was not reactivated until 1,400 years later. There were, of course, a number of reasons for this curious gap in Western exploration and conquest, curious when it is remembered that the rest of the world was being overrun by European travellers and adventurers. The obvious reason was the physical nature of the African desert. It was considered impassable. Standing on the edge of the great sand seas of Algeria and Libya the European traveller can see why. The fact that the Saharan tribesmen and their Arab masters crossed it all the time was unknown, or discounted, even though the caravan trade of ivory, gold, ostrich feathers, rhinoceros horn, and slaves had never ceased from the time of Carthage to the reign of Victoria.

Yet the armies, explorers, and travellers of the ancient world had no such psychological block towards the 'unknown'. Their patrols and flying columns went down into the desert from the

time of Cambyses the Persian in 525 B.C. Their ships sailed up
into the Arctic and down to the Equator. The Carthaginians are
reported by Herodotus to have circumnavigated the African
continent in 600 B.C., a voyage which was not repeated by
European sailors until 2,000 years later. Perhaps this enormous
gap in time is the reason why modern historians are still arguing
whether those old mariners actually did leave by the Red Sea
and return by the Pillars of Hercules, having seen the sun 'on
their right hand' as they entered the Southern Hemisphere. Yet
the record plainly states that they were gone three years, leaving
at one end of the Mediterranean and returning at the other.
Similarly, the evidence is clear that the Carthaginian admiral
Hanno sailed down the west coast of Africa and reported for the
first time in history the existence of 'gorillas', not seen again by
white men until the American missionary Dr. S. T. Savage
identified them in 1846.[1] Hanno, then, may have got down as far
as Sierra Leone. The trading posts he established along the West
African coast—Mehedia, Mogador, Agadir, and so on—are still
there; and one day archaeologists may find tangible evidence of
his settlements.

As for the Sahara itself, which Europeans had not penetrated
even as far south as Ghadames by 1800, the Romans had occupied, settled, and cultivated the northern zones before Christ was
born, and had sent flying columns right across the Libyan Desert
probably to Lake Chad by A.D. 100. There is even the possibility
that their patrols pushed down the Tripoli–Timbuktu caravan
route as far as the Hoggar Mountains in Central Sahara.

In other words, all of northern and Central Africa roughly
below the Atlas Mountains and the plains of the Mediterranean
littoral was far better known 2,000 years ago than it was at the
beginning of Queen Victoria's reign. And for a long time after
that the first European explorers either died on their travels
before they could accurately map their findings or were not
believed at all. Consequently, an area of the earth's surface larger

1. However, the apes that Hanno's men chased, losing the males but
capturing three females, whose skins were brought back to Carthage, were
certainly not Dr. Savage's gorillas. If they had been the chase would have
been reversed. The 'hairy men' were probably chimpanzees.

than the United States was lost to Europe for 1,400 years, even though large tracts of this seeming desert were once conquered and exploited by the white race. And even today the area of the Sahara actually settled and developed by the West is not comparable with what the Romans achieved in their 400 years of occupation. Indeed, the degree of cultivation attained by the Romans and the Romanized Africans was so extensive in view of the state of agriculture in the desert today that it would not be credited without the evidence of canals, irrigation channels, dams, and cisterns which the archaeologists are still finding.

There are a number of reasons for this surprising *lacuna* in the story of European enterprises. The principal one is the Sahara Desert itself, which stretches, in one form or another, right across the upper third of Africa, some 3,000 miles in width from west to east, and 1,000 miles in depth from north to south, the most formidable barrier to land travel in the world. Secondly, Europeans from the time of the fall of the Roman Empire have not been encouraged to try and cross it, as all the early travellers discovered to their cost. The desert was an Arab monopoly since its conquest in the seventh century by the armies of the Prophet; it was full of holy places; it was peopled by religious fanatics; and infidels were no more welcome in the oases—the stopping places of the Mecca-bound pilgrims—than they were in the mosques themselves. And without the consent and co-operation of the Moslem tribesmen no traveller could survive in the desert.

There were no such obstacles in classical times. True, the ancestors of the same tribes who still control the caravan routes opposed the penetration of the invaders from the north; but a Roman legion could make short shift of 'feathered Libyans' and negro cave-dwellers who 'squeaked like bats'. They could, and they did. In other words, the Romans went into the desert when and where they pleased, and just to make sure that their presence was permament they built forts and towns in places which Europeans had not even visited 1,400 years later.

The reason for the Romans' success in conquering the desert can be summed up quite simply: the efficiency of the legions; their characteristic disdain of the barbarians (non-Romans); and, most important, the psychological factor that their armies never expected to conquer any part of the world, whether hot, cold, mountainous, swamp land, or desert, except slowly and methodically on foot. Further, they never relied on the goodwill or co-operation of the natives. They obtained such co-operation eventually by the right of conquest. The rest was simply a matter of organization, discipline, and master-race mentality. Thus, the Sahara Desert was no greater an obstacle to the Third Augusta Legion than the moors of Northumberland were to the Twentieth Valeria Victrix stationed on the British Wall during the second century A.D.

The question may be asked why, if they had so little trouble in penetrating the desert, the Romans didn't extend their dominion farther south to the rich interior of Africa. Had they finally reached a terrain which appalled even their hard-bitten legionnaires?

No. In the first place we have abundant evidence to show that neither deserts nor mountain ranges ever stopped the ancient armies from their wars of conquest. The campaigns of the Persian Cambyses, the Egyptian Ptolemy Philadelphus, the Greek Alexander, the Carthaginian Hannibal, and the Roman Hadrian all prove that country was never an insurmountable obstacle to fighting-men whose daily marching quota was twenty miles a day, and twenty-five if accelerated. The fact is, the Romans had no interest in Negroland to the south of the desert and no practical reasons for adding Central Africa to their empire. They knew from their probes, like that made by Julius Maternus down to Lake Chad, that the equatorial regions were peopled by blackmen, pygmies, and cave-dwellers whom they put on the level of animals, and not, therefore, worth the trouble of civilizing. Central Africa provided gold, wild animals for the gladiatorial games, ivory, and precious stones across the caravan routes which they took good care to patrol and protect. Otherwise it was commercially unprofitable.

Secondly, the Romans were not especially interested in the romantic or adventurous side of exploration, leaving this pastime, or hobby, to subject people like the Greeks. It was, in fact, the scientific passion of Greeks like Pythias, Strabo, and Ptolemy that gave any recognizable shape to the world at all. The dabblings in geography of a Roman like Pliny the Elder were simply the busy work of an elderly pedant in comparison with the scientific methods of these Greeks. A sample of the hodge-podge of facts, myths, legends, and old wives' tales he calls natural history is typified in this extract taken from his sixth book on the geography of Africa:

> The Atlantes violently abuse the rising and setting sun because it has destroyed them and their plantations; they don't have dreams like other mortals. The Troglodytes dig themselves caverns in which they live on the flesh of snakes; they make noises but don't speak, and so can't communicate by language. The Garamantians don't marry, but unite themselves with women haphazardly. The Augyles only worship devils. Nobody ever goes near the naked Gamphasantes. The Blemonyes lack a head; their face and their eyes are on their chests. The Satyrs have nothing human about them but their faces. . . . The Himantopodes crawl along like snakes. . . .
> There is nothing else to report about Africa.

So the Romans were utilitarians: they took and exploited as much of the desert as they needed for supplying Italy with grain and olive oil, and abandoned the rest of Africa to the barbarians whom it was necessary from time to time to chastise. That entailed some hard fighting on occasions—particularly in the Atlas Mountains—but there was never any doubt of the outcome. One legion—the Third Augusta—was all that was needed for 300 years of occupation to control an area half the size of modern Europe. The surveillance of the area south of Africa Proconsularis was left to desert garrisons and an occasional flying column which seems to have gone farther and faster than modern units which have undertaken the same sort of punitive expeditions. The Sahara Desert was probably not as great an obstacle to a Roman centurion at the head of his cohort as the marshes of the Thames were to Julius Caesar on his first expedition to

Britain. If you had asked a Roman infantryman in, say, A.D. 150 where he would rather serve, in Britain or Libya, you may be sure he would have opted for Libya. The African climate was better, the natives were more friendly, and the desert cities were more civilized. The African service, in other words, was 'seldom disagreeable', and no mutiny was ever recorded in the Third Augusta Legion. Conditions were very different in Northern Europe. Writing of Britain 2,000 years ago, the geographer Strabo describes the climate exactly as it is today:

> It rains more than it snows; and most of the time it is foggy, so that the sun is seen only three or four hours a day.

Life on the Wall in Britain, therefore, or keeping watch on the Rhine, was banishment to the ends of the earth. What lay beyond these North European frontiers really did appal even the Romans. The Sahara Desert never did.

III

The salient facts about the desert are these: Its area is 3,000,000 square miles, which makes it the largest desert on earth. The next largest, the Gobi of Central Asia, is 500,000 square miles. The Sahara, however, consists of several contiguous deserts: the Sahara proper in the west; the Libyan in the centre; the Arabian in the east; and the Nubian to the south. This vast arid belt continues eastwards into Asia; and, passing through Syria, Jordan, Iraq, Iran, and Turkestan, finishes in the Gobi Desert.

The basic conditions of the Sahara is the meagre rainfall. The average annual precipitation is less than ten inches, and that is irregular and limited to certain favoured regions. When it does rain the torrential downpour runs off the rocks and sinks into the sands within a matter of hours. In many parts of the desert, no rain at all falls for several consecutive years.

With the aridity goes the heat. Temperatures of 136 degrees Fahrenheit have been recorded in Azizia in Libya. This was the road and rail junction to which Mussolini despatched groups of settlers in 1930.

Not all the Sahara is a desert of sand. It is broken up into mountain ranges with peaks as high as the Emi Koussi volcano in Libya, 11,204 feet; and the Hoggar Mountains in the central Sahara which rise to nearly 10,000 feet. In between the mountains lie the rocky uplands called the *hammada*; the gravel-covered plains, or the *reg*; and the shifting sand-dunes, the *erg*. The entire area is carved and gouged up by dry river beds called *wadis*, some of them indicating by their great depth and width the force of rivers in prehistoric times. The presence of rivers is also proven by the evidence of the rock drawings and engravings of aquatic animals found all over the desert. These lost rivers and streams were tributaries in a vast system linked with the Niger and the Nile, and they are still flowing in one form or another underground. Without them there would be no wells and no oases at all, and therefore no life, animal or vegetable, in all the 3,000,000 square miles of this part of Africa. As it is, or as it has been since recorded times, there is just enough water to enable the caravaners to get from well to well, which are spaced at frequent intervals in the north but are sometimes 200 miles apart in the Central Desert.

The Sahara has always been peopled by some race, and it is only modern Europeans who have regarded it as uninhabitable —an opinion that is rapidly changing. During the Ice Age of Northern Europe all kinds of animal life teemed in regions which are now utterly deserted, for the rivers then flowed above ground. Go back far enough, in fact, and we come to an epoch where the Sahara Desert was a jungle with enough vegetation to feed the largest animals that have lived on this planet. Tucked away in the Natural History Museum at Tripoli, collecting more dust than visitors, are the gigantic bones of a mastodon called Stegotetrabelodon Syrticus, a fitting name for a four-tusked beast twice the size and height of a full-grown elephant. His skull is as big as a bath-tub, and his tusks measure about eight feet in length. Since he was herbivorous, he must have eaten the foliage of an entire tree at every meal; yet he lived in what is now the Libyan Desert, just north of one of the hottest places in the world where nothing grows at all but a little coarse grass if there happens to be rain in the winter months. The only water for hundreds of miles in this part of the desert is found at the oases of Augila and of Kufra, 350 miles to the south. It is a very bad desert indeed, but here lived the Stegotetrabeledon and his companion of the forests, the Pentalophodon Sivalesis; and here at Sahabi in the Libyan Desert they left their bones, now on display in a castle built by the Crusaders.

When Man first came to the desert, he—or his descendants—covered whole hillsides with depictions of the successors of these behemoths—elephants, giraffes, ostriches, deer, rhinoceroses, and hippopotami. More and more of these strange and beautiful drawings are being found in remoter and still remoter regions of the desert, but who these artists were, or what their pictures represent—men with horses' heads, men with tails, women with heads like mushrooms—we still don't know. The prehistorians incline to the view that they could not have been drawn for aesthetic reasons, on the grounds that 'art' is a luxury of a leisured civilization. Their best guess is that they have a religious or magical significance, though it is impossible for us to see the world as it was 10,000 years ago through the eyes of hunters. Moreover, there are quite a number of so-called 'domestic' pictures which can have nothing to do with religious practices—unless, as in the case of the Song of Solomon, exegesis is able to give sexual intercourse (as depicted in some rock paintings) a hidden ritualistic meaning.[1]

But most of these drawings are of animals that no longer exist in the Sahara, and could not have existed there after 5000 B.C., unless a few giraffes, ostriches, and even hippopotami survived in the last islands of vegetation in the middle of the desert sea. Some of these animals did survive, of course, until quite recent times, and it wasn't the desiccation of the region that wiped them out. Elephants wandered happily all through North Africa till

1. For a further discussion of the Saharan rock engravings see Chapter One.

well into the Christian era, the Atlas Mountains being their favourite habitat. But first the Carthaginians captured them for military purposes, using up thousands of them in their three long wars with the Romans. Whether these pachyderms were worth the expense of their upkeep as military machines or not is arguable: protected by flank armour and carrying a bell under their neck to excite them, they were at first successful in panicking men and horses, destroying ramparts, and trampling down the heavy-armoured infantry. But the Romans quickly devised anti-elephant weapons: fire and trumpets. The Carthaginian elephant 'cavalry' was thus easily stampeded and was liable to end up by trampling to death more friends than foes. This classical military miscalculation necessitated an 'anti-anti-missile' device invented by the Carthaginian general Hasdrubal around the year 205 B.C. It consisted of a spike and mallet with which the mahout aboard his elephant could destroy his 'secret weapon' when it went out of control. Thereafter, the elephant became, like the battleship, more of a status symbol in warfare than a useful weapon, so that whereas Hannibal set out from Spain with thirty-seven of them, he was probably not over-disconcerted when only one survived to carry him personally over the Alps.

To the Romans the elephant was, as the poor beast is to us, a circus animal. Plutarch describes how they danced in a ring and adds, as an illustration of their sagacity, how one of them, a slow student, used to steal off to practise his steps alone in the moonlight. Some of the North African elephants danced, then, and some died in the arenas to amuse the circus crowds, so much so that the great Barbary herds were wiped out by the end of the Roman period. Three thousand five hundred African animals were slaughtered in three Games alone put on by Augustus—elephants, lions, tigers, and leopards. But far more sinister from the pachyderm's point of view than the circuses was the great demand for ivory in Roman times, so that hunters were out after elephants all the year round. The last of them must have died on the High Atlas Mountains in late Byzantine times. The ostriches, on the other hand, survived in North Africa and the Sahara within living memory. Now all that remains of the wild animal life depicted by the Saharan hunter-artists is a few mountain lions, an occasional leopard, and the dwindling herds of desert gazelle which are being systematically exterminated by tourists armed with machine-guns and transported in Land Rovers.[1] With the aid of these refinements the Christians are able to get among the deer and shoot them in comfort, while the Moslems can chase them until they drop with exhaustion and lie still waiting to have their throats cut.

The desert rock paintings do tell us one significant fact. If the Sahara in the Pleistocene Age was as well watered and wooded as they suggest it was a northern extension of the equatorial forests of Central Africa and therefore inhabited by the negro race. The earliest recorded history we have of the region suggests that this was indeed the case: the black men, in other words, have been driven back by the white towards the middle of Africa. Where the first 'white men' in northern Africa came from we don't know. From 'over the sea', say the first historians; and we first hear of such migrants, the Garmantians, or 'Garamantes', in the sixth century B.C. already hunting the negroes in four-horse chariots, probably of Mycenaean origin. The captives were used as slaves. The process of hunting the negroes and transporting them to the Mediterranean ports went on for the next 2,500 years. Millions of black men have been driven across the desert. It is estimated that the Arab traders brought 5,000 slaves northward from Kano every year, the survival rate being one in two. Over

---

1. From a letter to the editor of an English-language newspaper published in Tripoli. (*The Sunday Ghibli*, October 13th, 1963.)

Libya Letter Box

HUNTING FROM VEHICLES

I drove through a part of the pre-desert last week where several years ago I had seen large herds of gazelle. On this occasion I did not see any.

Back in Tripoli my enquiries led to my establishing that most of the wild animals living within week-end truck-range of the coast have been driven away by hunters.

I heard (and substantiated that it had taken place) of gazelle being chased by hunters in trucks and shot with machine-guns. One reliable informant told me that on one occasion he had been offered fifteen gazelle that had been so slaughtered.

a period of two centuries, during which the Arabs had a mono-poly of the slave trade, this represents a total on this one route alone of a million men, women, and children who crossed the most desolate and waterless region in the world. It is not sur-prising that, as late as 1910, travellers reported the vicinity of the wells on the Lake Chad–Murzuk–Tripoli route as being piled high with the skeletons of African slaves en route to civilization.

This was in 1910. But the records of the desert go back at least 7,000 years before that. They begin with pictures on the walls of caves, and simple monuments of stone which speak to us of life and death in the Sahara at the dawn of history.

ONE

In the beginning

I

IF YOU travel westwards along the Wadi el Ajal in central Libya you can see on both sides of the valley 10,000 years of Man's history—caves, cities, castles, forts, irrigation systems, tombs, and towers, a continuous array of monuments. The backwash of this tide of life is still seen in the present oases which support an existence of the most squalid kind. The contemporary inhabitants of the valley have wells, date palms, a few animals, huts made of mud bricks, and nothing much else. The number and size of the relics of the past speak of a different people and a different standard of life altogether. They speak of the empires of the Hunters, the Garamantes, the Romans, the Byzantines, and the Arabs. They speak, too, of eras when the valley was densely populated where the inhabitants today number only a few hundreds. If graves are any indication there are literally tens of thousands of them. They cover the sides of the rock escarpments which shut the valley in from the south.

Halfway along this valley is the oasis of Germa, the capital of a kingdom larger than Europe in the days of Herodotus; now a collection of mud hovels beside the washboard track which runs along the valley. Germa, the *Garama* of the Romans from which expeditionary forces set out for Lake Chad and Ethiopa in A.D. 70, is one of those 'lost cities' of the Sahara concerning which passing travellers write in vague, romantic terms and archaeologists are now making their first tentative explorations. Germa, Ksar Mara, Sharaba, Loroko, el Hatia, Zuila: their foundations are there under the sand as an occasional tower or turret or sudden stone wall reveals. To the unpractised eye they are

31

merely miserable palmeries hanging on to some semblance of life on the fringe of the lifeless desert. So with Germa, that mosquito- and scorpion-ridden oasis somehow typified by the abandoned village nearby where up to fifty years ago the north-bound caravans stopped for the purpose of castrating the negro slaves intended for the harems along the southern and eastern shores of the Mediterranean.

Overlooking Germa from the south is the Djebel Zenkekra, a high escarpment of black, crumbling rock on the sides of which one can almost see the processes of millennia of geology taken place under one's eyes. The huge slabs of volcanic stone tumble down the sides of the cliffs, chiselled neatly out by the extremes of temperature; break into boulders halfway down; disintegrate into black nuggets at the base of the mountain; drift away into cinders; and sift into the orange dust which ends up as yellow sand on the high dunes to the north. It is the slow, inevitable creation of a desert. But climb above the lower stages to the top of the mountain and you can get a glimpse of what life was like here 10,000 years ago. For here on the upper ledges of the Djebel Zenkekra is one of the 'art galleries' which the prehistoric Saharans left all over the desert and in which they depict, some-times in simple, easily recognizable ideographs, sometimes in mysterious symbols, the way the world looked on those morn-ings when a man went out with his comrades to hunt animals which haven't lived in this terrain for generations.

The Zenkekra rock faces on which these prehistoric artists worked are typical. Their 'canvases' were slabs of smooth stone on the upper ledges of a cliff from which they must have seen the herds of tropical beasts moving down the valley below. Their 'brushes' were flints with which they incised the rock and pro-duced, with who knows what effort, their curious record of a world that has disappeared. To a modern viewer up there in this wilderness of living rock the sensation is again typical of the strangeness and fascination of the true desert, at once so dead, yet so full of the presence of those who were here ten millennia before him. Nobody comes up to these ledges any more, of course. The oases-dwellers in the valley have no interest in such scratchings on the rocks. They have never seen these animals with the long, sinuous necks and the huge curving horns. Yet the giraffes and the cattle these pictures represent with the eye and skill of a natural artist roamed the land where now grow only date palms—and those thanks to the hundreds of water-tunnels dug by the descendants of these hunters.

The rock engravings of the Djebel Zenkekra are by no means unique. The Sahara is a veritable art gallery of prehistoric painting. There is almost no part of it which has not its examples, and almost every year new specimens are being found. In fact, it can be said that the discoveries have only just begun and they still are, in any case, largely fortuitous. While I was in the Wadi el Ajal a tribesman informed us that he knew of some 'pictures' in the mountains which nobody had yet seen. (Meaning nobody who was particularly interested.) The report was noted for future investigation, for at the present those who are working on the antiquities of the region already have their hands full in merely recording already known sites. It is not surprising, then, that most of these rock engravings were first seen by chance, originally by French camel-corps officers on their desert patrols, and recently by those travellers who visit one area of the desert with an objective in view as contrasted with those who are 'on safari'. Even so, the plotting and recording of the Sahara rock paintings have been, of necessity, haphazard and unsystematic, although we know that engravings appear in almost every corner of the desert from Morocco in the north-west almost to the Niger River in the south, and again east and south into the Fezzan and the Tibesti.

The evidence is enough to show that the Sahara was one of the well-populated areas of the prehistoric world, as it has become the least populated within historical times. It seems to have been inhabited, moreover, by a race of men whose domain extended from South Europe to South Africa, for the rock paintings found in Spain, Eastern Spain, the Sahara Desert, and South Africa itself have certain striking similarities, almost as though they belong to the same 'school'. Thus, they all depict long-horned cattle in a similar style; and, most curious, all portray men with the so-called 'mushroom' head and clad in ankle-length gowns. Sometimes the mushroom head disappears altogether, leaving a decapitated trunk with a longish neck; and sometimes the head is replaced by an animal mask. It is quite obvious, then, that these men were not only all hunters, but had some other cultural affinity. What is not so obvious, and not so easily explained, is why they painted or engraved rocks in such profusion; what some of their drawings mean; or who, for that matter, the artists were.

The mystery is deepened when the traveller first sees the type of terrain in which these rock pictures are found. 'Art' in such surroundings seems incredible, not counting the subject matter of the drawings themselves. And how did the artist manage the sheer physical task of engraving over such an area and such a surface? Yet there is his work, in the most inaccessible corners of the desert, literally thousands of figures of tropical and aquatic animals, enormous herds of cattle, hunters armed with bows and boomerangs, and even 'domestic' scenes of women and children and the circular huts in which they lived.

The most famous of the Saharan art galleries yet discovered is found in the Tassili-n-Ajjer, that region of the desert which lies in the south-eastern corner of Algeria. There are no roads, or even regular tracks through this wasteland, which is, as it were, a separate world in the desert, a vast plateau of grit and rubble, enclosed by high escarpments of rock. It is these escarpments which are the chief characteristics of the *tassili*: deeply eroded by by the wind and sculpted by vanished rivers, they rear up in strange shapes often resembling cyclopian cities, or Byzantine fortresses, or Crusaders' castles. In fact, it is the erosion of these once green and fertile regions that has produced the *ergs* (sand seas) and *regs* (rocky plains) of the Sahara.

Here in the Tassili-n-Ajjer where barely a handful of Tuareg herdsmen survive, and where nobody now goes unless they have to, a race of hunters and the animals they hunted flourished in a remote period of prehistory, presumably contemporaneous with the cave-painters of Eastern Spain. And here, the Saharan 'dawn' men left us a record of themselves in hundreds of drawings in the grottoes which they inhabited 7,000 years ago. The story they tell us is, in some ways, quite clear, in others, veiled in mystery.

What is obvious is that this part of the desert was once not only habitable, but as teeming with life as the great plains of Central Africa today. Indeed, many of the same animals now found a thousand miles to the south were then living in the Tassili. These prehistoric Saharans saw them, hunted them, and drew them: elephants, hippopotami, giraffes, buffalo, deer, and wild cattle. It is therefore indisputable that this arid region once supported a rich life thanks to rivers and lakes which have since vanished. The earliest viewers of this lost world were hunters who stalked their prey in animal masks and skins, armed with stone-tipped lances and boomerangs. Some of their number depicted what life was like on the walls of the caves and grottoes where they lived and from which they must have observed the gradual fall of the rivers and lakes and the departure of the great herds to the south.

For these geological changes—the drying up of the rivers, the shrinkage of the lakes, and the erosion of the hills and river beds —are facts which are implied in the rock paintings themselves. Thus, the earliest drawings depict the great pachyderms—the elephants and hippopotami—who were the first to leave in search of better grazing grounds. We can tentatively date this period at 5000 B.C.—and it is called the Period of the Hunters. After the huger beasts had gone the men of the Tassili must have seen the need to conserve their food supply on the hoof, for they now begin to depict herds of cattle guarded by herdsmen. It is notable that the cows in these herds have no well-formed udders, so the cattle were kept for meat, not milk. The Period of the Herdsmen is put at around 3500 B.C. Next comes a third well-defined stage, that of the horse, the dog, and the wheel. It is the Period of the Garamantians and the four-horse chariot, datable in the first millennium B.C.

So much the geologist, the anthropologist, and the pre-historian can agree upon with some assurance. It is, in any case, a familiar pattern in human affairs—the evolution from hunting to herding to organized war. It is a pattern we can discern in the history of other tribes, notably in the Old Testament annals of the Jews. But at this point our facts come to an end and speculation begins. It begins as soon as we ask, as we must, why these prehistoric men painted so industriously on the walls of their cave-homes; and how are we to interpret what they were saying in their pictures? Here it is every theorist for himself.

There are two obvious explanations.

The first is that primitive men had the same artistic urges as civilized men have today. In other words, that they drew their scenes and portraits for aesthetic motives, to give pleasure to themselves and their viewers—not forgetting the other incentives which have animated artists from the beginning of recorded time: namely the expectation of a reward. Who knows, for instance, whether it wasn't the hope of praise, or applause, or some material compensation—an extra hunk of meat—which prompted some artist, not so expert with a bow or spear, to sketch the hero of the hour newly returned from the chase with the carcass of a deer? We have a great many portraits of this type, as well as other drawings which may well suggest that some of the artists, at least, were painting as 'entertainers'; for it is surely admissible that these cave-dwellers needed relaxation and amusement as much as their modern descendants seated in front of their television screens at the end of the day. If, therefore, these murals tell a story—as many of them seem to do—we are entitled to assume that their purpose was divertive rather than didactic. Indeed, even the greatest authority on cave art, the Abbé Breuil, admits that a great many of the Saharan drawings are comic both in execution and effect, provoking, he says, a gentle laugh in the manner of caricatures. So the humour of the Tassili paintings is expressed in the slightly exaggerated figures of men and animals, a form of comic art familiar to us in the fables of Aesop, himself an African. Perhaps, then, we shouldn't over-solemnize the function or meaning of these pictures, any more than we should the unsophisticated 'primitives' of children, or those adults who paint with a child-like vision. It is not the children, incidentally, who read the symbolism into their own work.

There is a second theory, and one much more in favour with

the academicians. According to this interpretation, the Tassili frescoes have a much deeper significance than mere aesthetics. The keyword of this theory is 'sympathetic magic'—a resounding phrase on paper, meaning, as far as it means anything, the practice of some form of necromancy, like sticking pins into wax *homunculi*. It is possible; it is 'scientifically' arguable on the grounds that men and animals were depicted in order to ensure good omens for the daily hunt, the success of the hunters, the efficacy of the witch-doctor, the safe birth of an infant, and so forth. Unfortunately, we have no evidence at all for such an interpretation of the rock paintings. True, if we scrabble around among the records left us by those who were closest in time to the North African primitives, we find an occasional reference to the practice of magic. The Greek historian of the Roman emperors, Dio Cassius, mentions the cult of rain-making (we are still at it, come to that); St. Augustine condemns the 'ritual bathing' of the pagans in one of his sermons; the same divine refers, as does Herodotus, to symbolic battles between young people who took sides and then pelted each other with stones, the idea being thus to expel their evil spirits. We see a survival of this rite in the smashing up of empty houses by young people today. Other writers of astonishing obscurity and dullness like Corippus hint at strange gods like one Gurzil, born of Ammon and a cow and worshipped by the Saharan aborigines. This is about all we have, and not one example of such magic, sympathetic or otherwise, can be positively identified in the Tassili paintings. Our 'reading' of these paintings, then, must remain intuitive, which is permissible, provided we recognize that we are trying to interpret the motives and intentions of men of another time and another world by the yardstick of our own physical and intellectual experience. On the other hand, what basis for comparison do we actually have?

Let us take some actual examples. What, for instance, are we to make of some of the more naturalistic *graffiti*? A man and woman engaged in the sexual act, she astride and facing him? What is the 'sympathetic magic' of this wall 'entertainment' piece? Is it merely casually pornographic, like a scrawl in a public

water closet? No doubt the phrase 'fertility rite' springs to the
lips of the more earnest student. It is a phrase, like 'sympathetic
magic', which smells of the lamp. We will come across this
'fertility rite' theory again when examining some of the goddesses
worshipped—or enthused over, rather—in later history.

Again, we have the scene of a father and mother playing with
their child. Is this a symbolic representation of the origin of the
world, the coming of spring, or a votive offering made by child-
less parents? Or is it a little family portrait such as we hang on the
walls of our own homes? Dancers, girls with exaggerated breasts
and thighs, queenly women? Are they symbolic of something?
Or merely the equivalent of prehistoric 'pin-ups'? It is instructive,
and amusing, to read the 'interpretations' of some of the more
puzzling drawings. One, for instance, which contains a total of
eleven figures, some with enormous headpieces like a sultan's
turban, is explained by the Abbé Breuil as:

> Scene of circumcision composed of eleven persons: on the
> left two operators and the one to be operated upon; in the
> middle, with legs crossed and beating time with their arms,
> singers ordered to drown out the cries of the victim; and on
> the right, members of the family turning their back on the
> scene.

A remarkable feat of imagination when one examines the
drawing for oneself. For the scene could be interpreted in half a
dozen different ways if the viewer's imagination is allowed free
scope. For instance, if the huge head-pieces of the 'white'
characters are turbans; and if the shock of crinkly hair over black
faces represent captive negroes, the gestures, knives, and the rest
of it might depict a castration scene, particularly in view of the
known custom of emasculating negro slaves for harem duties.
Or again, what we see could be a quarrel between three men; the
pursuit of one man by his enemy armed with a knife, a procession
of people bringing gifts or food; two men and a woman praying.
. . . Could this, then, be the life and death of a member of the
tribe, depicted from the initiation of a quarrel, in which he was

killed, to his burial when he might have been interred with food
for the journey into the other world? The answer is we don't
know. We can only guess.

In other words, anyone is entitled to look at these drawings
and deduce from them what he likes, despite the tut-tutting or
outright disapproval of the 'experts', who, humanly enough,
resent the intrusion of the outsider. We can remember in this
respect, however, the attitude of D. H. Lawrence towards the
Etruscan tombs: the experts contradicted each other so often that
he felt entitled to fall back on his own intuition.

Henri Lhote has done this in his survey of the Tassili paintings,
and he was richly entitled to do so in view of his immense labours
in recording for us so many of these almost inaccessible works of
prehistoric man. One painting, for instance, found in a cave in
Sefar, Lhote calls 'The Great God with Praying Women'. In the
centre of the picture is the so-called god, a huge figure some
ten feet high, with an eyeless face and the head of a frog (?)—his
whole outspread, flat-bodied stance, in fact, resembling a frog
spread-eagled on the surface of a pond. What is this monster?
What is the great bag between its legs? A scrotum? Or a tail?
What are these phallic protuberances on the creature's upper
forearms? We can't say. It could be a god, and the encircling
women could be holding up their hands in prayer. But who is to
assert that prehistoric women prayed in the *orante* attitude of
early Christians? Aren't we confusing levels of culture and religious practices of different millennia? Wasn't the Abbé Breuil
doing exactly this in introducing his circumcision *motif* into the
picture discussed above? We don't *know*. We can only follow
Lawrence's example and 'accept one's own resultant feeling'.
Beyond this, all we can say is that some of these frescoes are im-
bued with true genius, whereas others are the crude scrawlings
of the prehistoric ancestors of our own water-closet artists.

There are, however, certain conclusions that we can make with
some assurance. We can say, for instance, that these drawings are
a naturalistic depiction of life as it was lived in the Sahara for a
period roughly covering 5,000 years of history: from 5000 B.C.,
that is, up to the Roman period; and during that period, and for

long afterwards, the Saharans never progressed beyond the Iron
Age. Sallust's description of them as 'savages who lived on the
flesh of wild animals' is an accurate one. It is the modern historian who introduces his own enigmas and complexities into a
world in which hunger, procreation, and death were the only
problems men had to contend with.

II

The prehistorian's job in North Africa and the desert is not an
easy one, and the qualities he requires in addition to a vast knowledge are of the kind that were needed by the old explorers—
those travellers, in other words, who went to unknown places on
their own two feet and without the aid of machines. Even today,
when the visitor to this part of the world doesn't meet with the
overt hostility of the natives—a hostility based until recently on
religious fanaticism—he is liable to be discouraged in his search
for the monuments of the primitive inhabitants of what is almost
a lost world.

There is, for instance, a neolithic site in the Tunisian Sahel, at
a place called Menzel Dar-bel-Ouar, about thirty miles north-west
of Sousse, the old Carthaginian port from which Hannibal was
supplied in the Second Punic War against Scipio. Early travellers
in this region reported the presence at Menzel Dar-bel-Ouar of
prehistoric monuments in the form of dolmens or monolithic
erections familiar to us from the British site at Stonehenge.
Dolmens, in fact, are found all over north-western Europe, and
they are found, too, in parts of North Africa. They were to prehistoric cultures what the pyramids were to ancient Egypt and,
perhaps, the cathedrals to the Middle Ages. But who erected these
monuments here on the fringe of the desert?

It is not easy to find out. You can get to Menzel Dar-bel-Ouar
by road, and you arrive at a collection of huts obviously built
from the stones taken from the dolmens themselves. These huts
are thatched, but the village has no resemblance to those quaint
English hamlets beloved of the Sunday motorist. You stop outside a broken-down caravanserai where the usual crowd of

Tunisians sit in the dust. Communication with these curious yet silent observers of your arrival is the first problem. Do they know where the big stones are—the very ancient ones placed one on top of the other?

They are puzzled. Stones? It is a world of stones hereabouts. The peasants spend their life removing stones from the cracked, dust-dry land in order to plant a little grain which may, or may not, sprout in the spring, provided there is rain. But who wants to look at stones? And why?

You explain that these stones are very old and they were the tombs of a race who lived here several thousand years ago. Ah! The Romans! No. Not the Romans. Before them. They are now more puzzled than ever, with reason, perhaps, because, in the first place, time means nothing to them; and in the second they don't speak a recognizable French, and you don't speak their Berber dialect.

However, a small boy is brought forward to represent the community. He is, presumably, a schoolboy, because he wears a pinafore and carries a satchel. He is supposed to speak French, but conversation is limited to smiles and hand-waving on my part to which he sees no reason to respond. A serious lad, and let's hope he goes far—at least farther than Menzel Dar-bel-Ouar. We march in silence across the vast empty plain which is not strictly desert, for the terrain consists of rubble rather than sand. After twenty minutes' tramp it becomes clear my guide has no idea where we are going or what we are going for. But then I see in the distance what I am looking for. There are, in fact, several small dolmens still left standing, so I make for these. My guide follows stoically.

We arrive at the dolmens, and from a hut built of the stones themselves emerges a turbaned tribesman to whom I am quick off the mark with fraternal greetings. He appears to be the occupant of this place, and stands by as I examine what is left of this neolithic site. It has, of course, been almost totally destroyed, the stones thrown down and, where possible, broken up to make material for the walls of the thatched hovels in one of which this man lives with his son, a camel (this beast stands hobbled in the courtyard), and, presumably, his wife. Those dolmens which remain standing are in the form of three-sided tombs covered with a flat roof, the monoliths having been brought from the mountains fifteen miles away. A coin passed to the guardian leads me to a hole in the ground. It has just been discovered by workmen who are digging holes in which to plant olive trees. I am lowered down into the bowels of the earth and find myself in a circular tomb chamber, twelve feet in diameter, hacked out of the rock probably with stone axes and antlers. The ancient gravediggers have done a good job under the circumstances, and in view of the labour involved, this must have been the resting place of a person of importance. It appears that someone in authority has been here before me, for the bones found in this rock tomb have been removed. Where to? Impossible to find out. All the guardian knows is that the bones were those of a woman and that other 'holes' have been discovered; and it slowly becomes apparent as one examines the site that Menzel Dar-bel-Ouar was a vast neolithic cemetery. Some day, no doubt, the archaeologists will get around to excavating it; and then we shall know more about the prehistory of the region. In the meantime the local farmers knock down what remains of the tombs above ground.

Menzel Dar-bel-Ouar is typical of the prehistoric sites of North Africa, including the desert itself. These simple and unexciting monuments of primitive men have, understandably, been neglected by comparison with the splendid remains of those who came after. Thus, while we know almost everything of the Africa Proconsularis of the Romans and something of the Africa of the Phoenicians, we are in almost total ignorance of who and what went before them. We have now entered a phase of the time zone which no longer conforms to our neat divisions into the reigns of kings and the duration of empires.

III

'In the beginning', says the historian Sallust writing around the middle of the first century before Christ, 'North Africa was inhabited by the Gaetulians and Libyans, savages who lived on the flesh of wild animals and fed, like cattle, on the plants of the fields. Wandering aimlessly about, they stopped where night found them.'

Sallust was describing what he had seen with his own eyes as a military commander in Africa and later a governor of the new province. He was, incidentally, a much better historian than he was an administrator. But what he tells us in those few words is the essence of Saharan prehistory. Our present knowledge of the first inhabitants of the desert, though augmented by a hundred years of archaeological research, doesn't add very much to Sallust's observation.

Of course, a Roman was not interested in prehistory in the modern manner. For him the word 'savage' embraced about all that needed to be said on the subject. The rest was myth—good enough for epic poetry, but nonsense to the practical scholar. So we don't know whether Sallust in the course of his travels ever saw the monuments erected by stone-age Saharans, or gave them much thought if he did. The Roman soldiers had spotted dolmens all over Europe in their long marches across the lands of the barbarians, but how old they were, or what they signified, was of no more importance to these campaigners than ruins are to the average infantryman today. A modern soldier marching along the Appian Way en route to Rome is reported to have remarked on the amount of bomb damage to the line of once-splendid tombs where the great and the rich lie buried.

What Sallust didn't know, then, was that the North Africans, like their fellow men in prehistoric Europe, erected tombs in the form of dolmens. And what nobody knew until recently was that whereas such megaliths don't appear to have been set up in Europe after 1500 B.C., the North African aborigines were erecting them as late as the Roman occupation. For not only have Roman coins been found in some dolmens but Roman methods have been used to build them; or, alternatively, Roman squared-off blocks have been used to support the characteristic roof slab of unhewn stone. In other words, a monument which, in Europe, manifestly belongs to the prehistoric age (Stonehenge, for instance, dating from around 2000 B.C.) has no 'date' in North Africa, for the very obvious reason that the desert people themselves had not radically changed with the passage of the millennia. They were still at the cultural level of savages up to and beyond the Roman occupation.

As far as the actual archaeology of the Sahara is concerned, the prehistorians have not yet been able to systematize their findings, or even to date the majority of them. The terms palaeolithic, megalithic, neolithic, bronze, iron, and so forth really have no particular meaning as applied to the innumerable stone piles of one sort and another strewn over the desert. That most industrious and conscientious of archaeologists, Maurice Reygasse, in fact, wisely abstains from all attempts at precise dating—on the basis of his many years' experience. He tells us how an examination of a circle of stones deep in the desert may give the impression to the unpractised eye of immense age—a veritable prehistoric 'temple' made by the hands of men dead for 5,000 years or more. Knowledge of desert ways and closer examination may show that the stones have been placed *in situ* a week before by a herdsman pitching his round tent within their circle, as a Boy Scout might hold down the sides of his tent with the nearest available rocks. The stones, of course, are prehistoric! The design typical of primitive man's ritualistic practices. But what a blunder the over-enthusiastic amateur could make on seeing such a 'site' from the seat of a Land Rover, particularly as there are hundreds of genuinely ancient stone circles throughout the central Sahara.

However, despite all the difficulties and pitfalls of Saharan archaeology, certain clear and specific conclusions can be drawn from the hundreds of 'digs' undertaken, for the most part, by intelligent and enthusiastic French army officers who, up to recently, were the only Westerners with the means of reaching the more remote sites. Isolated in desert villages, many a young French lieutenant or captain has ridden out with his goum or camel patrol and dug into earth mounds and piles of stones, sending back a well-written report to the archaeological societies in Algiers or Paris. Their findings can be briefly summarized:

(1) The graves are nearly all of the most primitive form of inhumation, the corpse being placed on the ground with

the knees drawn up and then covered with stones and rocks, sometimes in a loose pile, sometimes in the shape of a low cylindrical tower, sometimes in the centre of a stone circle, or an avenue of stones.

(2) Such graves, with the absence of all but the poorest and most primitive artifacts, indicate the extreme poverty of the Saharans right throughout history, from the stone age up to the recent past.

(3) The existence of 'cities of the dead' in regions now largely abandoned proves that such areas of the central Sahara once supported large and fairly settled communities.

(4) Nothing in the manner of burial, and none of the objects found in the graves, give us any clue as to the religious beliefs and practices of the desert population before their conversion to Islam.

(5) The most curious and mysterious of the monuments are patterns of stone laid out rather in the manner of a giant keyhole, with two concentric circles of stone chippings, a mound of boulders in the centre, and an avenue of banked stones leading from the mound to the circumference. These keyhole monuments are found in the depths of the Sahara, on the side of mountains, the largest of them having a diameter of sixty yards. Excavations have sometimes unearthed a single skeleton under the central mound, laid on its side with knees drawn up. No accompanying artifacts, such as one expects to find in the burial places of even the most primitive people, have been found. In fact, many of the keyhole monuments are empty. Their purpose in such cases is unknown, their nearest counterpart being the stone avenues of prehistoric men in northern Europe.

(6) Where archaeologists have found artifacts in the Saharan tombs, it is not unusual to find articles, in the same grave, as far apart in time as flint arrow heads and Roman coins. Obviously the one item was as functional and treasured as the other. It is therefore possible that the central Saharans were, culturally, still in the neolithic age as late as the third century A.D. In other words, the period and dates by which we measure European history have no relevance in this part of the world. M. Reygasse concludes: 'From the anthropological and archaeological point of view, we find ourselves faced with a hiatus.'

IV

Among all these voiceless mounds and rings of stones which mark either the poor graves or simple shrines of the central Saharan people only one monument speaks to us in a language we can partially understand: that is, the language of the Roman civilization. This monument, certainly the most exciting archaeologically in the desert south of the Roman *limes*, is the fortress and tomb of Tin Hinan, at an oasis called Abelessa near Tamanrasset in the Hoggar. The name Abelessa itself has a Roman sound, which has led some historians, notably Henri Lhote, to go so far as to suggest that it may be a variant of 'Balsa', a place actually recorded in written history. Pliny, in fact, mentions a 'Balsa' in connection with the African campaign of Cornelius Balbus, conqueror of the Fezzan. From this supposition—that Abelessa is Balsa—it is only one step for the more daring, or imaginative, of theorists (that is, those who have no academic prestige to maintain) to suggest that the fortress of Tin Hinan was an actual Roman outpost halfway to Timbuktu. The shadow of the Third Augusta Legion falls at this point on central Saharan history.

Be that as it may, there is no doubt at all that the fortress, or castle, is unique; that its architecture bears no relationship to the monuments erected by the savages, or the later barbarians who inhabited the desert wastelands. Tin Hinan, in fact, is the work of quasi-civilized hands, and was certainly occupied by people who had contacts with the civilized world; for when it was excavated, it was found to contain artifacts which we associate with an advanced culture: e.g. a wooden bed, Roman coins, jewelry, lamps, and utensils that were certainly not made by the natives of the surrounding desert. Tin Hinan, therefore, was built and occupied by foreigners. Who were they? And what were they doing a thousand miles away from the centres of the civilized world?

To the practised eye, the appearance of the fortress suggests some of the possible answers. We can see in it, for instance, some resemblance to the Roman farm-forts along the northern frontiers of the desert. The walls, on an average four feet thick, are built of basalt blocks, some of which have been squared off in the Roman manner. There is only one entrance, leading to eleven rooms which open out one from the other—again typical of the farmhouses along the *limes*. The room farthest from the entrance was found sealed off in the Franco-American excavations of 1926. Breaking in, the archaeologists found themselves in a rectangular chamber measuring about sixteen by twelve feet with walls eight feet high. The floor of this room was covered with soil and, under the debris, a layer of stone chips; and under this flooring six large monoliths, the biggest of which measured nearly seven feet long, a foot wide, and five inches thick. When these stone slabs were removed, the excavators looked down into another chamber, seven feet long, four feet wide, and four feet high. It was the tomb of Tin Hinan, the first 'queen' of the Hoggar, the legendary ancestress of the Tuareg. Her skeleton was still *in situ*.

She was lying on her back, with her arms lightly folded. She had evidently been laid to rest on what appeared to be a ceremonial bed of ornamented wood, or perhaps a chair-throne. Only a few pieces of this bier remained. The jewels buried with her had survived: on the right forearm were seven silver bracelets and on the left seven gold bracelets. The number seven may have had some symbolic significance, as it did in classical numerology. Lying beneath the neck of the queen was her pendant of a hundred silver beads. Another pendant of white and red pearls was in place on her ribs; on her right shoulder two safety-clasps with the remains of her dress attached; by her side several baskets containing date stones, some wheat, wood faggots, a little gold ring, fragments of glass, and the figurine of a good-luck charm. This statuette appears to be of great age, belonging to the dawn of mankind's religious beliefs, for it has a featureless head, a shapeless body, with the whole emphasis placed upon the hips and female pudenda: not an idealistic reproduction of an anthropomorphic divinity, then, such as the Greeks and Romans worshipped, but a fetish whose symbolism is the female counterpart of the phallus, or Priapus of other cults. And just as phallic

amulets were, and still are, worn as lucky charms, so no doubt
this palaeolithic Venus was worn by Tin Hinan.

What else do we know about this queen or princess? Dr.
Leblanc, of the Faculty of Medicine at the University of Algiers,
who examined the skeleton, describes her as: 'a woman of the
white race. The formation of the skeleton strongly recalls the
Egyptian type as seen on the pharaonic monuments, characterized
by height and slimness, wideness of shoulder, smallness of pelvis,
and slenderness of leg.'

The Tuareg for their part give us some additional information
—or, rather, a choice of two legends. One merely says that Tin
Hinan is the maternal ancestor of all the noble tribes, the first
mother and the first queen. The second has a more historical
significance, for it tells how the fort was originally constructed
by a foreigner who lived at Abelessa before the advent of Islam.
(That is, before A.D. 700.) This man's name was Jolouta, and he
was a soldier. Driven from the region by the Arab invaders, he
returned with an army and fought a battle in which he was killed.
His soldiers remained in the desert and married negro women.
Their descendants are the serfs of the Tuareg who, if noble, are
the progeny of Tin Hinan who came from Tafilalet in south-
eastern Morocco, a journey of 1,000 miles across the desert. Why
she came is not known. All that the legend records is that she
arrived with her followers and lived and died in this castle.

There are a number of curious implications in this account—
assuming that we are willing to accept the idea that legends have
a basis in fact.

First, the statement that a foreigner built the fortress accords
with the archaeological evidence. The aborigines of the Central
Desert were not able then (and are not able now) to construct a
building of this size and character. The only masons who could
have done so were invaders from the north, either Roman
legionaires themselves; or, more likely, one of their African
detachments. Why was such a massive stronghold considered
necessary this far down in the desert?

The answer is not as obscure as it may seem. Abelessa was,
and is, on the north-south caravan route from the Mediterranean

ports to Central Africa. The trade coming out of this latter region was always considerable and always important to the cities of Proconsular Africa. We remember that cities like Sabratha in Tripolitania had their own shipping agencies in the Roman port of Ostia. Such North African ports were shipping not only oil and grain to Italy, but also the produce of the African interior. This produce came up the ancient caravan routes from Lake Chad and the Niger River, to both of which places Roman columns had already penetrated on punitive and exploratory raids across the desert. The big Roman forts at Bu Ngem, Ghadames, and possibly Ghat were not built solely as military establishments. They were also Customs stations. Could it not be, then, that Roman patrols were policing the desert as far down as the Hoggar, with military posts along the caravan routes, comparable to the posts established by the French during the nineteenth century? And was the fortress of Tin Hinan one of these military Customs posts, actually built by the long-range desert patrols of the Third Augusta Legion? For those who like speculation, there is a parallel case to be found in the activities of the British-based legions beyond the Hadrian and Antonine walls in Britain. We still don't have all the evidence either for the extreme northern or the extreme southern provinces of the Roman Empire. All we know for a certainty is that the legions in the heyday of the *pax romana* were continuously patrolling beyond the fixed frontiers.

The fortress of Tin Hinan, then, could be evidence that the Romans, through their mercenaries, were much farther down in the desert than we know, since the monument was either a strongpoint proper, or a fortress-warehouse, strategically placed on the Tripoli–Ghadames–Abelessa–Niger River route. Whether it was ever garrisoned by a regular detachment of the Third Augusta Legion we may never know; nor whether Jolouta (a Syrian name?)[1] was the last officer to command the forces cut off

1. For those who think that etymology may contribute something to solving the mystery of 'Jolouta', a rota of common names among the Third Augusta legionnaires is available. Very popular was the *nomen* Julius. Cognomens were Datus, Tertius, and so forth. Could 'Julius Tertius', then, become, through the processes of linguistic attrition, 'Julouta'?

from his home base in Ghadames or Ghat by the Arab invasion of the seventh century.

It seems reasonably certain, however, that Tin Hinan was an exiled 'princess' from the Berber kingdom of Tafilalet, who lived in the abandoned castle, died there, and was buried with her personal treasures, including odds and ends, like Roman lamps and coins, which were either left behind by a previous occupant or which she brought with her. Why she made the long and difficult journey from her homeland to the wilderness of the Hoggar Mountains will never now be known. There are, however, comparable legends of queens and princesses driven from their native kingdoms to distant places, for such was the origin of Carthage, founded by Queen Dido of Tyre. And for those with a powerful imagination there is the theory of the American enthusiast who helped finance the excavations of Tin Hinan in 1926 and who joyfully announced after the discovery of the tomb and the exhumation of the skeleton that here, in the middle of the Sahara, reposed the mortal remains of Antinea, last queen of Atlantis.

TWO

'Carthage must be wiped out'

So FAR, then, the history of the desert has to be read in the
evidence of drawings on rocks and piles of stones, for nothing
resembling writing has been found there prior to the Carthaginian period. This absence of a script supports the supposition
that the Sahara was occupied up to recorded times by a negro
race who were driven farther south by the invasions of north
Mediterranean peoples, notably the Garamantes, that still
mysterious nation who, Herodotus tells us, 'chased the Ethiopian
troglodytes in four-horse chariots'. These 'Ethiopians', then,
meaning black-skinned people, were presumably the aboriginals
of the desert, surviving (some anthropologists say) as the 'Rock
Tiboos' in the mountains of the Tibesti. They were, and still are,
said to be the fastest runners known to man, as they have reason
to be, since they have been hunted by slave-raiders as far back
as 500 B.C. up to the recent past.

As for the Garamantes (or Garamantians, as we may as well
call them), archaeology is only just beginning to reveal something about them. They left, for instance, at least 40,000 graves
in the neighbourhood of their capital at Garama, the modern
oasis of Germa. Their capital itself, a small metropolis of stone
temples, forts, and outlying houses, is even now being slowly
excavated from under the rubble of an Arab village abandoned
to the mosquitoes and scorpions. It is an eerie place, with its
crumbling mosques, Roman wells, and malarial marshes; but not
as eerie as the nearby necropolis of el Hatia with its hundred or
more pyramid tombs lying out there untouched in the desert.
If you approach this cemetery from the east when the rays of
the morning sun are level with the sand, you see these tombs

standing up in the desert like the miniature skyscrapers of a prehistoric city. Tombs, forts, watch towers, and irrigation tunnels speak of a sizable community in what is now a waterless and abandoned wasteland. But this, too, was a pocket of the Gara-mantian kingdom which the Romans eventually conquered, but probably never completely subdued.

What is also notable in Herodotus's description of these pre-Roman Saharans is his reference to horses and chariots being used this far down in the desert, now the undisputed province of the camel. But we should remember that the camel, the heraldic beast of the desert, is a late arrival on the North African scene, and the first we hear of this animal is at the Battle of Thapsus where Julius Caesar defeated the followers of Pompey and acquired, among the other spoils of victory, forty-three camels which had been used in the army of the Numidian king Juba.

The Romans, in fact, never made much use of the camel, an oversight which was to cost them dear in the final invasions of their North Africa colonies from the east and the south. But when it came to horses, their attitude seems to have been that of a fox-hunting man towards his favourite hunter. The African mosaics depict the most splendid horses, drawn with all the verve of nineteenth-century prints: beautiful horses immortalized by their names, which themselves bespeak the affection and pride of their owners. 'Adorandus' and 'Crinitus', a handsome pair of Barb stallions, stand beneath a date palm. 'Amor' and 'Dominator' still show the whites of their eyes. 'Pupillus', 'Amator', 'Cupido', 'Aura'—we are clearly told by their magnificent portraits how greatly they were prized on the stud farms of Africa.

We can't be so sure about the Carthaginian attitude to the horse. It was typical of the Phoenicians that they preferred the elephant and hired Numidians for the cavalry wing of their army. Still, they must have needed horses for transport, for even though they were sailors, they still had a flourishing trade with Central Africa across the desert. Carthaginian merchants undoubtedly crossed the Sahara with horse and donkey caravans that brought back gold and ivory from the Niger, as well as black slaves, always popular in the courts and seraglios of the Mediterranean.

Eastern potentates, in particular, liked a negro eunuch to run their harem, an arrangement that was apparently quite satisfactory to their wives and concubines, judging from some of the episodes in *The Thousand and One Nights*.

But the Romans did such a thorough job of wiping out Carthage that our records of the Phoenician exploration of the desert are sparse. The traveller who makes the pilgrimage to Carthage or the other Punic cities along the south Mediterranean coast will find almost nothing left on which to base his opinion of this mysterious semitic people. If there is anything remaining of one of the greatest cities of the ancient world it is deep underground. Everything Carthaginian above ground was either smashed into rubble by the Romans or used as the foundations of their own immense city. Ironically, most of their own buildings have suffered the same fate. A lot of Roman Carthage, for instance, went into the foundations of the embankment across the Lake of Tunis. The electric trains which run from Tunis to Carthage along this causeway rattle along on the debris of who knows how many Roman temples and baths, not to omit the rubble of the oldest synagogue in North Africa. The archaeologist has little chance when the bulldozers get going.

All the same, one is irresistibly attracted by the very name and descends in an expectant mood at the little station. Carthage! Where is this capital of an empire among these jerry-built villas and parched fields? The station-master hasn't the slightest idea what you are talking about if you ask for the naval dockyard whence the Punic ships sailed to Spain, Britain, and West Africa. The touts who run up with coins and little oil lamps know, for they are still digging in the rubble for souvenirs. But if you don't buy you don't get any directions, or get wrong ones; and there is nothing to show you the way—the signs, like the cross over the memorial to St. Perpetua in the Roman amphitheatre, have been removed—perhaps by Moslems who disapprove of the whole business. For the ground hereabouts reeks of alien saints and martyrs.

However, you climb the hill on which stood the Carthaginian citadel. On all sides you see the remains of the later Roman city and, surmounting the summit itself, that great white elephant of

Christendom in North Africa, the Cathedral of Saint-Louis, a monument as bizarre (the guide-books call the architectural style 'Moorish-Byzantine') as Cardinal Lavigerie's dream of converting Islamic Africa to Christianity.

But of ancient Carthage absolutely nothing. Not a vestige of even those encircling walls nearly sixty feet high regularly spaced with watch towers—the admiration and envy, according to Greek writers, of every nation. It is the same throughout the Phoenician Empire. Everything they built has gone. Carthage was literally wiped out.

The archaeologists are really the only ones who regret this deletion; and even they will admit that these Phoenicians were a reactionary, mercenary, cruel, inartistic, and unsympathetic people whose disappearance from history was a boon to mankind, like the wiping out of other evil political systems, ancient or modern.

The observer who stands in the two great museums of Carthage —the Bardo in Tunis, the Lavigerie in Carthage itself—will quickly sense the soullessness of a people whose religion permitted them to burn children alive to ensure victory in war. Moreover, while it was axiomatic with the Greeks that they civilized their gods as they civilized themselves, the Carthaginian deities didn't change fundamentally in a thousand years or more. The old Jews knew the horror of the Phoenician Moloch, or M 'ilk; and proclaimed their disgust at his hideous rites. The vases full of children's bones taken from the sanctuaries of Baal Hammon and his consort Tanit indicate that the Phoenicians had not changed their cult of religious murder since the time of Moses. Standing in the Punic room of the Bardo gallery, confronted with these rows of small vases and the wedge-shaped votive tombstones which commemorated the child sacrifices, the visitor finds it hard to grieve at the disappearance of an empire founded on that much senseless cruelty.

And even without the evidence of their chilly religious practices, there still remain enough odds and ends of their everyday life to give us a glimpse, if nothing more, into their Asiatic mind. Rich and successful though they were, they didn't have the flexibility to adapt themselves to the new world which was being created under their very noses. Socrates, Plato, Sophocles, Pythagoras, and Demosthenes could never have existed as far as they were concerned. They closed their minds to the art, philosophy, and science which was spreading across the Mediterranean world—the greatest renaissance in the history of mankind. The Carthaginians were so penny-pinching that they never even used marble in their public buildings; and so aesthetically dead, they couldn't apparently produce a single beautiful building, monument, painting, or sculpture of their own. The Greeks had to do it all for them. The native Carthaginian efforts, seen, for instance, in the carving on the tombstones, are invariably shoddy in conception and technique. The figures look as though they have been hacked out by a stonemason, certainly not a sculptor. And the few large monuments which survive show an amazing ignorance of the architectural laws of balance and line. Every style and fashion of the Mediterranean—Babylonian, Egyptian, Persian, Ionic, Doric, and what-not—is mixed up together, so that one is reminded of Victorian Gothic in its most outlandish manifestations. In fact, the Carthaginians and the Victorians had much in common, for both were a merchant people whose energies were directed towards overseas commerce.

Even so, standing in the ruins of Carthage, the observer has this sense of wonder and strangeness that a people, once so renowned, could leave so little behind. Almost everything that the White Fathers have unearthed in a century of excavations fills only one room in the Musée Lavigerie; and of all the exhibits there displayed in the home-made show cases—coins, lamps, odds and ends of jewelry, sarcophagi, and figurines—nothing gives us a clue to the might and wealth of their empire. They seem to be a people of grinning masks, or stony faces, with large, fleshy noses, down-hanging ears, and narrow eyes. The one lovely sculpture that remains, a priestess holding a bird in her right hand (no doubt Greek-executed), seems to be the only touch of humanity they left us. In all other respects, they remain a mystery.

But no one can doubt that they were the greatest sailors and explorers of the ancient world. We know some of the places they went to. We even have a reference to their Saharan travels, for

we are asked to believe by the Greek physician Athanaeus that
they made regular crossings of the Great Desert. Athanaeus
states that he knew of a Carthaginian merchant-adventurer who
made the trip living entirely on barley, without requiring any
water at all. This tall story was intended to prove the Greek
physician's theory of the efficacy of a barley diet; but it also
suggests that the Carthaginians accompanied their caravans on
the trans-Saharan routes from the trading posts along the North
African coast into Central Africa.

Even if the Phoenician merchants occasionally went with a
train, the actual command of the expeditions was then, as now,
in the hands of the tribesmen whose profession was desert navigation. Like the captain of an ocean-going ship, the chief guide,
or *kebir*, was the supreme commander of the venture, with his
officers and crew. Often the caravan commander had two
thousand travellers in his care, for it is a rule of the desert that
no one can be denied a passage, nor, in theory, does a traveller
have to explain who he is, where he has come from, or where
he is going. In the great days of desert travel, the chief danger
(provided one wasn't a Christian infidel) was not so much the
scarcity of water as the desert bandits, which explains the punitive
raids the Romans were constantly making deep into the Sahara from
the time of the Governor Cornelius Balbus until the withdrawal
of the Third Augusta Legion from its headquarters in Lambaesis.

The Carthaginians, however, were quite content to leave the
control of the desert in the hands of the Saharans who knew it
backwards and forwards. Some of these tribes had been crossing
the wastelands from earliest recorded history, and we still have
in Herodotus an unusual account of five young Nasamonian
tribesmen who did so. They were taken prisoner en route by
pygmies whose language was wholly unintelligible to them; then
taken south and westwards through forests to a large city on the
banks of a great river which abounded in crocodiles. Was this
the Niger River? And was the city Timbuktu?

We can never tell now how much was fact and how much
fancy in these old travellers' tales. The historians recorded them
for what they were worth, and geographers tried to make them

the basis for their maps. The results, even where longitudes and latitudes were given, were often wildly wide of the mark, as a look at these old maps of the world will show. Ptolemy, for instance, tried to fix locations by direct astronomical observations; but this being physically impossible in most cases, he fell back on determining distances by calculating and comparing the itineraries of travellers. This was hopeless when it came to plotting the locations of the African rivers, mountain ranges, and cities, since the trans-Saharan caravaners were not relying on map-readings then, any more than they do now. They found their way largely by instinct and intuition.[1] It was therefore obvious that these desert itineraries, as reported second-hand to Ptolemy by travellers and merchants, were useless for purposes of fixing precise locations. In fact, even approximate locations in the Sahara were not fixed until well into the twentieth century when desert explorers used astronomical observations to plot their positions.

It has already been pointed out that the Romans had no interest in these, to them purely theoretical, aspects of geography; and this explains why they produced no accurate maps of the territories they conquered.[2] They could have done so if they had taken scientists along on their expeditions. But these expeditions were wholly military and the records of them have puzzled geographers ever since.

The campaigns of the generals Septimius Flaccus and Julius Maternus in A.D. 70 are classic examples. The former of these commanders marched south through Libya for three months into the land of the Ethiopians, which was the name for all of Negro Africa. The latter went even farther, for he was gone four months and reached a country called Agisymba 'where the rhinoceroses foregather'.[3]

1. If you ask a desert guide how he finds his way, he may still say by keeping such and such a star in the corner of his eye.

2. There was an official map of the Empire set up in Rome under Augustus, but it was a generalized or pictorial map, probably made for prestige purposes. The practical Romans preferred itineraries, like modern road guides, giving the approximate distances between towns, state of the roads, and so on.

3. Reported by the Greek-Egyptian geographer Ptolemy, greatest of classical astronomers. Unfortunately most of his latitudes are 'educated' guesses as a result, and often quite inaccurate.

For those interested in detective work, the following are the known data on the Julius Maternus expedition: the general set out from Germa, the ancient capital of the Garamantians, 500 miles south of Tripoli. He then marched southwards for 120 days. We are told that the Roman columns covered the 500 miles from Tripoli to Germa in twenty days. Their rate of marching was, then, twenty-five miles a day, which was the standard accelerated rate of the Roman legion. We cannot expect Maternus's column to have kept up this speed across the Air, but we have a basis of comparison in the times of other travellers along the same route. The first Europeans after Maternus to go south from Germa were Major Denham and Captain Clapperton, who travelled the 1,000 miles to Lake Chad in sixty-eight days on the outward journey, sixty-one days on the return. Denham and Clapperton, therefore, moved at an average speed of just over fifteen miles a day, which is a normal day's journey in the desert. If, then, we can assume that the Roman patrol also covered an average of fifteen miles a day (and they would have no reason to linger en route in view of the wasteland they were traversing), they went 1,800 miles, which could have taken them as far as the Congo River. But this is straining credulity too far. Allowing, then, for periods of rest, reconnaissance, and detours, the column could easily have reached Lake Chad marching by way of the old caravan route Murzuk–Madama–Bilma–Agadem, a distance of just over 1,000 miles due south, as the text says; or, if they went south-west by the Ghat–Hoggar–Adrar des Iforras route, a distance of some 1,300 miles, they could have reached the Niger River at Bourem. The former route was the one taken by the Oudney-Clapperton-Denham expedition in 1822; the latter roughly that of Major Laing in 1826. The important fact, which must not be overlooked in a report of this kind, is that rhinoceroses did not 'abound' north of Central Africa. Julius Maternus must, therefore, have crossed the Sahara Desert.

Alternatively, the report might have been confused, and the four months' march might have been a 'round trip'. Most commentators don't permit the Romans to have gone farther than Lake Chad, though when one remembers how they marched through the bogs, marshes, and forests of Northern Europe there is no reason to underestimate the distances they would have been capable of covering in Africa.

The Carthaginian conquest of the Sahara, in contrast, was negligible. The Carthaginians were primarily mariners; their empire, since Phoenician times, was the sea. Wherever they went, which was farther into the unknown than European explorers ventured until the Middle Ages, they were after one thing only: trade. Territorial conquests were undertaken only if absolutely necessary. Those colonies which they did establish in North

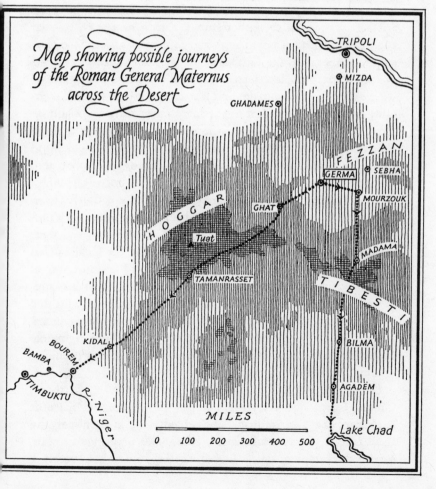

Map showing possible journeys of the Roman General Maternus across the Desert

Africa, Spain, and elsewhere, they did not even administer properly. The usual procedure was to establish a trading post on the coast, fortify it, and leave it in charge of a factor and a small garrison. The proof that the Carthaginians were not true colonists is evidenced by the fact that they left nothing of themselves behind but the names of the towns they founded—Tangiers, Cartagena, Cadiz, and Tunis among them. They left very little in Africa itself apart from their barbarous gods. Typical of a nation of business men, they left the fighting of their wars to mercenaries, though they did have a soldier class from which their famous generals were drawn. The 'Sacred Battalion' was an aristocratic, decorative, rather stupid, and, if necessary, suicidal band of young men, bored with the commercial life of the city-empire. Otherwise, the Carthaginians were anti-militarist on the grounds that wars interfered with trade and mercenary armies were expensive to maintain; and it is characteristic of their mentality that on the occasion of the invasion of their homeland by the Greek tyrant Agathocles, the Carthaginian leaders tried to save military expenditure by making a deal with their chief god M 'ilk (or Moloch), the monster with the face of an old man and, for some reason, the horns of a cuckold. M 'ilk got 200 children tossed into the furnace of his belly in return for a Carthaginian victory. The bribe seemed to work, because the Greeks, victims of an error, fought their Numidian allies by mistake and were then cut off from their home base in Sicily by the Carthaginian fleet. The practice of sacrificing children to M 'ilk in times of national crisis naturally continued. All the same, this venal and, at the same time, mingy attitude was eventually to cost the Carthaginians dearly, especially when they came up against a people like the Romans who went through the pious rigmarole of dabbling with the entrails of the sacrifices while depending wholly on their strong right arms.

Before the Romans decided to wipe out Etruria, Carthage, Greece, Egypt, and every other empire or kingdom, civilized or barbarian, the Carthaginians undoubtedly had a monopoly on the Central African trade: gold, ivory, skins, precious stones, ostrich feathers, and dates. In exchange the black men received the usual trumpery which modern traders have always found most effective in their bartering: cheap finery, weapons of inferior quality, gaudy clothes, and knick-knacks in general. African slaves were not yet needed in any numbers, as there was always a vast supply of manacled labour in classical times as a result of the wars, the prisoners filling the mines, quarries, farms, and homes of the victors. Alexander the Great, for instance, after he had reduced Tyre, mother-city of Carthage, first slaughtered 8,000 Tyrians on the spot, selected 30,000 for slavery, and then liquidated the remainder. The Carthaginians and Romans followed the same practice, so there was no shortage of forced labour until Christian times, when the enslavement of white men was considered degrading, except where permitted by law as in the European colonies and the southern American states.

In 149 B.C. two Roman consuls with an army of 80,000 infantry and 4,000 cavalry waited outside Carthage, ready to wipe the city out in accordance with the politician Cato's slogan: *delenda est Carthago*. The Carthaginians were in no mood and no position to sustain a war or a siege. They surrendered unconditionally and asked what they could do to expiate their 'crime'. Their crime, of course, was to have defied Roman imperialism for a hundred years or more. The consuls promised them their liberty, laws, territory, and retention of all their possessions, both public and private, provided they sent, within thirty days, 300 hostages chosen from the families of the Carthaginian senate. The terrified Phoenicians concurred: 300 young men were handed over. The second Roman demand followed at once. All weapons and engines of war must now be turned over. This, too, was done. Next condition. Send thirty of the Carthaginian senators to the Roman camp. Thirty were sent. Next demand—the last one.

(1) The citizens were to evacuate their city, which was to be razed to the ground.

(2) The population would be allowed to go where they pleased as long as their new town was not less than fifteen miles from the sea.

In other words, Carthage and its half a million population was to be annihilated.

The people decided to fight. Instead of stoking children into the furnace of the god, the citizens manufactured every day 1,000 shields, 300 swords, 500 lances, and 1,000 projectiles for the catapults which were corded with women's hair in the absence of rope. There is a curious confirmation of these figures—at least as far as the projectiles were concerned. For in the little green courtyard outside the Lavigerie Museum at Carthage, some monkish gardener, puzzled by what to do with literally hundreds of these beautifully rounded stone missiles left over from the siege of the city, has placed them lovingly in the mouths of the Roman wine and oil jars, one per jar, so that the whole courtyard is lined along its paths with this ammunition of a 2,000-year-old war. Some of these projectiles are monsters, weighing fifty or sixty pounds; and these have a place of honour among the flower beds. The probability, of course, is that these 'shells' are actually Roman, since they were inward bound from the besiegers' catapults; and this theory seems supported by the neat rows of Carthaginian tombstones which the White Father archaeologists have set up in serried ranks, like shark's teeth. But before the Romans broke into the citadel which stood where now stands this garden full of flowers and small birds the Carthaginians must have heaved back many a twenty- or thirty-pounder from those catapults corded with their women's hair.

It did them no good. Their commanding generals defected to the enemy in order to save their own lives; the city was breached; the fire and pillage continued for twelve successive days. When Carthage was finally reduced to rubble, the symbolic plough was passed over it and the site condemned by solemn imprecations to lie desolate for ever, as Roman piety required.

Thus the religious and patriotic scruples of the Romans were observed, and continued to be observed until the business men decided there was a limit even to piety—and the loss of the rich trade from the African interior was that limit.

The Sahara Desert was about to be conquered and exploited for the first and, up to now, the last time in history.

THREE

'The Third Augusta Legion erected this monument . . .'

I

ABOUT a hundred miles eastwards along the coast from Tripoli stand the ruins of Leptis Magna—or *Lepcis*, as British archaeologists prefer to call it more accurately on the basis of inscriptions. The accepted name, however, is Leptis—not a great name in the annals of the Roman Empire, but the appellation of a city that is, in some respects, the most remarkable monument the Romans have left us.

To begin with, though Leptis was never more than a provincial town on the wrong side of the Mediterranean, it became one of the largest cities of the ancient world—and large even by the standards of modern urbanization. Yet today its vast ruins stand in the middle of nowhere in particular. For this reason, more than Rome itself, it is symbolic of the decline and fall of an empire.

As soon as the visitor walks down the Via Triomphale and through the arch of Septimius, he has the feeling that he is in a city not of a dead civilization but a place which has suddenly been abandoned as though after a war. With repairs and rebuilding, the port would be ready for its old activity; the people would come back. The river still flows down to the sea; the wharves await the ships; the warehouses line the quays; the custom-house is open for business; the great markets are strategically placed; the shops need no signs to announce their wares, for the poultry slab is marked by its marble cockerels, the fish slab by its tunny and octopuses, the oil and wine counters by jars, all in the form of exquisite carved legs supporting the tables on which the shopkeepers displayed their wares. The theatre holding 40,000 people

63

is ready for the next production. The forums and the temples, Christian and pagan, need considerable tidying up, of course; and somebody has to find the water springs which filled the dozens of fountains, cisterns, horse troughs, public baths, and the rest. So far they haven't been able to locate them.

It is all quite fantastic, difficult to believe, and impossible to visit in the course of several days' exploration. The Dutch historian I meet tells me this is his fifty-second visit: he hopes to see and to photograph all of Leptis within the next few years. Even so, neither he nor the archaeologists can keep up with the amount of material they are uncovering week after week and year after year. The museum in the Castello at Tripoli has no more room for the gigantic statues of gods, emperors, the wives of gods, the wives of emperors, and the Greco-Roman sculptures which filled the hundreds of niches in the series of triumphal arches and the many temples. The mosaics, most of which still lie under the sand-dunes, dazzle the eye: they are unbelievably rich and gay, and speak of a life that could have had no rival in ancient or modern times. Leptis Magna, in fact, is the most stupendous abandoned city in Africa; it makes the Roman cities of Italy look drab and lifeless in comparison. Ostia, by contrast, is a dull little port; Pompeii, a city of the dead. But at Leptis the sea is so lilac-coloured, the sky so madonna-blue, the air so clear, that the vast buildings sparkle with life, and the long streets with their latticed fountains and marble benches lead the visitor enchanted down to the sea through a series of triumphal arches.

Several hundred thousand people lived here, then, and lived with every known luxury of civilization—in a country which today supports a few hundred shepherds and farmers who inhabit wattle huts or houses of uncemented rubble. Yet there is no place called Leptis Magna on the local maps. There is a Libyan village called Lebda. So with at least a dozen of the great and flourishing seaports of Roman Africa. They are now only names on the archaeological maps. Gigthis has been replaced by a village of a half a dozen fishermen's shacks called Bou Grara. Sabratha was not inhabited at all until 1922 when Mussolini resettled it with disconsolate South Italian colonists, though it was

a full colony in Roman times and the birthplace of an empress, as Leptis was the birthplace of an emperor.

The cessation of life in a city the size of Leptis, then, is puzzling until the visitor finds his way down to the sea which gave the metropolis its reason for being. The breakwaters are still in place, but the channel which the Romans dredged into the river which runs through the town is silted up. The river itself could no longer carry triremes. The herons stand knee-deep in it fishing; the fallen wharves and bridges have dammed it up; and the sand has blown into the river bed. In fact, across the entrance to the river, a barrage of white sand has finished the sea commerce of Leptis for ever. No ship will ever sail in again.

History gives us some clues as to the causes of this desolation. By the time the Vandals came with their mania for destruction the great African port was already getting old and enfeebled. It was, after all, a thousand years old by then. Moreover, it was involved in the shrinkage of the Roman Empire. It had reached its peak of prosperity and civic splendour during the reign of its native-born son, Septimius Severus, who was to die at the northern extremity of the Roman world, in York, England. Soon after Septimius's death in A.D. 211 the port began a slow decline, as though the life was being drained out of it. The citizens could no longer keep up appearances; and they were frightened, as they had good cause to be. The Third Augusta Legion was no longer in control of Roman Africa; it had disappeared as a cohesive fighting unit; and its outposts, where they were manned at all, were garrisoned by native mercenaries whose allegiance was no longer to the eagles. The barbarians from the desert were now coming in always closer. They had already sacked the sister port of Sabratha. The surrounding country of these great commercial cities—the immense olive groves, palmeries, and wheat fields—was now incapable of supporting hundreds of thousands of city-dwellers; and these same people, exporters, merchants, business men, and bureaucrats, found it more and more difficult to justify their existence. Leptis began to shrink behind closer and closer walls which left the immense suburbs unprotected. The rest of the story of the decay and final death of the metropolis is obvious.

First the Vandals in 455, then the desert barbarians for the remainder of that century, and finally the Arab invaders in the sixth century, finished it off. It was now the turn of nature, which quickly covered the enormous ruins with sand.

Leptis was to receive one final despoliation in modern times. The European consuls in Tripoli spotted the number and variety of the columns that still reared up from the dunes and scurried off with as much as they could. Over 600 marble pillars were despatched to Paris for the Sun King's new palace at Versailles. Scores of other columns were pillaged for the British King George IV's fake ruins at Virginia Water near Windsor. Even so, there is enough left above ground at Leptis to build, or remake, a city the size of a European provincial town; and there is enough left under the sand to occupy archaeologists for the next hundred years.

The place to see all this, and for some future Gibbon to reflect on the significance of ruins, is down on the sand-bar which now separates the sea from the river which still winds, in shallow pools, into the centre of the city. The sea stretching to the north and Europe, the river flowing from the hinterland of Africa, and the narrow strip of sand dividing the two tell most of the story of the vast buildings which lie behind. It is then that the traveller ponders on the rise and fall of empires and asks why cities the size of Leptis, Sabratha, Gigthis, Appolonia, and many whose names are only memories, flourished in Roman times. Where did their wealth come from? Not from Europe, certainly, and not all from the desert which lay immediately behind them. It must, therefore, have come from Central Africa, the produce of which was brought along the great trans-Saharan caravan routes from Timbuktu and Lake Chad for export to the European markets.

Hence the Roman trading posts and forts at Germa, at Bu Ngem, Garbia, Ghadames, possibly Rhat, and westwards along the fringes of the Sahara to the Atlas Mountains and the Atlantic. The Romans built these strongpoints as frontier and customs-stations from which their expeditions and patrols could set out into the desert on reconnaissance or punitive campaigns against

the bandits who interfered with the caravans. The system, making due allowance for climate and terrain, was comparable to that used in Britain and Germany, except that the frontier fortifications in the latter countries were eventually built up into a solid and unbroken wall owing to the impossibility of civilizing the northern barbarians. The Saharan tribesmen gave the legions less trouble, though we have records of several campaigns in the desert itself. One of them was commanded by Suetonius Paulinus, the future victor over Boadicea in a battle of annihilation between the Britons and the Ninth Legion. Suetonius crossed the Atlas Mountains[1] and plunged on into the desert for ten days, 'across a torrid belt of black dust to the River Ger'. The River Ger is unidentifiable; but the black dust obviously refers to the *reg*, so characteristic of this region of the desert.

II

The exploration of North Africa by the Romans took a long time, for the curse put upon Carthage was a solemn one: it forbad the rebuilding of the Phoenician city in any shape or form for all time to come. In fact, it was well over a hundred years before the Romans knew what to do about their new province of Africa. Arguments as to whether to abandon it altogether raged back and forth in the Senate; the conservative view was summed up by a senator who stated that it would cost more to keep the African colony going than Rome would get out of it on account of the size of the military force needed to keep the barbarians in check.

But this spokesman was a conservative business man of the old school. Times changed, and the new men of the Empire saw that it was time to exploit Africa as they had exploited the other Mediterranean provinces. The Roman mob needed bread, and Italy no longer grew enough wheat to supply them. A man with the authority and prestige to challenge the old imprecation laid

1. One thousand seven hundred years later the French general de Saint-Arnaud, who thought he was the first commander to cross the range by this route, found an inscription commemorating the Roman military road through the same defile.

upon the site of Carthage was called for. The man was Caesar Augustus.

Colonies were now established in Numidia (Tunisia) whilst Mauretania (Algeria and Morocco) was provisionally assigned to the African kings loyal to Rome. This was shrewd politics since the Romans were not yet in a position to subjugate the tribes who lived in the Algerian and Moroccan mountains; so, for the time being, they left them alone under their native chieftains. One of these was the Moor, King Juba, who took the wrong side in the Civil War and paid for it with his life. The last we hear of him is his wandering around the Tunisian countryside with his companion, the Roman soldier Petreius, trying to find a haven. But no city would let Juba enter—understandable in view of the fact he had announced he would burn his capital with everybody, including himself, in it. Defeated, denied sanctuary, and knowing what would happen if Caesar's men caught them alive, Juba and Petreius decided to kill each other in a duel. It must have been quite a fight, since both men were professional soldiers. Juba the Moor had been in the field since he was a child; Petreius the Roman was the son of a chief centurion. Who killed whom in this duel we are not told, only that the survivor was finished off by a slave.

Caesar, then, was disappointed in his expectation of including King Juba in his triumph, but he had some compensation in being able to parade the children of his dead enemies before the populace. Thus Juba's son, Juba the Second, was exhibited at Caesar's triumph, along with the children of another of his enemies, the twins, Sun and Moon,[1] offspring of Mark Antony and Cleopatra.

These three royal children were kept in Rome under the imperial aegis and were, in fact, reared as Romans of Rome. In due course Prince Juba was married to Princess Moon (Selene) and the royal couple sent off to Africa to rule over the old kingdom of Mauretania. They chose as their capital the ancient Carthaginian colony of Iol, renamed it Caesarea in honour of Julius and Augustus, and soon made it one of the most splendid cities of

1. That is, Helios and Selene.

the Mediterranean. Today Caesarea is a fishing village called Cherchel lying about a hundred miles west of Algiers and there is very little left to remind the traveller of King Juba II and his queen Selene, daughter of Cleopatra, unless it is the Greek statues now housed in a modest musum on the site of the ruins. For the palaces and public buildings of Caesarea were once adorned with hundreds of statues, many of them copies of famous Greek originals, including those of Alcamenes, Phidias, and Praxiteles. A number of these sculptures somehow survived the axes of both the Vandals and the Arabs, notably a most glorious Venus—the Venus of Cherchel, as she is now called.

Indeed, it seems to have been this African king's passion as a collector which may have been responsible for the greatest underwater find of classical archaeology—the Mahdia shipwreck. The treasures taken from this sunken vessel fill two of the largest halls in the Bardo Museum, and they represent perhaps the finest collection of Greek bronzes in the world. But to get an idea of the tonnage of the cargo this ship was bringing to Africa from Greece one should begin by looking at the two huge lead anchors; the impression is that they would hold the *Queen Mary* at a pinch! Such, then, was the size of the trireme loaded with marble columns, statues, furniture, household utensils, and bronzes. We don't know what happened. Perhaps she was putting into one of the many Roman ports along the shallow coast between Sousse and Sfax—ports which are no longer used today—and ran aground. Perhaps she was attacked by pirates, or sunk in a storm. We only know that she was loaded with the treasures of the Greek ateliers for which King Juba was the best customer in Africa. The bronze statue of the young wrestler, nude, bending forward as if to get his first hold on his opponent, his head raised, his expression wary yet quite fearless, is surely one of the finest works of art of ancient or any other time. The little bronze dancing dwarf, too, with her big head, her short arms raised as she clacks her castanets, her stumpy left leg raised in a dance step, is unique. Very few people see these treasures, for the Bardo Museum out of season is almost empty. The Tunisian guards' children run around playing among the show-cases. And fewer still see what is perhaps the most extraordinary Greek bronze of all, since it is discreetly set aside in the manner of the *oggetti pornografici* of Pompeii. A pity! Hercules Drunk is a masterpiece of art, combining in one twenty-inch-high figure of all the humour and ribaldry of Suetonius, Rabelais, Fielding, Hogarth, and all that company who saw man at his most comic—the hero leaning back at such a perilous angle that his calves bulge, his club held behind as he staggers out of some tavern to relieve himself—the lord of the earth in his cups.

So we see from these reminders that Juba's capital was once a great centre of art and culture. For, by one of those rare chances in history, King Juba II was a scholar who devoted himself to art and science as other monarchs to war and venery. He wrote equally well in the Punic, Latin, and Greek languages and immersed himself in the study of geography, botany, history, archaeology, and philology. Scholars and artists were always welcome in his domain; and from all accounts he was a happy, peaceful, and much-loved monarch. He appears, however, to have been slightly henpecked. (Was Selene as beautiful as her mother? We are not told.) For there seems to have been some dissension between the royal couple as to whose blood was the bluest—hers by descent from the Pharaohs; his by descent from King Masinissa.[1] Evidently Queen Selene won this argument, because we find King Juba falsifying geography by making the rivers of his Mauretanian kingdom tributaries of the Egyptian Nile—a piece of chicanery comparable to the genealogists of the British royal family tracing their ancestry to King David. Certainly Selene never forgot her birth or her homeland. She insisted on setting up a temple to Isis, which housed a sacred crocodile expressly brought from the Nile. She also had her way in the naming of her first-born son: he was called Ptolemy. But neither Isis nor the sacred crocodile was able to save the African prince from the insane rage of Caligula who had him murdered in the dungeons of Rome.

1. The Numidian who conducted a cavalry charge and begot several children at the age of eighty.

III

So ended the day of the African kings in A.D. 40, when the
Romans decided that Africa was too rich a province to share with
local monarchs. Now, 200 years after the destruction of Carthage,
they wanted undisputed possession of all of Africa, down to the
land of the Pygmies: Mauretania, Numidia, Tripolitania, Egypt,
and the deserts below.

Once Rome was ready to take over the administration of a
territory she went about it in her usual efficient manner. The
limits to the province were provisionally marked with a ditch;
the legions set up camps in strategic places; and a network of
roads and forts was built by the army engineers. This enormous
task was principally the work of the Third Augusta Legion, a
body of 12,000 men, including the native auxiliaries, or *goums*.
This fantastic corps was to control an area of roughly a million
and a half square miles for the next two and a half centuries. They
fought the wars, pacified the tribes, built the roads, forts, and
cities, patrolled the mountains and deserts, and policed the
desert. The story of North Africa in Roman times is the story
of the Third Augusta Legion.

This story can be followed thanks to the Roman legions' habit
of commemorating their work, however small and inconse-
quential it may have seemed, with a dedicatory plaque. Thus it
is that deep in the desert—at Ghadames, for instance—the French
explorer Henri Duveyrier found an inscription which read: *To
the Emperor Caesar Marcus Aurelius Severus, and Julia Mamaea,
Mother of Augustus and of the Legion, a cohort of the III Aug. Leg.,
commanded by its Centurion, erected this Monument.*[1] A rather sad
little stone, in view of what life in that part must have been like.
For Ghadames, literally a one-horse town in Duveyrier's day
('There is only one horse (a mare) in the entire town,' he
writes under the date August 12th, 1860), could not have

1. Marcus Aurelius Severus Alexander: emperor A.D. 222–35; son of
Mamaea; murdered with his mother by the legions on the Rhine. Not to be
confused with Marcus Aurelius, the emperor-philosopher (A.D. 121–80).

been a particularly desirable post for a Roman centurion in A.D. 225.

On the other hand, a Roman legionnaire had very little time to feel sorry for himself. He knew no other life and had no other home but the camp. In a great many cases, from the rank of centurion down, he had been born into the army—meaning that his father was a legionnaire and his mother a respectable camp-follower who would have become a legal wife on the completion of the soldier's term of service.

In short, the Roman legion was a complete little world in itself, with a corporate mind and, indeed, a corporate soul. A soldier from the start to the end of his twenty-five years' service knew of no other world but the camp, for he had no home, no wife, and no family. No military unit in history has ever been so efficiently organized for its function: the legion, in fact, was almost as infallible as a machine. It is only seldom that we find its component parts behaving otherwise than as cogs in a powerful engine of war. When they rebelled against the system the punishments, as we shall see, were ferocious.

The organization of a Roman legion can best be seen in the table opposite. The English titles are, of course, only rough equivalents.

The Roman army, then, was the most efficient military organization that mankind has ever devised, for not only was it, in general, invincible on the field of battle, but also indispensable in peacetime as a corps of engineers, builders, colonizers, and civilizers. In comparison, modern professional armies are largely supernumerary. In the event of war, civilians of both sexes are required to bear the brunt of the fighting, with the participation of children in a semi-passive role; in peacetime a standing army often does nothing more useful than escort dead monarchs to their tombs. The Roman legion, in contrast, was the most productive single unit in society. It literally built Western Europe from the ground up, and almost every important city of that continent was first founded, then given law and order, by the Roman legions, as nearly every city built by them has since been destroyed several times over by modern armies.

The actual business of combat to a Roman legion, then, was

The Organization of a Roman Legion

Roman Title	English Equivalent
Legatus (Augusti) (legionis)	Commanding General
Tribunus (laticlavis)	Senior Staff Officer
Praefectus (castrorum)	Quartermaster
Primus Pilus (Chief Centurion)	Brigade Commander
59 Centurions	Company Commanders
Signifer (Standard Bearer)	Regimental Sergeant-Major
Optio	Sergeant-Major
Tessevarius	Sergeant(s)
Armorum custos, medicus, etc.	Corporal(s)
Miles	Private soldier

only incidental to a way of life which consisted for the most part of a pioneering experiment comparable to the conquests and colonizations of the New World, except that the Romans were less ruthless in their treatment of the aboriginals. The wars that were a necessary part of conquest were, of course, equally relentless and, from the point of view of the conquered, equally disastrous. 'They make a desert and call it peace,' said a British chieftain—or Tacitus has him saying so. But the wars and campaigns undertaken by the Romans were at least relatively 'clean' (man against man), having little, if any, resemblance to modern warfare with its incredible confusion of military, scientific, and civilian theory. To a Roman commander a battle was an engineering problem: clearing and levelling the ground, removing the debris, and preparing the site for rebuilding.

So, in a sense, the legion marched out of their camp en route to battle more like a company of engineers and road builders than a division of fighting-men. There was no comparison with a modern military unit on the move. The Romans, on the whole, moved much quicker. There was no waiting around for transport. The legion marched its regulation twenty miles a day, twenty-five if accelerated, day in and day out. In the vanguard rode the cavalry scouts; behind them came the engineers and road-makers; next the artillerymen; then the commanding general with his staff, followed by the banners and trumpeters; then the infantrymen drawn up six abreast with a centurion in the rear of each company to keep discipline; then the baggage of the legion carried by servants and beasts of burden; then the rearguard of mercenary troops; and finally a detachment of picked cavalry troops. Cavalry units also rode reconnaissance on both flanks of the column.

In the event of an attack by an enemy the infantry formed a hollow square into which the baggage train was moved for safety. It was the function of the light infantry to attack the enemy from the flanks, pinning them against the wall of shields until the cavalry could get amongst them. No barbarian troops ever found a method of breaking this formation, and it can be generally said that where the legions were defeated it was because of rashness, or cowardice, or disobedience.[1]

Thus the Third Augusta Legion marched out from its permanent camp at Lambaesis during the 300 years that it controlled the mountains, rivers, and deserts of North Africa from the Atlantic Ocean to the shores of Tripoli, from the Mediterranean in the north to the Saharan outposts in the south. Like the legions in other parts of the Roman world, it settled down to a civilized community life without ever losing its identity or changing its *raison d'être*. Its organization remained the same from the beginning to the end. Rank, conditions of service, food, duties, privileges, and pay varied only slightly. The principal change was in the nationalities of the recruits. In the beginning only a Roman

---

1. There are, of course, numerous examples of such incidents in the history of the Roman army, as in any other army. See Caesar's *Wars*.

citizen could enlist in the legions. In the end enlistment automatically implied citizenship. The Third Augusta Legion's ranks
were increasingly filled by native Africans, the sons of legionnaires whose common-law wives lived in villages outside the
main camp.

But irrespective of nationality a legionnaire was dedicated to
his unit like a priest to his order, and the relationship was not
dissimilar. It was a quasi-religious one and entailed swearing a
sacred oath. The chief deity of the army was, in theory, the
Emperor; in fact, it was the regimental spirit, or *numen*. This 'soul
of the legion', as Tacitus calls it, was symbolized in the Eagle
which was bestowed by the Emperor himself. The Eagle, then,
was the godhead of the division and was worshipped as such. It
protected every individual soldier by its divine emanation and
was carried into battle by the bravest and most distingushed of
the officers. As the position of the Eagle marked divisional headquarters, it follows that its loss pretty well signified the defeat
and annihilation of the legion.

The other hodge-podge of gods and goddesses which the
soldiers collected in their campaigns were of minor importance.
The oriental gods were popular with the soldiers since most of
them personified a 'good-time' cult. The Carthaginian Astarte,
for instance—equivalent of the Hebrew Ashtoreth, the Cyprian
Aphrodite, and the Roman Venus—was neither more nor less
than a deified harlot who tolerated sexual licence, whether in or
out of wedlock. Modern writers who dignify such goddesses with
symbolic attributes (fertility rites, and so forth) seem to forget
that the ancients accepted sex, in all its manifestations, as an inescapable fact of life. Judging by what went on in the venereal
temples all over the classical world, the shrines of Venus and her
sister-goddesses were neither more nor less than brothels sancti-
fied by the odour of incense. We are told that the Carthaginian
women sacrified their virginity within the confines of Astarte's
temples, and we can assume that those who took advantage of
this practice were not deeply concerned with fertility rites. For
Astarte's altars were also served at all seasons by sacred prosti-
tutes, both male and female, which makes it difficult to believe

that the worshippers went to 'church' in the same frame of mind, or with the same object in view, as, say, an English Baptist on his way to Sunday Service.

The other gods adopted by the legions were mainly local deities which the soldiers probably regarded as mascots, or good-luck charms. The legions in Britain picked up some pretty odd-looking deities, including one old fellow with a club who goes under the name of Taranis. Similarly, the Third Augusta Legion during its long sojourn in Africa acquired a collection of minor deities whose attributes and functions now escape us, though we know their names from their dedicatory altars—Thasun and Motmanius and Jorchobol. These vulgar deities were the mascots of the men. The officers favoured the more aristocratic Mithras, whose cult of austerity, trial by ordeal, and all-male membership has a curious resemblance to the war-cult of Prussia and Nazi Germany.

Very important to an Africanized legion like the Third Augusta were the priests and snake-charmers.

The priest's job was to examine the entrails of the sacrificed animals for the auguries, but it is highly unlikely that the commanders of a Roman legion took the slightest notice of a corporal-priest and his mumbo-jumbo, any more than the general of a modern division would do more than go through the motions of closing his eyes and bowing his head when the chaplain prayed for victory before a tank battle. Conversely, we may be reasonably sure that the *haruspex* found nothing to displease his superiors as he raked over the offal of the sacrificed animals.

The snake-charmer, on the other hand, was a useful man to have around in a land of scorpions and snakes, and his prestige in a practical unit like a corps of fighting men must have been higher than the priest's. No doubt his prestige depended upon the efficacy of his anti-venom remedies, because something has to be done, and done quickly, when either pest strikes. We are not told much about this side of campaigning in Roman times— whether scorpions, for instance, were the plague they are today in the oases. Today you can see settlements which have been recently abandoned because of the child mortality caused by snakes and scorpions. There is not much sleeping parents can do if a restless baby brushes away a scorpion in the night. What did the Roman soldiers camping out in the sand do if they were stung by these loathsome arachnida? What did they do about the myriads of flies and mosquitoes that cover the face and hands? How much typhoid, dysentery, and malaria did they have to cope with?

Of course, every legion had its hospital with a medical staff, including surgeons, dentists, and oculists. These low-grade specialists were certainly busy men during active campaigning, and it is not surprising that classical medicine has little to say about minor problems like snake and scorpion bites and emphasizes rather the treatment of wounds. One of the most important books in the Hippocratic Collection concerns 'Wounds of the Head'. Another is devoted to surgery.

> When operating [says Hippocrates], the surgeon, if sitting, should raise his feet in a direct line with his knees so that they are practically together, with the knees raised and far enough apart for the elbows to rest on them. The attendant is to hold down the patient and listen to the commands of the surgeon.

'Listening to the commands of the surgeon' was important enough for Plato to recommend that a doctor take a course in oratory to persuade his patient to accept the treatment he recommended. Understandable, inasmuch as Greek (and hence Roman) surgeons were liable to open the larynx in order to remove a fish-bone from the throat. These operations were skilfully performed, the obstruction being cleanly removed; but, as the Greek epigram says, though the operation was successful, the patient died. Moreover, 'holding down the patient' in an age without anaesthetics was sound advice in view of the classical surgeons' partiality for trepanning, their principal instruments being carpenters' saws, brace and bits, mallets, and forceps. In the case of head wounds, the procedure was as follows:

> Make an incision proportionate to the size of the wound and fill the whole opening with a tent [?] which will expand the

wound very wide next day; and along with the tent, apply a dressing of flour powdered in vinegar. The next day remove the tent and scrape the bone, and so on until the mischief be discovered. If the bone is broken, trepanning will be required.

IV

When he wasn't actually fighting, the Roman legionnaire was kept constantly occupied in both military and peaceful pursuits which convinced him of his usefulness as a Roman citizen as well as a soldier. Naturally his primary function was his professional fitness, and all his training was directed to this end. That training was almost identical with the Commando tactics employed in the Second World War, since the Roman soldier had to rely on his own physical prowess in combat, much as the Commandos did in their raids on the enemy coast. The legionnaire, then, began his training with route marches intended to condition him to covering twenty miles in five hours with full pack. Next came barrack-square drilling and formation exercises, with special emphasis on running, jumping, and swimming. A Roman soldier was expected to swim a river, vault a ditch, and, on order to attack, to finish the last stretch between himself and the enemy at a run. Arriving in the enemy lines, he was required to overpower his opponent in physical combat. For this purpose target practice with dummies was undertaken in exactly the same manner as bayonet drill in modern armies, including the same ferocious yelling as the recruit was exhorted by the sergeants to strike at the vital organs of his enemy.

These were the exercises which the men of the Third Augusta Legion performed so competently in the presence of the Emperor Hadrian that the Commander-in-Chief issued a special order of the day complimenting both officers and rank and file. The Emperor notes in particular how well the infantry performed the most difficult of manœuvres, which was simultaneously to hurl both the javelin and shield at the enemy on the word of command. Anybody who cares to try this feat will appreciate the Emperor's praise. Hadrian also complimented the cavalry on the way they jumped into the saddle fully dressed. True, the Roman horses were smaller than the modern charger, but vaulting on to a horse in full armour would now be limited to circus acrobats. It is no wonder that the Emperor was pleased with his African legion, and no wonder that the Third Augusta commemorated his visit and his words of praise on a marble plaque which still survives.

The Romans, then, had a simple formula for victory: training and discipline. Both were strict to the point of ferocity. They had the advantage that they made defeat on the field of battle a crime for which every soldier was responsible. Defeat could only be due to cowardice, desertion, mutiny, or insubordination, the punishment for which was death as it has been, theoretically, ever since. But whereas modern military law concerns itself with the individual, Roman law held the entire unit responsible. If it had been practicable a whole legion would have been put to death for any one of these crimes; instead the system of *decimatio* was enforced whereby the death penalty was inflicted on every tenth man in the company, regiment, or whole division, if need be. The method was for the nine to beat and stone to death the tenth. Caesar, Antony, and Augustus all resorted to the *decimatio* in their time. A cohort of the Third Augusta Legion was 'decimated' after its defeat by the Berber chieftain Tacfarinas in A.D. 18, so it is not surprising that the dead men's comrades eventually hunted down and killed the rebel. Nevertheless, it was not easy to enforce the decimation, since even under a totalitarian military system like that of the Roman army, soldiers were disinclined to murder their comrades in cold blood, and we have examples of where they refused to do so. The commanders sought alternatives to this practice and eventually hit upon an effective substitute. Mutinous or disobedient troops, together with their officers, were left outside the fort to fend for themselves and, in enemy territory, to fight for their lives by night as well as by day.

Apart from the decimation, the other punishments were similar to those enforced in all armies up to our own times. Stealing, giving false witness, and slacking were punished by flogging, this being the job of the centurion. Flogging was particularly resented by the soldiers, and the centurions usually got themselves hated in consequence. They could sometimes be bought off, but the infantryman's pay seldom stretched to the luxury of bribes. He drew about £10[1] a year, from which was deducted the cost of his food and clothing. He was supposed to save £3 of what remained and deposit it in the legion's Savings Account Bank; but judging from the letters home of the private soldiers they found difficulty in even making ends meet, let alone putting something aside. One recruit by-passes his parsimonious father, who gave him nothing on his visit to the camp, and addresses his mother:

My dear Mother, I hope that this finds you well. On receipt of this letter, I shall be obliged if you will send me £2. I haven't got a farthing left, because I have bought a donkey-cart and spent all my money on it. Do send me a riding-coat, some oil, and above all my monthly allowance. When I was last home, you promised not to leave me penniless, and now you treat me like a dog. Father came to see me the other day, and gave me nothing. Everybody laughs at me now and says 'his father is a soldier, his father gives him nothing'. Valerius's mother sent him a pair of pants, a measure of oil, a parcel of food, and £2. Do send me some money and don't leave me like this. Give my love to everybody at home. Your loving son.

If the common soldiers were as penniless as this it is understandable that they resented having to bribe the centurions, who were getting £150 a year, and, in the case of the chief centurion, £1,000.

Yet dissatisfaction with the pay, food, or conditions of service was not, on the whole, serious, due to the second function of the legion, which was its peacetime role of civilizing occupied territories. In Britain the Second, Ninth, Fourteenth, and Twentieth Legions brought law and order, cities and towns, roads and bridges, to a barbarous and inhospitable land under conditions of great difficulty. In Germany, where the Watch on the Rhine

1. In view of the variations in the actual purchasing value of modern money, no particular 'rate of exchange' can be given for the Roman soldier's wages.

needed a holding force of eight to ten legions, or one-third of the entire Roman army, the process of improving the country by roads, bridges, and the Saône-Moselle canal was continued under a succession of governors, though none of them had much success in civilizing the Huns to the east of the river.

But it was in Africa that the army accomplished its greatest achievements, turning one of the most backward areas into one of the most civilized and prosperous provinces of the Empire— a region which was to produce emperors, soldiers, saints, philosophers, and writers until it was destroyed by the Arabs and returned to its pristine state of barbarism. All this metamorphosis of Africa from a land of 'feathered Libyans' and 'cave-dwellers who squeaked like bats' and tribesmen whose principle diet was crushed locusts into a land of splendid cities, villages, and farms was largely the achievement of the Third Augusta Legion. This dedicated band of soldiers not only brought law and order to the habitable regions of North Africa but they pushed the desert back to a line which had never been attained before or since.

It is with the conquest of the desert by the Third Augusta Legion with which we are now concerned.

FOUR

The lost cities

To GET a true idea of the extent of the Roman occupation of
what is now quasi-desert, abandoned except for Berber shepherds,
the traveller should visit those Roman cities which are off the
tourist route—perhaps with the old guide-book exhortation in
mind:

> For the following excursions, fatigue and the absence of
> comfort are compensated for by the strangeness of the country
> to be crossed.

The country which lies to the east of the Great Western Sand
Sea is an example, especially that region of salt marshes along the
coast which the Greek geographers called the Lesser Syrte. Here,
at a fishing village of a half a dozen huts, stands the Roman city
of Gigthis, about which we know practically nothing except what
the ruins themselves can tell us. There is certainly nobody there
to give the visitor a pat commentary of what it was all about.
Naturally, from the brown tent of a shepherd family a small boy
soon appears with his handful of Roman coins. But the coins are
not interesting. What is interesting is the existence of such a large
city in such a desolate and abandoned country. But there rising
up out of the sand-dunes are the temples, the curia, the court
house, the public baths, the forum, shops, and houses of a city
which must have supported twenty to thirty thousand people.
And all over the barren ground for hundreds of yards in every
direction lie the broken pots, vases, lamps, and kitchen utensils
of a once busy and thriving community.

It seems that sixty years ago some amateur French archaeologist with the aid of the French officers isolated in their camps in this region did some haphazard digging at Gigthis, so that today the bare outlines of the city emerge, with its well-defined public monuments centred around the spacious forum. The forum itself has been cleared with its surrounding portico of columns; and contingent to the forum, the more important public buildings, all built of massive stonework covered with a variety of marble, of deep red marble predominating.

Gigthis, then, was obviously one of the principal Afro-Roman ports, and its history parallels that of Leptis Magna, Sabratha, and a score of smaller maritime cities through which flowed the trade of Africa. As with Leptis and the other ports, it is difficult today to see how the old ships came up to the piers and warehouses lining the now empty wadis which meander through the centre of these land-locked ruins. The answer is that the Romans dredged channels from the sea and banked the wadis so that the triremes could be brought right into the heart of the city. All these engineering works have since been destroyed by Man and nature.

The urbanization and exploitation of Africa, then, was made possible in the beginning not merely by military conquest, but more by the peacetime contributions of the legions to the new provinces. For once the job of pacifying the region had been completed, the army engineers and architects set about building roads, aqueducts, and cities. Thus by A.D. 50 the major work of pacification was finished. From then onwards the fighting elements of the legion were only engaged on punitive expeditions against recalcitrant tribesmen in the desert to the south and Moorish bandits in the Atlas Mountains.

Now began the second great task of the Africa-based army, the control of the frontiers by a line of forts, observation posts and signal stations and the building of advanced bases deep in the desert to protect the caravan routes. Behind this frontier shield called the *limes*, the cities, towns, hamlets, and farmsteads lived in peace and prosperity for the next three to four hundred years. Thanks to the legion, a hundred flourishing centres of civilization sprang up all over North Africa with the usual refinement of Roman life in the form of temples, libraries, baths, and theatres.

It is almost impossible, even when standing in the centre of a city the size of Gigthis or Leptis Magna, to visualize the order, prosperity, and, indeed, splendour of this civilization whose ruins are still scattered over tens of thousands of square miles of a continent. In comparison, subsequent invaders of North Africa have left so little behind. The Arabs left their mosques, forts, and souks, but some of their buildings wouldn't have stood up this long without the massive pillars and squared-off foundation stones pillaged from temples, amphitheatres, and public buildings. The alleys of the medinas all display their Roman columns and cornice stones helping to prop up the gimcrack buildings above; and as far down in the desert as the southern oases, Roman wells and dams and irrigation tunnels make life a little more practicable for the modern inhabitants. Arabs, Turks, Spaniards, French, and Italians have all left their imprint on this land—but it is a superficial mark compared with the civilization the Romans left behind. That civilization was smashed to pieces, of course, by subsequent invaders, but it is still visible in literally thousands of towns and villages right down into the wasteland of the central Sahara. In a sense, it is also still functioning, for Roman aqueducts, Roman wells, Roman tunnels, and cisterns are still supplying some cities and some oases with water.

A small boy named Ali takes me to see the ruins of some forgotten Roman city we think was called Uppena. Ali comes out of a hovel among the olive groves, akin architecturally to the thatched huts of the savages so despised by the Romans. We eventually find Uppena among the groves, and it is clear that this, too, was once a well-built and well-organized provincial city, with its fortress, church, theatre, and baths, and an efficient system of aqueducts and water tunnels no longer found anywhere in North Africa outside the big cities. The public buildings and private homes of Uppena also provided the museums with some of the magnificent mosaics portraying the richness and beauty of life 1,800 years ago. Yet what must life be like today to Ali and his parents? They have nothing but their hovel, a mattress, and a few cooking pots. For water they depend on a Roman well of such horrendous proportions and depth Ali, with much rolling of the eyes, tells me that it is death to approach it. One sees why. The mouth of the well is nearly twenty feet across, and its depth some eighty feet. It is beautifully constructed of fitted stones, and quite obviously Roman. The wells the Arabs made in the desert are usually only holes in the ground without proper walling, and they fill up with sand as soon as they are neglected. But when the Roman engineers went after water, they built an aqueduct or well as they built a temple or a fort.

But despite all that remains above and below ground—the hundreds of cities, the thousands of miles of roads, the frontier forts and farmhouses—we still cannot fully estimate, or even comprehend, the extent of the Roman conquest of North Africa and the desert to the south of it. At the present state of our knowledge, we can only assert that the Romans had at least 2,500,000 acres of what is now full desert colonized and under cultivation in South Algeria alone. If we assume, as the evidence suggests, that the Romans followed the same practice of building roads, forts, and irrigation networks in Morocco, Tunisa, and Libya, as in Algeria, the total area exploited under the Empire and now abandoned would be 10,000,000 acres at the lowest estimate.

Until recently this was impossible to believe in view of the almost complete desiccation of these desert zones today. How could any kind of settled communities survive in this desolation of rock and gravel, where not even a blade of grass is now growing?

Part of the answer was provided by one man who spent three years looking for the evidence. This was Colonel Jean Baradez, of the French Air Force, specialist in aerial photography and an amateur archaeologist, who spent three years, from 1946 to 1949, surveying the desert of South Algeria for traces of Roman occupation.

The results of his work is one of the most astonishing achievements of archaeology. Flying continuously for three successive years back and forth along the fringes of the desert, Colonel Baradez took hundreds of high-altitude photographs of the Roman frontier as far as it was known from the Roman road maps which give us the names of the forts along the frontier, together with the distances between them and the principal cities.[1] Baradez was not after particular or isolated ruins which could have been better studied by low- or medium-level photography; but vast expanses of country which could be examined and studied to give the kind of general picture needed for a large-scale map of Roman occupation of the desert. What he found will keep the historian and archaeologists busy for the next hundred years if it were decided (or were even possible) to explore every piece of evidence that his photographs clearly and sharply reveal. In short, Colonel Baradez's survey suggests, for the first time, the full extent of the military and civil organization along the desert frontiers—an example of colonization that has no parallel for planning, efficiency, and success in all history. For the construction of ditches, roads, forts, castles, observation posts, and signalling towers along a frontier of 1,500 miles was not undertaken simply to keep the Saharan nomads from attacking the great and prosperous cities of Africa Proconsularis but to prepare and exploit the ground for a large settlement of farmers. That this policy succeeded is proved by Colonel Baradez's magnificent aerial survey which shows the remains of hundreds of villages and farming communities where today there is nothing but eroded rocks.

Even the experts are still puzzled as to how the Romans accomplished this seemingly superhuman task of erecting so many outposts in the wasteland, let alone bringing in water without which any work of settlement was a waste of time. Arguments also continue, and will continue for a long time, as to whether the *limes*, or frontier, was a military zone intended to keep the barbarians out altogether, or, conversely, to let them come in through customs-control points. The same argument is still going

1. For instance, *The Peutinger Table*, a probable road map, and *The Antonine Itinerary*, both of the third century A.D.

on in regard to the precise function of Hadrian's Wall across Northern Britain.

In short, we know next to nothing of why, how, or when the Saharan fortifications were built, for, as in the case of the occupation of Britain, it is difficult to see why the Romans bothered with such inhospitable territory. Just as they got nothing except a little tin and leather out of Britain in return for their immense labours in pacifying and civilizing that province, so the produce of the Saharan settlements was negligible in terms of the great export-import trade of the North African littoral. Why did they trouble?

We don't really know—though the most plausible theory is that imperial Rome in the first century A.D. badly needed a new source of supply to feed the overcrowded cities. From the time of Augustus Caesar the Italian countryside was being depopulated as people flocked to the towns for free bread and circuses. The feeding of these mobs was an integral part of imperial policy. North Africa, then, was considered and looked at with a view to exploiting it as the granary of Italy. And this was what it eventually became, for once the Roman military and administrative machine had been put into motion, nothing seemed able to stop it, or change its course. The machine began its operations with the road and fortification works of the Third Augusta Legion which was sent to Africa in the reign of Augustus, and immediately set about building a road from Gabes on the coast inland to their winter quarters at Haidra. For the next 200 years when the legion was not actually campaigning its engineers continued to construct a network of roads right across North Africa. At the same time they, together with the veterans of the legion, built a score of cities which were to become among the largest and most prosperous urban centres of the Empire. It was an engineer of the Third Augusta who specialized in constructing water tunnels and was constantly loaned by his commander to communities short of water. We see an example of this kind of engineering in the Roman water tunnel bored deep into the mountain from the Blue Grotto on Capri where the Emperor Tiberius took up his residence.

There were in the Roman provinces two kinds of roads, both built by the legion, one type considered civil, the other military. The civil roads were main highways, wide and well paved, used for public transport and the swift movement of the post. The military roads were narrower and more direct and usually cut straight across country from fort to fort. In their usual methodical manner the legion erected a stone signpost every mile—or, more precisely, every 1,480 metres—of the way along their vast network of main roads. Well over 2,000 of these milestones have been found and recorded. One can imagine how many more lie under the sand and rubble of North Africa.

As the legion pacified the mountains and deserts of Africa Proconsularis, they built forts at all strategic positions and linked them up by a series of turrets and towers which resembled the mile-castle system used along Hadrian's Wall in Britain. In other words, the system was designed to keep every unit of soldiers, however small, in visual touch with each other, both by night and by day. Hence the series of hundreds of castles, turrets, and observation posts along the military roads and desert frontiers. Signalling at night was done by fires; and by day either by smoke or semaphores. It was an efficient, almost foolproof system of controlling vast areas of wild country, and it explains how the Romans were able to occupy 1,500,000 square miles of North Africa for several centuries with a corps of some 12,000 men.

Once the great fertile regions south of the coast had been secured by the system of roads, forts, cities, and villages, so that oil and grain supplies by which Africa helped to feed almost the whole of Italy were assured, the army was free to push deeper into the desert. First it established camps and forts at the principal oases on the caravan routes which went down into the interior of Africa. These forts, like that at Ghadames, were built and garrisoned by detachments of the Third Augusta Legion. They were next linked together by a ditch which gradually ran right across the northern fringes of the Sahara Desert proper. Behind this ditch ran a road, or track, for the use of the army patrols. Inside, and in some cases outside, the frontier grew up in a series of fortified farmsteads designed and built under the direction of army engineers. It is probable that these farmhouses were turned over to veterans of the legion, together with the necessary slaves and servants to farm the land. From the reliefs carved on the tombs of these colonists we can get a good working picture of the activities of these frontiersmen. Horses and, later, camels are used for ploughing, and crops are harvested under the eye of the master who directs the work from his camp-chair. This frontiersman, then, can be almost directly compared to his counterpart in the Southern States of America during the eighteenth and nineteenth centuries where large plantations were hacked out of the wilderness by slave labour. And as in the case of the Romano-African colonist, the American planter belonged to an organized militia which was an integral part of a professional army. Thus new lands were developed despite the threat of the local tribesmen. The principal difference, of course, was the abundance of water in one case and the almost total absence of it in the other.

How, then, did the Romans overcome the problem of aridity in the desert?

Excavations and, in particular, Colonel Baradez's aerial survey have given us some of the answers to this key question.

The main camps and forts, of course, were always built where there were springs or wells on the theory that whoever controlled the water supply controlled the country for miles around. But the colonists who pushed farther and farther south into the actual desert—the *hammada* or *reg* as the case might be—did not always have access to springs or wells. They had to depend on the rainfall and the wadis, the nearest thing in the desert to rivers or brooks. The Arabic word *wadi*, or *oued*, is the proper word, since it implies a fissure in the earth which channels off water when there is any, and is otherwise dry, baked hard by the sun. As a source of water and irrigation, the wadis of North Africa and Tripolitania are practically useless today. Some of them which drain off the springs support life for a few inhabitants clustered nearby in huts or tents. Those which have no drainage apart from the spring rainfall are merely ravines which split up the land into cracks and fissures. But they were not so in Roman times. To the contrary, millions of acres were cultivated by means of a highly efficient system of hydraulic works and soil conservation which has never been equalled, let alone surpassed. So that one could say that of all the aspects of civilization that the Romans left us their agricultural theory and practice are the most valuable and important.

The Roman system of using the wadis, then, was simple and, as we would expect, exceedingly thorough. They harnessed the wadis by building dams and by controlling the rainfall *before* it ever reached the water-courses. This was the secret of their success. In view of this, all discussions as to whether the climate of the desert has changed within historical times are irrelevant. The matter has been summed up by an expert: 'the prosperity of Africa [in Roman times] was not a question of meteorology: it was the prize of hard work'. This hard and continuous work was directed to conserving every precious drop of water that fell from the sky, not necessarily in the water-courses (wadis) or dams, but in the soil itself and, of course, in cisterns. This is what Colonel Baradez's remarkable photographs reveal *all along the Saharan frontier*—namely a system of walls, terraces, ditches, barricades, dams, and cisterns both natural and artificial, which captured the rainfall before it could rush down the rocky escarpments and flush down the wadis to be lost in fissures in the earth. In other words, the rain was retained where it fell by means of terraces and retaining walls; that which tried to run away through gullies was directed into reservoirs for future use. The flow in the wadis themselves was controlled by barrages of stones. Particular attention was paid to the erosion of the wadis' actual channels along their whole length to prevent a heavy downpour of rain from flooding the dry ground on either side and running useless into the earth. In addition irrigation channels led off from the wadis and reservoirs to the fields which were divided up into rectangles by ditches. The water flowing along these ditches seeped gently into the soil instead of gushing away. This is a system which is still used in Southern Italy. The modern Berbers and Arabs who inhabit the wilderness where the Romans built these magnificent hydraulic works are completely ignorant of their meaning and use, but they continue to sow a little grain along the Roman ditches which retain moisture after the rest of the soil is completely arid. Apart from this, the entire irrigation system which made cultivation not only possible but profitable has now completely broken down and the desert has reclaimed its own. The similar deterioration of agriculture has occurred throughout the desert regions of the Middle East, once cultivated by Roman colonists, so that the loss of arable land and the resultant food supplies to mankind is incalculable. For those who are interested in the process of destruction by erosion, the 'dust bowls' of the United States present a modern parallel.

The question next arises, as it does to some extent in the case of Britain, as to why the administration, or Central Government of Rome, troubled to colonize and civilize the desert at all. The reasons why modern man should, and soon may be obliged to, look to land reclamation and soil conservation are obvious. The expanding population of the world demands more room and more food. Emigration to other planets is a quixotic solution to the population problem when there are 3,000,000 empty square miles in this part of Africa alone. But the Romans, while they had population and therefore food supply problems, were not humanitarians; and the opening up of the African frontiers was not undertaken out of ethical considerations. It was simply a practical solution to the overall problem of holding together a vast empire by strengthening the frontiers against the only enemy the Romans knew—the barbarians. They also knew from long experience that the first step in civilizing the savages who resided within their confines was to settle them first in agricultural communities and eventually in villages, towns, and cities, which grew naturally from such settlements. The frontier forts and farms along the limits of the Saharan Desert, then, served three main purposes: first, they were the outer defence line in the complex military system which covered the whole of North Africa; second, they were custom- and passport-control points which regulated the movements of travellers; and third, they demonstrated to the barbarian nomads to the south that Romans were stronger, richer, and more civilized than they were.

We know that to the end of the Roman Empire, and for a long time after, this system worked so efficiently that the Saharan outposts and farms which they protected were the only organized survivors of the universal destruction which followed the Vandal invasions of North Africa. In fact, these desert colonies hung on for a time even after the Arab conquest and the utter collapse of Roman-Byzantine Africa, and continued as long as the hydraulic works on which they were founded were kept in repair. But gradually the knowledge, skill, and will to work which marked the Roman period faded and disappeared altogether. Today there remain nothing but ruins which are sinking deeper under the sand every year.

The last we hear of these frontiersmen[1] is in the letters exchanged between African bishops concerning the spiritual welfare of those colonists who were now Christians. One such letter is instructive. Writing to St. Augustine, the correspondent says that he is concerned with the way in which the guards were accepting the pagan oaths of those barbarians who crossed the frontier to work as farm labourers or porters. These nomads swore to respect all the laws and regulations of the Roman province and to report back at the end of their service at the control post. They swore by their own gods. St. Augustine replied: 'It is worse to swear falsely by the true God than to swear truly by false gods,' and he took the occasion to remind his correspondent that the safety and peace of the Afro-Roman world depended on the sincerity of these barbarian oaths.

From this we know that, as late as A.D. 400, the frontier with the actual desert was still intact, and the whole system of colonization was working well enough for the farmers to need seasonal labour from 'across the border'. The movement of these desert barbarians was still carefully controlled by military police in their forts and stations, which the archaeologists are still finding deep

1. Called in Latin *limitanei* after the *limes*, or frontier.

in the desert. The discovery in 1949 of such a fort in the Wadi Merdum, near Mselletin, tells the last phase of the story of 500 years of Roman occupation. This particular fort, though it is comparatively well preserved and is still used by the local nomads, escaped the notice of earlier travellers. The interesting thing about it is that within a radius of five miles from this blockhouse over thirty Roman farmhouses have been located, though most of the region has not been explored and excavated at all. Today there is not a single farm; the wadis which were once highly cultivated are completely desiccated.

The fort at Mselletin is much bigger and stronger than would seem necessary in view of the nearby forts garrisoned by the regular army. Inside the quarters are restricted, allowing for no more than twenty men and their horses. It is axiomatic the more massive the forts and blockhouses, the weaker the garrison within and the greater the danger without. Such was the lesson of the French Maginot Line in the 1939 war; and such seems to have been the fate of the desert forts and the farms they protected. The barbarians finally broke through here as they did in Britain, and that was the end for the time being of civilization. The northern Sahara was again the domain of those nomads whom the Roman legions had driven back into the mountains of the Central Desert.

Here is the conclusion of Colonel Baradez after his three years' intensive study of one section of the frontier:

I must stress for the last time the fearful contrast between what this whole zone was like once and what it is like now. The region is terribly eroded today by ravines which are growing deeper and spreading out in all directions owing to the abandonment of the Roman soil conservation works. The impression that one now gets of the area is of a desert wasteland more stupendous than the Sahara itself: the desolation is even more depressing.

In these vast expanses of desert, there are no longer any inhabitants: the only thing that moves in that landscape are the long-distance caravans. . . .

In other words, tens of thousands of square miles of cultivated land, painfully wrested from the desert by the patience, skill, and hard work of men almost 2,000 years ago when the actual population needs for space and food were far less than they are today, have been abandoned and lost through the characteristic processes of destroying one culture without replacing it with another.

FIVE

'Enemies of the Roman gods'

THE guide who takes you to see the catacombs at Sousse in Tunisia tells you a horrendous story that appears at first hearing to be apocryphal, though he ends by convincing you that it is true. All the facts tally.

The story is that during the war three German soldiers went down into the catacombs, probably in search of the art treasures that the French were said to have hidden there before they evacuated Tunisia. These three looters never came out alive. In fact, they died of hunger and thirst going round and round in the maze of tunnels and passages without ever finding the exit. They were found forty days later, and the guide solemnly shows you the place where they died. It is now walled up.

Once you enter the catacombs and, with candle in hand, follow the flickering light of the guide, you quickly realize how this fate of the Germans was not only possible, but inevitable. The tunnels hewn out of the rock by the early Christians of Roman Africa wind in all directions for nearly a mile underneath a hill above ancient Hadrumetum. You are faced here with not a single gallery, but a veritable maze in which thousands of the faithful were buried, by families, singly, old and young, the free and the enslaved. It is a subterranean city of the dead, comparable to the catacombs of Rome, and somehow more mysterious out here in a country which has broken nearly all ties with the Christian world for the last 1,300 years.

Only an occasional tourist comes this far to see this monument of early Christianity which, like so many other Roman sites in Africa, was discovered by accident. For we are told that fifty

years ago the horse of a French colonel of the Fourth Tirailleurs
fell into a hole at this place and so revealed the original entry of
the Christians to their secret burial place. The catacombs were
then carefully excavated by the Abbé Leynaud, with the help of
the White Fathers and the soldiers of the French African regiment. Over a long period they excavated some 1,500 yards of
subterranean passages, progressing like miners deeper and deeper
underneath the hill and the houses above. The three Germans
must have got to know every inch of those galleries and have
passed the same niches and the same chapel hundreds of times
without ever finding the single exit.

The grizzled Tunisian guide who takes you on the tour of
some of the tunnels is probably the only man alive who can find
his way about this maze, and sometimes he pauses to get his
bearings by one of the more familiar landmarks, or waits for the
flame of his candle to take hold. He knows where what he calls
the 'rich' were buried in decent levels of three, one above the
other, with a plaque to mark their name and resting place. Deeper
in the mine, he comes to the graves of the 'poor', who were
buried *en masse*. Now he points to a niche where a child was
buried. You are asked to observe where the head lay, where the
arm, and where the imprint of the feet and toes. Even the bones
of these Christians have turned into a sort of red clay, which
crumbles between the fingers. For the dead were buried not in
coffins, but in a sheet; then interred in niches in the rock and
walled up. What we see is the outline of their bodies impressed
into the rock face. The plaques on which their names were in-
scribed—Gudulus, Heraclius, Sorica, Renata, Victorina—have
been removed to the museums, the best tiles depicting doves,
fish, peacocks, and lambs—emblems of the Christian faith. What
is left, then, is this underground city, proof of what it was like
to be a Christian between A.D. 50 and A.D. 300 when it was no
longer dangerous to confess publicly the new faith. The catacombs of Hadrumetum tell one part of the story.

There is also another side to that story. For how much did
this secret society called Christianity contribute to the collapse of
Roman civilization throughout North Africa?

Up on the ledges of Djebel Zenkekra you can get an idea of what life was like in the Valley 10,000 years ago. The author looks at an engraving of a giraffe

Writing in the fifth century B.C. Herodotus speaks of the four-horse chariots of the Garamantes. A Garamantian artist etched this drawing on a rock face

An elephant hunt. One man has just fired his arrow; another lies dead on the ground

Top: A Carthaginian mask. Bottom Left: A Romano-African frontiersman of the sixth century A.D. His descendants, 1,400 years later, still wear a similar hooded robe. Bottom Right: Hercules leaning back at such a perilous angle that his calves bulge...the lord of the earth in his cups

The little dancing dwarf...her short arms raised as she clacks her castanets....A Greek bronze recovered from a sunken galley off the coast of Africa

The young wrestler...his expression wary yet quite fearless....Another bronze recovered from the sunken galley

The necropolis of el Hatia, with its hundred or

The forgotten fortress
of Ksar Mara, the loneliest
building in the Sahara
Desert

A miniature African
Stonehenge: a dolmen of
the type found in northern
Europe

more tombs standing untouched in the desert

A typical oasis

The Romano-African city of Sufetula. The Byzantine civilization in Africa ended here with the final defeat of the Roman army by the Arabs in the seventh century A.D.

Top: Leptis Magna...the theatre, holding 40,000 people, seems to be awaiting the next production of Euripides....*Bottom:* The visitor has the feeling that he is in a city not of a dead civilization, but a place which has suddenly been abandoned....A quiet street in Leptis Magna

An abandoned castle in the desert. It is typical of the 'lost cities' of the central Sahara

The Arab fort at Murzuk on the old slave route

We must remember that before Christianity became the state religion under Constantine, the Christians in the view of officialdom were worse enemies to law and order than the barbarians themselves. This official view is constantly being stated by the authorities in specific and absolutely uncompromising terms, and was stated over and over again in the charges made against the early martyrs of the African Church. The sentence of the Governor Galerius Maximus in the case of Cyprian, primate of the African Church (martyred A.D. 258), is typical. Though 'given most reluctantly', it was final and said:

> You [Cyprian] have long lived in sacrilege; you have gathered round you many accomplices in unlawful association; you have made yourself an enemy of the Roman gods and their religion and our most pious and sacred princes. . . . Therefore your blood shall be the confirmation of the laws.

Sacrilege, of course, was refusal to admit the godhead of the Emperor—and Cyprian's crime was comparable today to a refusal to sign an oath of allegiance in many states in the United States. The Romans were not especially interested in religion, except as an aspect of *pietas*, or good citizenship. They certainly didn't care what god, or gods, a man worshipped; but they did expect loyalty to the state, and this is the reason for the accusations against Cyprian of 'sacrilege' and 'unlawful association'. The fact that the bishop had also made a vow of perfect chastity also alarmed not only officialdom but all reasonable men—as one gathers from the sheer incredulity of the bishop's biographer St. Pontius who was led to exclaim 'Whoever saw such a miracle!' But to the Romans pagan chastity wasn't a miracle; it was further evidence of the pig-headedness of these pesky Christians who were undermining the political and economic system of the Empire. So no compromise was possible with such revolutionaries, whether young or old, male or female, from the time of the first martyrs, among them the twenty-two-year-old St. Perpetua, murdered in the arena at Carthage in A.D. 203. Perpetua, following the dictates of her conscience, 'refused to offer a sacrifice for the prosperity of the emperors' (sacrilege). For this she was thrown into prison and her baby taken from her:

> What a day of horror! [she writes] Terrible heat, owing to the crowds! Rough treatment by the soldiers! And to crown all, I was tormented by anxiety for my baby. But later, due to my father's intercession, my son was given to me, and I suckled him, and obtained leave for him to remain in prison with me, and my prison suddenly became a palace for me. . . .

We should note that in the case of these early martyrs the authorities were most anxious to treat the accused Christians not only with justice but with mercy. Often the governors, as in the trial of St. Cyprian by Galerius Maximus and in that of St. Perpetua by the procurator Hilarian (substituting for the Governor, who was away), pleaded personally with the accused to make some gesture of compromise which would satisfy the law and avoid the awkward and unpleasant consequences of defying it. The martyrs preferred to die. St. Perpetua flatly refused to wish the Emperor's health and prosperity and was condemned to death in the arena on the occasion of the games in honour of Geta.[1] She was exposed to a savage cow and tossed on to her back, but she sat up and gathered her tunic around her 'lest she should seem to be mourning'. Her fellow Christian, Felicity, was likewise tossed by the cow until the spectators had had enough of the sport and shouted for the two women to be taken away. Outside the arena orders were given to a gladiator to despatch the two women. The nervous athlete assigned to the job bungled his sword-thrust so that Perpetua 'shrieked out in pain', but she was then quickly killed, together with her companion.[2]

1. Brother of Caracalla who later murdered him while their mother was trying to protect him. This Geta was once Governor of Britain with his headquarters at York. By order of Caracalla his name was struck off all inscriptions throughout the Roman Empire. An example of this deletion can be seen in the crypt of Hexham Abbey, Northumberland.

2. St. Perpetua's tomb was unearthed in the Basilica Majorum at Carthage with an inscription bearing her name and the date March 7th, 203. The full story of her martyrdom is told in a contemporary report.

The amphitheatre where SS. Perpetua and Felicity stood on March 7th, 203, is just a short walk from the station called Carthage, and the visitor is likely to have it to himself. Or perhaps the boy who sits there all day snaring birds will follow him around. This boy has a linnet in a cage, and one asks him how much he wants for it, so that it can fly away—in atonement, perhaps, for the martyrdom of a girl who was caged here nearly eighteen centuries ago. The linnet has been in its prison for two years, says the boy, and can't fly. One gives up and wanders around the huge oval, not incomparable in size to the Colosseum itself. The White Fathers have done a meticulous job of excavating it in view of its associations, so you can walk down the tunnel to the subterranean den where the wild beasts were kept for people like Christians. From the height of the guard walls round the arena, some of these animals must have been as ferocious as even an African Roman mob could want, for the dens are twenty feet below the ground, with slots high up in the walls to allow food to be dropped down to them. When the iron gates were removed at the end of the tunnel, they must have slunk out into the full glare of the sun, but it is not clear why they should have attacked the people who hadn't signed the loyalty oath, though no doubt they were goaded enough by the spectators behind the guard walls to turn at last on their victims.

One hundred and one Christians died that day or in the course of the games, comforted, according to the chronicle, by the courage of Perpetua and Felicity. Naturally these two saints meant a great deal to the first Christians to come back to the scene over sixteen centuries later, and Cardinal Lavigerie himself, as primate of Africa, had a little chapel erected in the amphitheatre and a large cross placed over it. For some reason or another the cross has disappeared, and the White Fathers, up at their monastery on the hill, aren't in a position to do much about it. One feels, however, in looking down on the arena where two innocent women were tossed by an enraged animal, that they are entitled to their memorial, for in these surroundings one has no need of a Hollywood epic to evoke that spring day in 203. A visit to the animals' dens beneath the arena is enough.

Still, the courage and faith of the Christian martyrs did not atone for their dangerous attitude in the eyes of the Roman authorities responsible for the administration of a province the size of the whole of Western Europe—with only one legion to keep the peace. And their point of view can be better appreciated by a study of what was to happen when Africa, together with the rest of the Empire, became officially Christian and the pagan persecutions ceased. The Christians now began to persecute each other, and of all the provincial dioceses, the African Church seems to have had the most heresies and schisms. The list is a long one and includes Arianism, Manichaeism, Maximianism, Rogatism, Circoncillianism, and, the greatest and fiercest of all, Donatism. It was this last which sowed the seeds of that discontent and rebellion which finally opened the way to the destroyer of Roman Africa, the Christianized Vandal King Genseric, or Gaiseric.

Of all the ridiculous religious controversies that Christianity has indulged in Donatism is perhaps the most fatuous—or it seems so when the origin and cause of the fraticidal struggle it brought about are examined.

The trouble began in about A.D. 300 with the persecution of the Christians by the Emperor Diocletian. During this period there were so many Christians eager to be martyred that the authorities forbad public meetings to celebrate the actual or potential martyrdoms and ordered all the sacred objects and books of the cult to be surrendered. Those of the clergy who obeyed the imperial edict—and they included some bishops— were called 'traitors' by those who deliberately went to the magistrates, declared they had copies of the scripture, and challenged the authorities to 'persecute' them.

The struggle now was more between the two factions of Christians than between Christians and pagans. On the one side, the 'traitors' who, naturally, preferred to call themselves 'traditionalists' refused to honour as martyrs those co-religionists who made unnecessary trouble with the authorities; and their leader,

Bishop Mensurius, went so far as to say that many of these 'Christians' were people of dubious morals, crippled with debts or guilty of crimes, who got themselves arrested and incarcerated in the expectation of escaping their just retribution on the one hand and of enjoying what he calls 'the delicate attentions of their brothers' on the other.[1] He may have been thinking of Juvenal's statement that 'one bears a cross for his crime, another a crown'. Mensurius declared that imprisonment, and even death, in these cases was more a deliverance than a sacrifice. Moreover, this shrewd old prelate offered a solution to the whole problem, or dilemma, of the Christian conscience. He advised his adherents (the traditionalists) to collect all those sacred books *tainted with heresy* and/or proscribed by the Church and to deposit them in a basilica, the authorities being notified accordingly. The Governor Arulinus was delighted with the bishop's stratagem as lives (and faces) could now be saved on both sides. The future Donatists, on the other hand, were incensed at this compromise and stepped up their rate of martyrdom to show what they thought of Mensurius and his followers, so that we find African 'martyrs' by the hundred in this period (300–305). The village of Abitina[2] alone supplied a priest, a deacon, and fifty of its flock for the sacrifice—probably almost the entire adult population of the hamlet.

By this time the two groups were now poles apart—the 'traditionalists' on one side, the 'martyrophiles' on the other. The controversy was aggravated by the latter party accusing Bishop Mensurius of actually surrendering *all* his religious books to the authorities and making up the story of the heretical documents in order to absolve himself from the charge of betraying his conscience. The quarrel was now serious, splitting, in fact, the African Church into two rival sects for the duration of its existence. The martyrophiles, now led by Bishop Donatus, were supported by all the dissident Christians and particularly those who were tired of the aged prelates who ruled the Church and

1. The 'brothers' included the 'sisters' of the congregation.
2. Abitina appears to have been somewhere in the vicinity of Medjez el Bab, thirty miles west of Carthage.

kept out the younger and more ambitious priests from the best jobs in the Establishment. According to the ecclesiastical historians of the time, a widow called Lucilla was largely to blame for a great deal of the acrimony and bitterness of the schism, though one has to remember that women have been blamed for men's woes by religious writers from the time of Genesis. At all events, this Lucilla, who was described by St. Augustine himself as 'a most mercenary and quarrelsome woman', had been publicly rebuked by Bishop Caecilianus, successor of Mensurius, so it is not difficult to believe, since she was both rich and fashionable, that she was eager to revenge herself for being branded, in ecclesiastical language, a shrew—not the best recommendation for a widow, even a rich one. Anyhow, Lucilla is said to have done everything in her power to make trouble for the traditionalists now led by Bishop Caecilianus, the man who had had the temerity to rebuke her.

It is too complicated and tedious to follow the various ramifications of the schism which was now to occupy the attention of the European as well as the African Church for many years to come. Ecclesiasts from the Pope down were now so deeply involved that conference after conference was called to try and decide who was in the right: Mensurius, Caecilianus, and the party of 'tradition'; or Donatus, Lucilla, and the party of the 'martyrs'. There was a Council at Rome in 313, another at Arles, 314, and one in Milan, 316, at which the Emperor Constantine himself was present. At this last convention the vital decision was finally given: both parties were pronounced right.

Unfortunately this satisfied neither faction. To the contrary, the hatred of the rivals for ecclesiastical power now became so fierce that real warfare broke out between them. At this stage the Imperial Church (as it now was) had to take definite sides in suppressing one group or the other, and it opted for the traditionalists. The Donatists were told to submit or be punished with exile. They chose to fight it out, this time with swords and spears instead of words and arguments. They formed armies, or rather bands of dissidents recruited from slaves, colonists, small landowners, debtors, and malcontents in general who were not in the least interested in Bishop Mensurius or Bishop Donatus, but were interested in overthrowing a political and social system which exploited them. However, in deference to religious feeling, both sides, though they were now openly killing each other in cold blood, kept to the rules and committed their murders in the name of God. Thus a battle cry of the Donatists was *'Deo laudes!'*, which they yelled as they pillaged the homes of their enemies and beat their fellow Christians senseless, while that of the orthodox churchmen was *'Deo gratias!'*

The killings and burnings soon reached such proportions that the orthodox Christians called on Rome to send troops to take care of the 'bandits', as the unorthodox Christians were now called. In 320 we find a Roman general fighting against the Donatists on the one hand and the barbarians on the other. This is perhaps the most significant date in the history of Roman Africa, for it hints very clearly at the inception of the eventual ruin that was to destroy civilization in Africa for the next 1,600 years—a long time in the history of any region. For the ominous fact that a Roman army had now to fight the barbarians after two centuries of the *pax Romana* throughout the province and that African Romans sided with the barbarians suggests that it was the quarrels and subsequent wars between Christians themselves that brought about the ultimate destruction of a thousand cities and 10,000 farms and millions of acres of good arable land. We can, then, date the end of Rome in Africa to the year 320, when the Roman general Ursacius had to divide his forces in order to fight Christians on the one hand and barbarians on the other. It was the latter who killed him; the former who gloated over his death, rejoicing that his body was denied a tomb and was left to be eaten by dogs and birds. This, of course, was what was to happen to their own grandchildren.

In fact, the Donatists never gave up their war against the orthodox church until both sides were wiped out of existence by a third and stronger religious force, that of Islam. But before that was to happen, the Donatists were to do everything in their power to undermine the Catholic Church, which was the same thing by this time as undermining Rome itself.

They succeeded just 130 years after the beginning of the quarrel between Bishop Mensurius who wanted his fellow Christians to save their lives and his adversaries who wanted them to lose them—both parties for the same reason, of course: namely, the greater glory of God. So in the year 430 the Donatists threw in their lot with the Vandal King Genseric who invaded Africa from Spain with an army of 20,000 men. Genseric, himself an ardent Christian (when he killed his enemies or sacked a city he used to say he was destroying 'the dwellings of men with whom God is angry'), paid back the Catholic Christians for the wrongs they had done the Donatists with a vengeance. He banished all the reigning bishops, persecuted their adherents, vicariously supported the Arian heresy, and devoted himself to piracy. If he hadn't called himself a Christian one would almost take him for a heathen. But whatever he was he ended Roman rule in Africa, for he and his warrior caste were not interested in trade and agriculture but in piracy and loot. Once the Vandals had sacked a city they lost interest in it, which is what happened to the great ports of Tripolitania—Leptis Magna, Sabratha, Oea, and the rest: Genseric knocked down their defensive walls, and so left them open to the barbarians who were already coming up from the desert and attacking them. Leptis Magna was now finished as a great and prosperous city. In fact, all of urbanized Africa was finished, so that when the Arabs invaded in 642–3 there was no resistance worth mentioning.

Yet so powerful, so efficient, and so deeply rooted was the old Roman culture that even after the motherland had collapsed under the weight of anarchy and corruption and Rome as the active master of the world no longer existed, the provinces of the Empire continued to live by the old laws; speaking the old language and following, as if by instinct, the old customs. It is, in fact, this twilight period of the Roman Empire which is in some respects the most fascinating, and in others the most terrifying, era, whether we observe it down along the fringes of the Sahara Desert or along the frontiers of Scotland. It is not easy to reconstruct this period in either Africa or Britain for the simple and obvious reason that not many people have the philosophical calm to sit down and record the end of their world. In other words, our historical authorities are now so few and far between that we can only guess at what life was like in the provinces after the disappearance of the law and order once so firmly maintained by the legions. What must it have been like in the town of York in Britain, for instance, when Hadrian's Wall was left unmanned and the last legion was withdrawn? It was quite clear to any intelligent citizen that civilized life was doomed, whether in the big cities or on the country estates, for the barbarians were always waiting at the gates. In Britain they poured into the peaceful and well-ordered country from the north across Hadrian's Wall and into the east and south-east coasts which the Romans had never needed to defend. Within fifty years civilization in Britain had been destroyed and the barbarians were in complete control.

The process took much longer in Africa. In fact, the Roman culture might never have been wiped out altogether in this province of the Empire if it had not been for the Arab invasions of the seventh century. The Arabs were to Africa what the Saxons were to Britain. Both were innate barbarians hostile to a civilized society: both wanted instinctively to smash it to pieces. Consequently the destruction of Roman-British cities by the Saxons and Roman-African cities by the Arabs was an almost methodical and even disciplined procedure. Saxons and Arabs, for instance, had the typical barbarians' horror of nudity—especially of the male genitals, whence the total castration of so many statues. Scarcely a single statue of a nude male in the North African museums is not mutilated. (The pudenda of the nude females, however, all seem to have been crudely decorated with scratchings and daubings representing the pubic hair—apparently a recent addition.)

But if the Arabs, spurred on by religious fervour, had not decided to destroy the Greco-Roman civilization in Africa, it is unlikely that the autochthonous tribes would have succeeded in doing so. For these tribes—the people we now call, generically,

Berbers—were half civilized compared with real barbarians like the Huns, Goths, and Arabs. They had been under Roman supervision for over 500 years and had been beaten in battles by the Roman army scores of times. Even in the desert, which they shared with the wild animals, they were under the stern eye of the legion: their piracy against the caravans was never tolerated. Moreover, close association with a civilized people like the Romano-Africans had introduced them to many of the refinements and some of the luxuries of life. In other words, they had the sense to know that they were culturally an inferior breed.

On the other hand, a sense of inferiority has never prevented people from hating their superiors; to the contrary, it has usually led to outright revolt, which it did in North Africa. The opportunity of the Berbers came during the 150 years that the Christians fought each other with books, tracts, sermons, edicts, threats, swords, spears, sticks, stones, and appeals to Almighty God. There is a curious story which illustrates the bewilderment of the Berbers in the face of the Christian behaviour. According to the Byzantine historian Procopius, a rebel chieftain who was about to be attacked by the Christians is reported to have said: 'He was ignorant of the God whom the Christians worshipped, but it was probable that if He was as powerful as He said He was, He would wreak vengeance upon those who insulted Him and defend those who honoured Him,' for which reason this chieftain, whose name was Cabaon, had detachments of his agents follow the Christian armies to repair the damage the Vandals and Donatists had done to the Catholic Churches *en passant*.

A curious story, then, and one which also gives us a further clue to what was happening in North Africa at this time (A.D. 520). Cabaon used camel cavalry against the Christians who were still using horses. It was these great camel armies which now enabled the barbarians to come up out of the desert, by-pass the Roman forts along the frontier, raid the cities, and fade back into the desert without the horse-mounted troops being able to follow them. The camel, in short, was to desert warfare what the tank was to be 1,500 years later.

What, then, had happened in Roman Africa by the end of the sixth century, just before the armies of the Prophet were to arrive and wipe it out completely, was the gradual sinking of the province into a state of pastoral nomadism. The big ports like Leptis, Sabratha, Sfax, Gabes, Tunis, Carthage, Cherchel, Tangiers, and others were no longer prosperous, or even necessary: there was no longer enough trade between Africa and Europe to justify their existence. The big farms of the coastal plains, once rich in wheat, barley, wine, and oil, had been attacked and destroyed so often that farming was no longer safe or profitable. Those citizens who could afford it moved away from the small towns to the capitals of the different regions where there was some sort of security—a regiment of professional soldiers and thick city walls in a good state of repair. Romans and Italians —merchants and officials—went back to their homeland as soon as they could manage.

As the force was drained out of the province by the slow process of depopulization, the irrigation system on which the whole of North Africa depended for its former wealth began to be neglected and then abandoned. This is the explanation of the extraordinary phenomenon of so many large Romano-African cities sprawling today across acres of ruins in a vast landscape which seems devoid of a single blade of grass, let alone fields of wheat. Such cities are Timgad (*Thamugadi*), El Djem (*Thysdrus*), Djemila (*Cuicul*), Haidra (*Ammaedara*), Lambèse (*Lambaesis*), not to mention large forts and settlements like *Gemellae*, Ghadames (*Cydamus*), and Germa (*Garama*) which are in the desert itself. How did this arid and bleak countryside, we ask, support such large populations? The answer is by irrigation; and once that system broke down, vast areas of Africa were turned back over to the desert from which the Romans had snatched them.

There is one curious aspect of the final days of Roman Africa: the last region to collapse was the desert frontier where life was hardest and the margin of survival slimmest. This frontier which, as we have seen from the aerial surveys of Colonel Baradez and the actual excavations of the archaeologists since 1945, thrust far deeper into the Sahara than was thought possible, was occupied, defended, and farmed by the *limitanei*, or frontiersmen, who may be compared to their American counterparts of the last century in the United States. The only real differences were climatic and topographical; otherwise the conditions were remarkably similar.

In the beginning when the frontier scheme was first put into effect, the *limitaneus* was a veteran of the Third Augusta Legion—an African or Syrian who was used to the desert and was prepared to retire along the new frontier, provided the government gave him land and protection. This is exactly what Rome did offer its veterans all over the Empire; and, in return, the veterans, inured to hard work and trained in every handicraft, built their own houses, villages, and communal forts. This is what had been done along the edges of the Sahara for a distance of 1,500 miles, and done at the cost of enormous labour. Most of these desert outposts had become in time oases, or belts of agricultural land, depending on 'dry farming' and an elaborate irrigation system. The soldier-farmers and their children who had developed this land were, on the one hand, much more rugged colonists than the town-dwellers to the north and much less inclined, on the other, to be intimidated by the tribesmen to the south. It is not surprising, then, to find that the frontier system of farming, irrigation, fortification, and Romanization was the last bulwark against the barbarians. It may even have survived for a while the Arab conquest of North Africa; but, of course, very little that was orderly and civilized could survive Arab fanaticism for long. The Arabs, a nomadic people, saw no prospects of either profit or pleasure in dry farming, and since these *limitanei* were Christians, they were due to be liquidated by the Moslems.

Thus by the end of the seventh century the last vestiges of Roman rule in Africa had been expunged; the province was plunged into a new form of barbarism; and it was not to move out of the seventh century for the next thousand years. All that was left of Scipio and Caesar and Augustus and Hadrian and the Third Augusta Legion and St. Augustine and a thousand cities and towns and a magnificent network of highways and acres of waving corn and vineyards and olive groves were the columns of temples and the triumphal arches which were too ponderous for the soldiers of the Prophet to knock down. This is what we see of Roman Africa today. The rest, the desert, depopulation, poverty, and squalor, is the work of barbarians ancient and modern.

SIX

Gaiety and songs across the Sahara

I

THE Libyan politician, business man, and intellectual sipping his
fruit-juice in the bar of the oil men's hotel in Tripoli is explaining
the philosophy of Islam; and he can evidently explain it equally
well in English, French, Italian, Arabic, or Turkish—whichever
language you prefer. Because of his intelligence, education, and
political skill he is one of the inner circle who runs Libya, a
curious composite state of three almost separate countries,
Tripolitania, Cyrenaica, and the Fezzan. If anybody knows the
answers to the future of this newly created nation it is this sort
of man whose resemblance to an Arab aristocrat of the old school
is undoubtedly carefully cultivated. The fringe of black beard
which outlines his jaws and chin are more characteristic than his
expensive Western suit. For his ideas and his thinking are not
European at all; they are Arab; and the difference between his
political, religious, and social philosophy and that of the Westerner
is profound. The listener gradually realizes in hearing him expound his views that the changes in this part of the world are
relatively superficial: the number and diversity of Western gad-
gets in a city like Tipoli have little to do with what is being
thought and with what will eventually happen in the Moslem
world of North Africa. Libya, together with those Moslem states
which lie within and around the Sahara Desert, is not looking to
either Europe or the United States or Soviet Russia for salvation,
but rather backwards into the past, to the great days of Islam.

Inasmuch as every other nation glorifies its territorial conquests, it isn't surprising that this spokesman for pan-Arabism
emphasizes not the atrocities of the invasions of Roman Africa

in the seventh and eighth centuries but the enlightenment brought
by the armies of the Prophet—quite a pill for a Christian to
swallow; for if there is anything that the first European travellers
into Moslem Africa underscore, it is the ignorance, prejudice,
and cruelty of the Arabs and their religion. In short, these
travellers, without exception, depict this whole vast region as a
world of hunger, thirst, bloodshed, slavery, and fanaticism. They
had plenty of experiences to prove it; and, for that matter, a great
many of them proved it with their lives. A reader of their accounts
of the slave trade and the treatment of slaves, as well as of women
and prisoners of war, then, is startled to hear a modern Libyan
defend these old masters of flaying men alive. What about the
razzias and the tens of thousands of negroes who were driven
across the desert? The scholar doesn't appear to hear the question.
He replies with fervour and apparent sincerity how it was a true
believer's duty to object if he saw one man ill-using another; but,
more to the point, how it was imperative to intervene actively if
he saw a master mistreating a slave—unless, he adds in fairness
to logic, the slave had misbehaved. At this point one remembers
Captain Lyons's account of his journey with a slave caravan in the
Fezzan in 1819 when scores of women and children died on the
journey and, says the English captain, 'none of the slave owners
ever marched without their whips, which were in constant use'.
The misbehaviour of the slaves in this instance was their inability
to survive a march of a thousand miles across the desert from
Lake Chad to Tripoli.

So much for the Moslem theory and practice of slavery.

It would be totally unfair, however, to suggest that the Arabs
invented the institution, or that their exploitation of the system
was any worse than that of other nations, ancient or modern. The
classical world, and the world into which the Prophet was born,
was firmly based on human bondage, a fact which Plato himself
took into account in his blueprint of the ideal society—ruled by
philosophers, worked by slaves. Here again, the Libyan spokesman for Islam makes his point. Mohammed was not concerned
in making a revolution by overthrowing society. He was concerned in improving it by sensible and practicable reforms: his

aim was to protect the rights of men—and even of women—and even of slaves. To denounce slavery in the sixth century was like advocating the emancipation of women: it would have led to the collapse of society. What was needed was what the Greeks called 'right thinking' on these and related problems. This is the basis of Koranic law: property must be respected; alms must be given, up to one fortieth of a man's annual surplus; women's security must be provided for; and slaves must be accorded certain rights.

All this was, in its way, a new and dynamic concept of society, impregnated by a religious fervour which was to shake the foundations of the then-known world for centuries to come. It undoubtedly marked the end of the old classical world. Rome was to follow Greece and Egypt and the other Mediterranean empires into dust. And part of this process—following, that is, the destruction of Roman Africa by the Arab invasions of the seventh century—was the relapsing of the desert into its pristine state of empty wasteland supporting the bare minimum of life. In the midst of this vast ocean of sand and rock stood the green islands of the oases on which the entire economy of the Sahara was dependent for the next 1,200 years. For not even the soldiers of the Prophet were fanatical enough to destroy these palmeries which provided just enough food and water for their handful of inhabitants and the trans-desert caravans. One thing the Arabs did respect was water; so the wells, most of them built by the Romans or by natives who had learnt the art of well-digging from their conquerors, survived the almost universal destruction. They are still being used today. And thanks to the negro slaves who worked the date plantations there were still green places in the desert.[1] However, for a century or more these oases disappeared from the map and lost most of their *raison d'être* now that the trans-Saharan trade between Central Africa and Europe had dwindled to nothing. As a result, the whole of Africa was practically *terra incognita* to Europeans for the next thousand years.

But a new factor was to change radically this 'silence' of Africa.

1. Leo Africanus describes these negro farmhands in the oases as follows: 'They lead a beastly kind of life, being utterly destitute of the use of reason, of dexterity, of intellect, and of all arts. . . . They have great swarms of harlots among them.'

This was the slave trade which, under the efficient direction of the Arabs, was soon to involve the whole civilized world from the end of the Middle Ages to the beginning of the twentieth century. The ancient world, of course, was based on slavery, but not on African slaves. The exploitation of black labour was the contribution of the Arabs to mankind, for it was they who organized the vast traffic in human merchandise out of Africa to the Atlantic and Mediterranean ports. In short, the slave trade became the corner-stone of Saharan economy for the next thousand years. It made the desert an exceedingly busy place, with tens of thousands of men and animals crawling every day across the immense wasteland, since by the eighteenth century the demand for negro slaves had become insatiable in almost every corner of the globe. Who else was to work the salt mines in the Sahara Desert itself, who the sugar plantations in the Barbados, who the cotton fields in Virginia, who the American, British, French, Portuguese, Spanish, and Turkish mines and factories, if not the docile African negro?

The Arabs had the answer to the world's economic problem.

Yet it was a long time before they got the slave trade properly organized. First they had to conquer by fire and sword hundreds of thousands of square miles in one of the most amazing campaigns of all time, not excluding Alexander's conquest of Asia Minor. For the Arab armies started their invason of North Africa and southern Europe from Egypt, which entailed crossing the greatest desert on earth from east to west, a march of nearly 2,000 miles. It isn't surprising, then, that it took them almost a hundred years to wipe out the last vestiges of Byzantine authority in the coastal cities in addition to the Berber resistance in the desert and mountains. Overpowering the Christians was a relatively tame affair. The Christians collapsed almost at the sight of 10,000 Arab horsemen under their pennants and banners. The Berbers were a different matter. When the armies or bands of Arabs and Berbers joined in battle it was axiomatic that they fought until one side or the other was wiped out to the last man. So died the greatest of Arab generals, the first conqueror of Ifriqiyah,[1]

1. The name for North Africa borrowed by the Arabs from the Romans.

Okba-ben-Nafi, who was ambushed near Biskra, 'the Garden of Allah', and cut down with every man of his band.

But the Arabs had one advantage over all other armies of conquest: their religion made dying on the field of battle a relatively easy form of martyrdom, since it assured the warrior a passport into the most delightful heaven men had so far conceived. The posthumous rewards for Christian martyrdom, in contrast, were debatable: one is amazed at a young mother like St. Perpetua willingly leaving her new baby and electing to be tossed by a savage cow into eternity. The Mohammedans, on the other hand, had far livelier prospects, whence it follows that no other religion has served the cause of war so well as Islam.

Moreover, the Arabs had an additional advantage: they were absolutely pitiless in their dealings with their enemies and devised some very fancy tortures, punishments, and insults for those who fell into their hands. We read of a Berber chieftain, though badly wounded, being flayed alive, his skin stuffed with straw, and the dummy thrown into a cage for two monkeys to play with. The Berber had died, incidentally, when the flaying reached his navel —'this enemy of Allah', exclaims the Arab historian indignantly as though to underscore the fact that the punishment fitted the crime. It isn't surprising, then, that the Arab commanders and governors could put to death all their prisoners in cold blood and thus save themselves the problem of what to do with them. In fact, they often enjoyed doing the job themselves. The Emir Ibrahim after his victory at Tripoli in 894 sat on his throne, had his prisoners led before him, and personally plunged his spear into their hearts. The admiring Arab historian Noweiri reports that Ibrahim killed 500 defenceless men in this manner before he grew tired of the sport.

These were the people, then, who took over North Africa and the desert from the Romans and ended by imposing their religion, customs, and language on almost the entire northern half of the African Continent, as they had done, in fact, on an area greater even than the Roman Empire, an empire extending from the Bay of Biscay in the west to the confines of China in the east: that is, south-western Europe; northern Africa; and Western and Central

Asia. These, too, were the people who had no interest whatsoever in the welfare of the nations they had conquered except to force their religion on them by the sword. Otherwise, the conquered territories were simply sources of loot.

The loot of Africa was two-fold: slaves and ivory, one, in a sense, presupposing the other, since slave-porters were obviously needed to bring the ivory out of the Congo. The routes by which both 'products' were brought from Lake Chad to the Mediterranean ports had, of course, already been well travelled even in Carthaginian times. The Arab traders now took over these trans-Saharan trails and began business. Before their day was over they were estimated to be bringing out 5,000 slaves a year by the Fezzan route alone, losing half of them on the way. By 1900 the Lake Chad region from which these negroes were taken was practically depopulated.

In the pursuit of the slave trade the Arabs again had the advantages of religion and ferocity as they had had in war. Their attitude was extremely simple. 'Allah has created negroes as slaves as he has made their skins black, and you can change the one as little as the other.' This was the statement made to the British consul, Hanns Vischer, as late as 1910 by the sheik of the Kwaida tribe who could trace his descent from the earliest Mohammedan conquerors. The sheik further argued that Allah had created black men to be sold and had given to the Arabs the especial right to sell them.

Neither the fact that the negroes of his old hunting-grounds were fast becoming Mohammedans and as such by the laws of the Koran ceased to be lawful spoil, nor the damage done to the Negro countries by the continual raids, reconciled him to the new conditions. He was a true and pious Mohammedan and his alms attracted many poor to his village. . . .

The main trans-Saharan slave-routes were:
(1) Timbuktu–Taudeni–Fez–Tangiers.
(2) Timbuktu–In Salah–Biskra–Tunis.
(3) Kano–Agades–Ghat–Ghadames–Tripoli.

(4) Lake Chad–Bilma–Murzuk–Mizda–Tripoli.

(5) Lake Chad–Tibesti–Kufra–Libyan Desert–Benghazi.

The most travelled of these five main routes seems to have been the fourth, which is the most direct between Lake Chad and Tripoli—the route which Julius Maternus probably took when he set out from Germa, the capital of the Garmantians. The slave caravans that crossed the Sahara by this Bilma–Murzuk route were enormous, consisting of thousands of camels and thousands of slaves, for the Arab traders travelled together when they could as much for the sake of pleasure as of security. As far as the slave-trader's personal safety was concerned, he had nothing to fear but the hostility of the tribes whose country he was crossing. Otherwise he was in no danger of dying of thirst, for he knew the whereabouts of every well between Kano and Tripoli and, in any case, always carried enough water for his own needs. It was the slaves marching across the desert on foot who had to worry about water, and it was this very concern of the negroes which enabled the Arab slavers to herd their caravans across the desert with the minimum of trouble. In the first place, no prisoner was going to leave the train unless he wanted to commit suicide; in the second, the Arab guards had only to indicate the direction of the next well, or water hole, and the slaves would trudge in that direction. The system was to feed and water the negroes at the well, point out the road and landmarks to the next, and send the column on its way. The only difficulty was getting the slaves to leave the well and plod off into the desert. This was accomplished by blows and curses, and, in general, there was very little resistance at any stage of the journey. The Africans were always timid and their sufferings on the trans-Saharan journey reduced them to the condition of automata. A few of the younger and prettier women were kept behind to entertain the Arab masters until the arrival of the next caravan. The men, older women, and children were driven off along the road to Tripoli, to reach the next well as best they could. As a result, the route was well marked with the skeletons of adults and children, together with the grotesque carcasses of camels who died lying on their sides with their heads drawn far back and their legs tucked up. These avenues of bones and the stone circles marking the site of the temporary mosques where the pious slave-traders performed their evening rites still mark the ancient slave-caravan routes across the Fezzan, a route which was being used certainly as late as the 1920s. The last known (i.e. admitted) consignment of slaves to arrive in Murzuk was in 1929 after a two-month march across the desert. From Murzuk there was another month's journey on foot to Tipoli or Benghazi before shipment to Saudi Arabia, but the northern third of the journey was considered easy compared with what the slaves had endured before arriving at Murzuk.

You can still meet older men in the desert who remember bringing slaves back in the northbound caravans from the Niger. The white-robed Libyan who described this traffic to me in the oases of Greifa, not far from Murzuk, stated that in his day the negroes were given a trough of beer from which they drank until they were besotted, then shipped off, as sailors were once shang-haied in British ports. He remembered, too, when the nearby oasis of Germa was the stopping place that specialized in cas-trating selected negroes intended for the Turkish harems.

Officially the slave trade was prohibited long before 1929; un-officially it has never stopped. The chances of a European getting any information, however—apart from hearsay and rumours often padded out with lurid details for the readers of the Sunday newspapers—are slim. Slaving is nowadays a very private mono-poly of the Arab world whose potentates can very well afford the luxury on the strength of their oil royalties. Naturally, no one will ever see again the long columns of men, women, and children stumbling across the desert, as the nineteenth-century travellers saw and described them. In any case, the commodity is too ex-pensive to treat in this manner. But in those countries where oriental despots still maintain the system of Islamic feudalism, slaves are obviously needed for the courts and harems of kings and princes. Moral indignation doesn't enter into this sort of commercial enterprise any more than it does into, say, the international armaments business.

II

During the great days of the slave trade Africans were being brought out of the interior at the rate of at least 100,000 a year. In some cases we have fairly exact statistics: for instance, the records show that 300,000 African slaves were imported into British colonies between 1680 and 1700. Between 1700 and 1786, 610,000 were imported into Jamaica. The *total* number of Africans sent overseas as slaves from 1510 (when the first negroes were shipped to the Spanish gold mines in Hispaniola) to 1865 when the United States, last among the Christian countries, abolished slavery by a constitutional amendment, was, at a minimum, 12,000,000. If we accept Dr. Livingstone's estimate that at least ten lives were lost for every one that reached the coast the figure of Africans who were captured, killed, or exported during the four and a half centuries of the slave trade is almost inconceivable.

The Arabs were by no means responsible for the system, of course. They were merely the entrepreneurs, due to their conquest of the whole of North Africa and their control of the interior. They were also the conveyers as far as the Atlantic, Mediterranean, and Indian Oceans. The Christian nations took over the trade at the ports, with the British getting the lion's share in the trans-shipment of slaves to the New World, the national hero Sir John Hawkins giving his country a good start in 1562, so that the British-African Company, with the aid of parliamentary grants, was able to enjoy a monopoly of the African-American trade for many good years.

However, all the civilized nations at this time were involved in one way or another with the slave trade, and the demand for more and more Africans to work the mines and plantations of the West Indies, North, Central and South America was enormous. Everybody co-operated to supply the demand, except the negroes, whose feeble resistance amounted almost to a form of collaboration.

The initial rounding up of the tens of thousands of prisoners

was undertaken by the African chiefs in their inter-tribal wars—
first only in order to get women for their harems. Male slaves
were useless, so the men prisoners, later a valuable booty, were
disposed of. Dr. Barth, travelling in the Sudan in 1852, witnessed
one method of disposal:

> To our utmost horror [he writes] not less than one hundred
> and seventy full grown men out of one thousand prisoners
> were mercilessly slaughtered in cold blood, the greater part of
> them being allowed to bleed to death, a leg having been
> severed from the body for that purpose.

This wanton destruction of a useful work animal was, of
course, typical of those African chieftains who had not been
apprised by the Arab agents as to the value of the 170 full-grown
men. For where the Arabs had been able to organize the slave
trade, many thousands of lives were saved, or, at least, given a
one-in-ten chance of survival. This principle of selling people
instead of butchering them had long been recognized by the
Congolese, for instance, for we find a seventeenth-century Italian
explorer relating how one native Congolese was in despair
because, having sold his brothers, sisters, children, father, and
mother, he had nobody left to sell except his wife, and his
personal honour forbad him to sell her.

Once the Arabs reached the royal African courts, however, the
system of selling was soon organized on the usual basis—the
basis which the Carthaginians had used 2,000 years before:
namely, the exchange of European gew-gaws in return for valuable African products like a strong young man, good-looking
young negress, or boys and girls suited to the harems. Now it
was a question of getting enough prisoners alive, not of killing
them off when captured. For this purpose the Arabs organized
the *razzia*, an expression originally meaning in their language a
'raid against infidels'. Eventually it came to mean 'a manhunt'—
though the Moslems never forgot that an infidel, and especially
a Christian, was, from the moral point of view, a better slave
than a black believer.

The *razzia* was a very simple form of manhunt whether conducted by the Arabs or their negro converts. It consisted of a surprise raid on a village, or an oasis, of cutting down any resistance, taking off the young men and women for slavery, looting the settlement, and, if the loot was inadequate, of burning the houses and palm trees by which the inhabitants survived. The wholesale destruction in the desert oases of the date palms, which took a generation to grow, was typical of the Moslem invader from his first appearance in Africa; and though it is doubtful whether the Arab could teach the negro anything about cruelty, he could teach him something about looting and destroying.

Captain Lyon, who was the first European to travel in the Fezzan, describes a *razzia* against the Tiboos in 1819, and states that 'in the course of one morning, a thousand or fifteen hundred slaves are procured by two or three hundred men only. When the inhabitants are all secured, the camels, flocks, and provisions come into requisition; and these dreaded Arabs march on and conquer other defenceless hordes in the same manner.'

With the connivance, then, of the African chieftains, the Arabs were able to achieve a double purpose by their *razzias*. First, they did a useful service to some local monarch who wanted his neighbours weakened by having their men carried off into slavery; and secondly, they supplied the European traders with an African commodity these traders had not been able to acquire yet for themselves; for long after the end of the Middle Ages, explorers, traders, and conquerors had great difficulty in penetrating into the interior of the Black Continent, with the notable exception of the Portuguese, whose traders and missionaries had made some penetration in West Africa. But practically nothing was known of the African kingdoms lying along the Tropic of Cancer, between the Niger and Lake Chad, until Dr. Barth's explorations of just over a hundred years ago. Our only real source of information was from Arabic texts, notably the *Travels* of Al Hassan Ibn Muhammad, *alias* Leo Africanus. But how reliable Arab or Moorish historians are is pretty much open to question, though in fairness to Leo he is engagingly frank about himself. 'When I hear the Africans spoken of badly,' he says, 'I will affirm myself to be from Granada; and when I perceive the Granadans to be discommended, then I profess myself to be an African.'[1]

None the less, it was on Leo's entertaining account of his travels in Negroland that geographers, historians, and others had to rely for the next 300 years, because no European had been as far as Roman Cydamus (Ghadames), let alone Timbuktu, till the second decade of the nineteenth century. So all we know about the African kingdoms south of the Sahara comes from Leo who visited them in 1520, or thereabouts—or said he did. 'I myself saw fifteen kingdoms of the negroes,' he writes; and proceeds to give their names, pointing out that they are for the most part Niger River states.

Slavery was an integral part of life in all these African kingdoms, as the Moslem faith which they had now adopted (the Hausa chieftains calling themselves sultans) only strengthened and didn't question the institution. Slaves, in fact, were the currency of Negroland as they were of Barbary. Leo informs us that one horse was worth fifteen to twenty slaves, the latter being in abundant supply because of the wars and *razzias*. In fact, in a list of African exports which Leo conveniently prices to illustrate the state of the Barbary market we find both male and female slaves quoted lower than civet-cats,[2] eunuchs, camels, and ambergris:

a skin of the Addax gazelle	8	ducats
a man, or woman slave	20	,,
a eunuch	40	,,
a camel	50	,,
a civet-cat	200	,,

One notes that a eunuch is worth twice a slave in 1520, and it is surprising that he wasn't worth more, since the mortality rate

1. Al Hassan, or Leo, was born in Granada, Spain, in 1495 and taken as a child to live with his parents in Fez, Morocco. He lived and wrote for a time in Rome.

2. The civet-cat, found in North Africa, has a sac of civet situated between the anus and the genitals in both males and females. The malodorous sprayings of the domestic Tom (*Felis domesticus*) should not be compared to the musky odour emitted by the civet-cat.

among the boys and men who were forcibly gelded was extremely high. Only one out of ten at the most survived the 'operation' which was done without any kind of surgical skill, let alone an anaesthetic. Yet it was usual for the most healthy boys and youths to be chosen for castration, all these eunuchs being sent up the Lake Chad–Bilma–Murzuk caravan route to Tripoli for use in the harems of North Africa, Arabia, and Turkey, or retained at the courts of the African kings. Major Denham tells us that in these African wars 'no males were spared on either side, except on terms worse perhaps than death. The Sultan of Bornu had more than 200 youths under twenty in his harem as eunuchs; while the sultan of Begharmi (who was said to have nearly 1,000 wives) had treble that number chosen out of the most healthy young men who had fallen into his hands as prisoners. . . .' Since the survival rate of eunuchs was one in ten for the castration operation and one in ten for the trans-Saharan journey, the odds against a young *castrato* reaching the Tripoli market were, theoretically, only one in a hundred. But the slave merchants could not afford to risk such odds even in the transportation of human beings who were easier to capture and transport than civet-cats. So the *castrati* probably received the preferential treatment accorded the especially beautiful virgins who were carried in cages on the backs of camels. The other slaves, of course, walked and were driven from well to well, arriving at the coast in the form of living skeletons, there to be fattened up before being sold at the auctions.

We have an eyewitness description by Captain Lyon of a slave caravan which he accompanied from Murzuk to Tripoli, himself attending on many of the girls and children who were left to die on the road by their Arab masters. Of those who arrived at their journey's end after months of travelling across the desert, Captain Lyon has this to say:

Their good-humoured gaiety and songs had lightened to me many hours of pain and fatigue, and their gratitude for any little benefits I had it in my power to confer had quite warmed my heart towards them. Even when so exhausted as to be almost unable to walk, these poor creatures showed few instances of sulkiness or despondency; the first stanza of a song having been sung by one enlivened the whole *Kafflé*, who immediately joined in chorus. Their patience under fatigue and endurance of thirst was very extraordinary. Khalifa's girls were allowed to drink only once in twenty-four hours, yet they were always cheerful.

I was frequently amused by observing the pains taken by these innocent savages to adorn themselves. Though overcome by privation of every kind and by the fatigue of a long day's journey, they employed themselves into converting into neck ornaments snail shells, berries, or any other whimsical objects they could meet with. . . .

One of the women of the Fellata had a little male child, which was carried in turn by the whole *Kafflé*. Her milk had failed her, and this poor infant had nothing to nourish him but a mixture of cold water and flour, unless I sometimes gave him some cusscussou. . . .

None of the slave-owners ever marched without their whips, which were in constant use; that of Hadje Mohammed more so than the rest: in fact, he was so perpetually flogging his poor slaves that I was frequently obliged to disarm him. . . . No slave dares to be ill or unable to walk; but when the poor sufferer dies, the master suspects there must have been something 'wrong inside' and regrets not having liberally applied the usual remedy of burning the belly with a red-hot iron. . . .

III

Thus for more than ten centuries of the slave trade, the negro captured in the villages and forests of Central Africa became the cornice-stone of the Saharan economy—first, because it was he who worked the oases and the salt mines; and secondly, because he provided the Saharan tribes with a *raison d'être*. This was the convoying of the slave caravans across the desert. With the prohibition of slavery and, in the twentieth century, the introduction of motor transport, the Saharan tribes, their way of life, their villages, and their vast herds of camels were doomed. Today, like all primitive peoples, like the Australian aborigines, or the Borneo head-hunters, they are an anachronism: the 'veiled men of the desert' are a thing of the past. They no longer have any function whatsoever.

It is worth taking a look at the particular Saharan tribe which has ruled the desert, perhaps even from Carthaginian times—the Tuaregs, or 'Veiled Men'. It is possible that these people are the direct descendants of those Garamantians who ruled the Central Desert in Greek and Roman times. Whether this is the case or not, the Tuaregs until quite recently were, in a sense, a nation whose culture and language had survived relatively unchanged since classical times.

The traveller who visits one of their settlements, particularly an encampment near an oasis which has some connection with the outside world, soon has visual proof of this. If he is lucky (soliciting the aid of the local police is the best approach) he will be invited into one of the black tents which are open on all four sides to allow the breeze, if any, to blow through. At such a settlement, between what is called the Red Rock Desert and the Great Eastern Sand Sea in western Libya, I made off towards such a tent from whence came the beating of a drum. With the customary salaams and the smiles strongly recommended in all dealings with these tribesmen by Father de Foucauld, the greatest friend of the Tuaregs (who were eventually to murder him), I was invited to sit in the tent. There were five men present, two in the dark blue ceremonial gowns of the nobility, the others in white. All were veiled, and what was visible of their faces was stained purplish by the dye of the veil. What was most striking, however, was the curious combination of impassivity and ferocity in their dark, partly bloodshot eyes gazing unblinking through the slit of their veil. The two chiefs who sat enthroned on a bolster spoke not a word, and made no sign or gesture of either friendliness or hostility in response to my wishes for the happiness of the bridegroom, for this was a wedding party—or the male part of it—and the drum was announcing the fact. The drummer sat in a corner of the tent, and after he had drummed for a while, an answer came back from the bride's tent, where the women were preparing a wedding feast of couscous. The Berber policeman did his best to convey my message and to initiate some sort of communication between us. The two noble Tuaregs, the bridegroom and his friend, merely sat cross-legged on their cushions and looked. There was no recognizable human expression in their regard: their manner and posture were strictly ritualistic. It was obvious that they belonged to another world altogether; we had nothing in common, neither experience, language, nor, possibly, human emotions. My presence was tolerated as part of the courtesy of the desert. Their tent was open to anyone who wanted to sit in the shade.

One was struck above all by the archaicism of the scene: five men sitting in a tent doing nothing for hour after hour, yet concentrating with all their being on maintaining the tradition and ceremony of a vanished way of life. Custom required that they waited in complete silence and dignity, immobile behind their veils, the human equivalent of tribal gods. For the Tuaregs remember that they were once lords of the desert, from the extreme north to the extreme south and, like all other conquerors, they have become obsessed with a conviction of their superiority to other men.

It will be much livelier than this when the women's drum announces that the bridal feast is ready. The men will then mount their camels and ride over to the women's quarters, and there will be some fun and life, for the Tuareg women, in particular, like to be gay, and they are the musicians and the singers of songs. They have a single-string violin like a lute; they have pipes, drums, and cymbals, and they play, sing, and dance, and things will liven up for the guests, though the bride and groom will maintain this ritualistic calm as part of the ceremony. But at the moment the scene in the men's tent is oppressively solemn, perhaps because the visitor knows it is becoming an anachronism, and partly because similar customs and scenes will soon survive only as tourist attractions.

For those travellers who can get as far as Ghadames, once a capital of the Tuaregs and still frequented by them on the outskirts, a tribal dance can be arranged to the accompaniment of the non-stop clicking of cameras. An old blind pipe-player turns up with his all-women orchestra of drummers and timpanists, and they give a first-rate concert of what is still genuine Tuareg music, for there aren't enough tourists yet for them to know any better. Few Western jazz orchestras could rival the rhythm produced by this band of black-faced and merry old girls half hidden behind their face coverings, for their fingers and palms beat out the most thrilling contrapuntal rhythms to the accompaniment of the pipe-player. In the meantime a negro Tuareg serf glides slowly back and forth, approaching and receding, his lance held stiffly in his right hand. Even his eyes are hardly visible through the narrow slit of his veil. He becomes, for the moment, the 'spirit' of the desert itself, for the desert, during the last 1,500 years, has belonged to the veiled men he personifies.

All the same, there is something pathetic about it. The regime of the Tuaregs is over. His is a camelline economy. He is, or was, a caravaner. And both the camels and the caravans are almost a thing of the past. The principal use of the camel today is as a plough-horse, or a short-range waggon between villages unconnected by paved roads. There are still thousands of camels in the desert, but there are few long-distance caravans. Aeroplanes, Land Rovers, and heavy diesel trucks have replaced them. Tractors are replacing the plough-camels. Roads are reaching out across the full desert. Nobody depends on the Tuaregs for transport or protection; and these are the only functions he knows. It is not clear how those who reside in the vicinity of the oases live at all. They have a few goats, tents of goatskin, camels, and nothing else. They are still the best ones for going out into the desert to find odds and ends of fuel which they bring in on their camels—enough roots of trees to light the domestic fire. Otherwise they have nothing to do and do nothing.

The five men I found sitting in their tent in the desert were representative of the Tuaregs who have close contact with 'civilization'. A few survivors of the great days of their desert dominion are still to be found in the remoter corners of the Air, and they would be no more strange in appearance, accoutrements, and weapons to a Roman observer than they are to us. The camel is the same; so is the riding saddle; so is the rider's 'seat' and his method of guiding his mount with his bare feet (as the legs are used for 'aids' in riding a horse). The Tuareg's provision for a long trip into the desert are still one goatskin of meal and another of water, with a handful of dates to appease his hunger on long marches. His weapons are a sword, a spear, a dagger, and a large shield made of sun-dried hide—roughly the arms of a Roman soldier of the Republic.

But this type of fiercely independent, proud, and primitively armed fighting-man is disappearing, along with his basic culture and even his language. Language is an index of the rise or fall of an ethnic group. Temajegh, the language of the Tuareg, is an example. It survives in everyday usage; the written language, called T'ifinagh, is all but forgotten. It was once the duty of all noble Tuareg women to be able to write in the T'ifinagh script which is one of the most ancient of North African alphabets, going back at least to Carthaginian times and probably, like all other alphabets, derived from the Punic. But since in the old monuments it is written from left to right, right to left, up to down, down to up, and in the spiral, or boustrophedon, manner, it is not unnaturally difficult to read. In fact, within a few years there will be nobody left who can write it at all and it will take its place with old Cornish as an utterly 'dead' language.

In short, with the official abolition of the slave trade, the desert tribes, and the desert itself for that matter, practically ceased to play any part in human affairs, and the Tuaregs, who had been the only link for two and a half thousand years between Central Africa and the Mediterranean—in other words, between the Negro and the White World—began to pass from the stage of history. The Saharan tribes had survived as transport agents and conveyers of the caravans on the one hand, and as pirates and raiders of the same caravans on the other. These activities kept them alive and to some extent flourishing. The cessation of the trans-Saharan trade left them unemployed and purposeless with the result that they turned to inter-tribal war and oasis-raiding to keep some semblance of their nationhood.

Then, again, as the supply of black labour for the cultivation of the oases dried up, the palmeries were increasingly neglected and often, as the consequence of a *razzia*, completely destroyed. The size and number of the oases decreased, sand filled the wells and cisterns, many of which had been carefully maintained since Roman times, and the age-old trails became more and more hazardous and finally were hardly used at all. The sizeable cities along the caravan routes—towns like Agades, Bilma, Ghat, Murzuk, Germa, Ghadames, and Mizda—were soon lifeless settlements with practically no commerce at all to justify their size and population.

The student of Saharan history is particularly conscious of this change as he travels the old slave-routes familiar through the descriptions of Lyon, Denham, Barth, and Duveyrier. Murzuk throughout the nineteenth century, for instance, was a thriving, bustling town, crossroads of the main caravan routes of the central Sahara. Arab, Turkish, Egyptian, and even some European commercial agents had offices here to expedite the flow of goods southwards to the Chad and northwards to the Mediterranean ports. It was an especially favoured oasis since it stands between two fearsome deserts, the great sand sea to the south and the black stone desert to the north. It was important enough, in fact, for the Arabs, Turks, and Italians to have built forts here, all three of which still survive in varying degrees of disintegration: the Arab fort with its conical tower of plastered mud is about to collapse; the Turkish castle is abandoned; and the Italian fort, built in the best tradition of a Hollywood Foreign Legion epic, is only partially occupied by a detachment of Libyan police.

None of these forts any longer served any purpose once the slave trade was suppressed, for Murzuk, formerly the capital of the Fezzan, is now only a halt on the Tripoli–Lake Chad trail— an unmade and unmarked track which is used by an occasional truck convoy carrying supplies down to the oil camps in the Tibesti. It has no other function, and an air of decay hangs over the town, especially over the great square where the thousands of slaves who had survived the march across the Tibesti Mountains and Southern Sand Sea were auctioned off to the dealers. As in other Saharan oases, the streets are crowded with men and boys who have nothing to do, since women and donkeys cultivate the oasis gardens and women do all the selling in the market. Some of the older men, aloof in their white robes and hoods, seem to be remembering the great days of Murzuk, when a caravan of hundreds of camels and thousands of slaves arrived from the south several times a year and the town was full of Arab traders, Tuareg tribesmen, Turkish soldiers, and the riffraff of the desert. This was how the first European travellers saw Murzuk, including the first to get that far down into the desert, the twenty-five-year-old Joseph Ritchie who lies buried somewhere on the outskirts of this place. Ritchie died here of fever, 'expiring without a groan or a pang', and was buried secretly at night so that his companions could read the Protestant burial service over his grave. Wandering through the streets of Murzuk, especially after sunset when the desert night seems to swallow up the forts, mosques, and slave market of this doomed oasis, the traveller has the time and solitude to recall those who were here before him and their accounts of their trials, endured with so much courage and simple faith.

IV

Even after the slave trade had been suppressed, the old life of the desert survived in one form or another for one simple reason, if no other: the absence of salt in the Sudan. Nearly all the salt in Negroland had always come from the north across the Sahara on the backs of camels, donkeys, horses, and oxen. The salt mines in the middle of the most terrible wastelands of the desert—at Taghaza, Taodeni, Walata, and Bilma—had always been worked all the year round by negro slaves who died within a few years of their arrival at the mines, to be immediately replaced by new workers. The salt they mined was worth its weight in gold in Timbuktu, and its transport across the desert was a commercial enterprise of unbelievable size, involving the assembling of as many as 40,000 camels to make the quick dash from Bilma to

Kano. These immense convoys carrying salt on the outward journey and cloth and corn when homeward bound formed the basis of the Tuaregs' whole economy, since they had to breed great numbers of camels to replace those lost on the journey and to provide guides and escorts for the train. This caravan traffic continued right up to the beginning of the twentieth century, and would still continue today if it were not for the internal-combustion engine. For the motor truck has replaced the camel in the desert as surely as the tractor has replaced the farm horse in the prairies of the United States. The camel which once carried the entire economy of 3,000,000 square miles on its back is fast becoming a museum of zoo exhibits.

To the Western observer of a romantic turn of mind the disappearance of the camel from the desert is a cause for regret until, perhaps, he considers the amount and degree of suffering that the system entailed. There are certainly tens of thousands of human and animal skeletons now buried beneath the sand to testify to this fact. The loss of entire caravans consisting of 2,000 men and 1,800 camels, as in 1805, is not uncommon in Saharan history. On this occasion the whole convoy perished of thirst on the Timbuktu–Marrakesh trail. Other large parties wearily marching across the desert met the same fate before and have since. In fact, what with the sufferings of the Africans driven northwards to slavery, the horrible fate of the salt-miners, the torments of thirst endured by the caravaners, the terror of the dwellers in the oases subjected to continual raids by the desert bandits, not to mention the misery of the overladen and exhausted beasts of burden, the history of the Sahara trade is neither romantic nor pleasant. In a sense it is further debased by the ruthlessness and cruelty of the Arab bosses who controlled it from earliest times, since Islam always encouraged and gave religious sanction to slavery. About all that can be said in excuse, if an excuse it is, is that Christians exploited and profited from the same trade for 400 years during which the captive Africans were shipped out of the Slave Coast ports by the tens of thousands. Whether their conditions were any better on the ocean voyage than the desert journey is unlikely; or whether they were any happier on the cotton plantations of Virginia than in the palmeries of southern Tunisia is unknown. In all cases the black men were chased like animals, rounded up and marched away like convicts, and allowed to die like flies. Hanns Vischer, the British consul crossing the desert en route to Murzuk in 1910, gives this description of what the slave route looked like:

> The ground (near the well) was literally strewn with old ropes, baskets, and pieces of clothes, the remains of horses, donkeys, camels, human skulls and thigh bones, which certainly gave one an idea of the traffic of former days. It is always near a well that the greatest number of bones are seen. The young slave children, weary from the cruel march through the desert, had perhaps strayed from the caravan or fallen by the road. When sufficient force enabled them to crawl to the well, they had found the caravan gone—without food and too weak to draw up water for themselves, they had lain down to die, quietly, in company with some sick camel who, abandoned by the men, had with its last remaining strength followed in the track of its companions.

The sufferings of these slave children dying from starvation after they had crawled to the wells had long been justified by the Church, both Catholic and Protestant: the slave trade, said the divines, gave Christians an opportunity of saving negro souls. With the blessings, then, of both the Moslem and the Christian religions, the trade continued unabated until the British decided to abolish it.[1] The first result was that the slave ships, chased by Royal Navy gunboats, crowded on all sail and jettisoned their cargo. In the meantime the overland caravans plodded across the Sahara Desert under the whips of their Moslem masters. In both cases the priests were proved correct. The Africans bound for the Americas were converted to Christianity; those for the Middle East to Islam.

---

1. One clause of the Peace of Utrecht, 1712, gave England the monopoly of supplying Spain's American colonies with negro slaves.

SEVEN

'Geographers, in Afric-maps . . .'

ONE HUNDRED AND FIFTY years ago Europeans knew more about the surface of the moon than they did of North and Central Africa. What they did know of the Dark Continent, as they called it, was derived from classical and Arabic sources, both by the very nature of them unreliable. The Greek geographers, as we have seen, didn't have the science to make exact maps, though travellers from the time of Herodotus had explored most of the Sahara. So had the Arab and Moorish travellers and merchants. In fact, the Moors had actually sent an army of 7,000 men, 8,000 camels, 1,000 pack-horses, and six large cannon right across the desert from Marrakesh to the Niger River in the time of Queen Elizabeth I, the majority of the specialists among the fighting men on this expedition being Europeans, including the English gunners; but none of them brought back any new or useful information to their home countries, for the probable reason that, to soldiers of fortune, one part of the world was very much like another. It was left to the Arabs, or the Arabic-speaking Berbers, to write about North and Central Africa, and they did so quite extensively, the standard 'textbook' of the region being Leo Africanus's *History and Description of Africa*.

All the European geographers could do to bring Ptolemy's second-century map of Africa up to date was to use the additional information given by the Moslem travellers. The results were chaotic. The late-eighteenth- and early-nineteenth-century maps of Barbary and Negroland are fairy-tale landscapes drawn from rumour and imagination. Jonathan Swift summed up the state of geographical knowledge in his day in a characteristic jingle:

132

So geographers, in Afric-maps,
With savage pictures fill their gaps;
And o'er unhabitable downs
Place elephants for want of towns.

Yet at the beginning of the nineteenth century the European scientists, geographers, and anthropologists were just as eager to left the veil on the face of the Dark Continent as were the politicians and merchants. In fact, in England, France, and Germany in particular, such topics as the size and nature of Timbuktu; which way the Niger River flowed; where was its mouth; was it a tributary of the Nile; where were the mines which yielded so much gold; where was the country Leo Africanus called Wangara; these questions, and the whole subject of African exploration, were to the civilized world of that day and age what space exploration is to this. We shall see, however, in examining the life and work of the early African explorers, that there were enormous differences in the two types of enterprise.

Systematic inquiry began with the formation in 1788 of the *Association for Promoting the Discovery of the Interior of Africa*, an organization of men of learning interested in scientific fact, not merely trade or conquest. Hence we read in the Proceedings of the Association 'at an adjourned Meeting of the Saturday Club at the St. Alban's Tavern, on the 9th of June, 1788' the following resolution:

That as no species of information is more ardently desired, or more generally useful, than that which improves the science of geography; and as the vast continent of Africa, notwithstanding all the efforts of the ancients, is still a great measure unexplored, the Members of this Club do form themselves into an Association for Promoting the Discovery of the Inland Parts of that quarter of the World.

In view of the subsequent scramble for African trade and territory, the sceptic might question the sincerity of the St. Alban resolution, particularly as the British had just lost their vast

American territories by the disastrous events of 1770–6. Were they merely looking for new colonies to replace those they had lost across the Atlantic? This is not the conclusion the student who has read the early reports of the African Association is justified in making. To the contrary, the entire emphasis in the early proceedings of the Association is on the desire for knowledge, coupled with the first serious campaign for the abolition of the slave trade. These two objectives were never lost sight of in the Association's history.

We see, then, in that meeting of nine men in the St. Alban's Tavern the first stirrings of that humanistic and scientific zeal which was to bring Europe within less than a hundred years to the highest stage of culture that it had ever known.

The Association quickly discovered that little useful would be learned from the merchant-travellers who were wholly disinterested in the scientific aspects of where they went and what they saw. Thousands of Arabo-Moorish traders, for instance, had seen which way the Niger flowed—a question which had been argued for hundreds of years in the schools and academies of Europe; yet, not being interested, they were not sure, when questioned, whether it flowed to the east or the west. Leo Africanus, who had seen the Niger many times, states bluntly that it 'flows *westward* into the Ocean; and our cosmographers assert that it is a branch of the Nile . . . we navigated it, *with the current*, to the west of Timbuktu'. Leo, of course, was 100 per cent wrong, with the result that for the next 300 years map-makers made the Niger flow the wrong way.

The first decision facing the Association was the selection of suitable explorers to undertake the formidable task of penetrating into the *terra incognita* of Africa. The tremendous intellectual and physical attributes required by such travellers posed an unusual problem. In the first place, if the emphasis was to be on scientific discovery, the explorer had to be a man of exceptional ability—with a knowledge of geography, surveying, and cartography as well as at least an acquaintance with geology, botany, and anthropology. For every shred of evidence as to what human, animal, and plant life actually existed within the hinterland of

Africa was considered vitally important. And, in addition to a familiarity with the physical sciences, the ideal explorer would have to be something of a linguist, and, if possible, an artist, in order to record factually and vividly the places and people he would visit. Nor was the importance of a working medical knowledge overlooked, whence no expedition, or single traveller, neglected to take a medicine chest on a journey into the interior.

Such intellectual qualifications, then, were essential; but even more requisite were the personal attributes of physical strength, stamina, and courage. But whereas these last three qualities are, in a sense, commonplace, as the history of Man's conquest of nature has shown from the dawn of time, they needed to be sublimated, as it were, by the addition of another quality which can, perhaps, best be called 'moral fibre', or, to use an old-fashioned definition, 'character'. In some respects the term is indefinable, for it implies a much subtler quality than the strength, stamina, and courage associated, for instance, with the good soldier. In the case of the early African travellers 'character' has a certain connotation which, since it is essentially religious, tends to elude us today. The faith of these explorers, in short, was uncomplicated by any of the arguments, doubts, compromises, or scepticisms of modern theology. The attitude of the Victorian traveller towards his Maker is perfectly simple, so that there is nothing out of the ordinary in Dr. Walter Oudney, dying with fever in a Nigerian village, reading his bible and saying his prayers before lying down to sleep. In fact, this whole company of men, many of whom died on their journeys, were constantly thanking God for His mercies, never railing against Him, or anybody else, for their misfortunes and sufferings. It is quite obvious that few, if any, of them had the slightest misgivings about the reality of a divine power, the existence of heaven, and the certainty of redemption through grace.

This childlike and unquestioning faith, then, was characteristic of the early-nineteenth-century African travellers—a faith which transcends the other outstanding traits of the 'traditional' Victorian—that is, the smugness, pomposity, sentimentalism, and bigotry which we have come to associate with the later period of the old queen's reign. In fact, there are no Pecksniffs in the desert. But when it comes to actual religious beliefs, and, indeed, genuine religious *fervour*, there is never the shadow of compromise. Nor, for that matter, is there any doubt that their convictions enabled them to endure untold sufferings.

These, then, were the attributes of mind, spirit, and body which the African Association had in mind in selecting its representatives for the great enterprise of bringing a vast area of the earth's surface into the community of nations. The difficulty, of course, was to find the ideal explorer, for such a man could hardly be expected to exist. Eventually one was found—the greatest of them all, in some respects the greatest of all African travellers, not excepting the more famous and still remembered explorers of eastern Africa and the Nile. He was Dr. Henry Barth, a German scholar whose incredible adventures, discoveries, and histories constitute the epitome of nineteenth-century African exploration. That Dr. Barth's name is forgotten is an almost brutal example of the neglect of truly great men. But then this scholarly German never conquered a square foot of territory by the sword; he merely revealed to an ignorant world the truth about half a continent.

But the Dr. Barths were few and far between in the early days of the African Association; so we find the directors back in London choosing of necessity the only men who were available. The first volunteers were 'strange' rather than truly competent selections, though one of them, at least, had the elements of greatness in his make-up. This was John Ledyard, an American.[1] Ledyard's companion was one William Lucas, a Londoner, of whom history has little to say.

But John Ledyard was a remarkable man by any standards. He was certainly one of the greatest 'tramps' of all time, and at one period of his short life had walked at an average rate of thirty miles a day from Stockholm to Yakutsk in Siberia, as a sort of warm-up for his project of walking right across America. Obviously,

1. A New Englander who sailed with Captain Cook in 1776 and published an account of the voyage, *A Journal of Captain Cook's Last Voyage to the Pacific Ocean*, published in Hartford, Connecticut, 1783. Ledyard's book gives the only account of Cook's death by an eyewitness.

here was a man who had that strength of mind and body, coupled with an undaunted spirit of adventure, which was the first pre-requisite of future African travellers. William Lucas, on the other hand, had certain qualifications, vague though they were: after having been a slave for three years in Morocco where he had learnt Arabic, he wangled himself the British vice-consularship at Gibraltar. A wild pair of adventurers, in short, who got the job of being the first Europeans since Roman times to cross the Sahara.

> To Mr. Ledyard [says the first report of the Association] they assigned, at his own desire, as an enterprise of obvious peril and of difficult success, the task of travelling from east to west, in the latitude attributed to the Niger, the widest part of the Continent of Africa.
>
> To Mr. Lucas, in consideration of the knowledge which he possessed of the language and manners of the Arabs, they allotted the passage of the Desert of Zahara, from Tripoli to Fezzan . . . and that he should afterwards return by way of the Gambia, or by that of the Coast of Guinea.

Nothing—no other statement or evidence—could so reveal the complete ignorance of the academician-geographers concerning the nature of the Sahara Desert than these two proposals.

Not surprisingly the results of the Ledyard-Lucas expedition were disappointing. The American explorer got as far as his starting point, which was Cairo, where he took an over-dose of 'vitriol' for his dysentery and promptly died, aged thirty-seven—the first of a long line of African explorers who were to die young. The Englishman Lucas got a little way inland from Tripoli in the following manner, according to the African Association's report of 1790:

> The caravan was composed of the Sherriff Fuwad, and of three other merchants on horseback, all of them well armed; of the little old Sherriff who rode upon an ass; of Mr. Lucas, who was mounted on the mule which the bashaw had given

him; of Mr. Lucas's black servant, well armed, upon a camel; of twelve Fezzaners on foot, but armed; of three negroes and their wives who had been slaves at Tripoli, but having obtained their freedom were now returning to their native country; and of twenty-one camels with fifteen drivers, each of whom was armed with a musket and a pistol.

But despite all these preparations Mr. Lucas made very little progress, getting as far as the Roman city of Leptis (which he calls Lebida) and not much farther. He and 'the little old sherriff' were eventually turned back. The sherriff went back to his mountains 'where he had many acquaintances and could live at small expense', and Mr. Lucas returned to Tripoli 'where the Bashaw to whom with many acknowledgments he returned the mule, expressed his hope that better fortune would attend him another year'.

The African Association now recognized what had been obvious for a thousand years: namely, that Moslem fanaticism on the one hand and the Barbary pirates on the other made penetration of the interior from the Mediterranean ports of Tripoli, Tunis, and Algiers extremely difficult. It was hard to say which force was the greater enemy of European exploration: Islam, which declared Christians to be 'the devil's children', or the Morisco pirates who exacted tribute from every ship plying the Mediterranean. In other words, the Mediterranean as late as 1830 was a Moslem sea and the North African ports were pirates' capitals. There had, of course, been some improvement since 1680 when the corsairs from Salee, Algiers, and Tunis were raiding as far north as Britain, carrying off women from English coastal villages, and striking terror to the heart of the Irish colleens as the Moslem call to prayer came echoing over the water. But there had been very little change in the Mediterranean itself; and there was to be none until the European powers, in sheer desperation, co-operated to wipe out the pirates and their lairs along the North African coast.

Having now failed to penetrate into the interior of Africa from both the east (Ledyard's assignment) and the north (Lucas's), the

African Association decided to send another explorer in from the west, and Major Daniel Houghton, an Irish gentleman-adventurer harassed by creditors, was chosen as the man for the job. His mission was to reach Timbuktu, the mysterious negro capital whose very name was synonymous to the nine-teenth-century explorers with the 'secret' of Central Africa. Even today, when the place has been described a thousand times by travellers arriving by camel, car, truck, or aeroplane, its mystery dispelled and its glamour debunked, Timbuktu has a special connotation and its own private aura.

So, on November 10th, 1790, Major Houghton, unable to shake off his creditors despite the rich lady he had just married, set out from the Gambia with his horse, five asses, and a large amount of merchandise, and, as usual, immediately ran into in-credible difficulties, dangers, and hardships. Who would have thought back in London where his trip was planned that the negro concubines of the Arab traders would plot against a British explorer's life, for instance? But such was the kind of hazard these lonely travellers were to experience for the next hundred years and more; and the African Association, though sincerely regretful to lose still another explorer, could not have been surprised when the news came through a year later that Major Houghton had died somewhere on the road to Timbuktu.

The next to go in, again from the west, was perhaps the greatest of them all, the twenty-year-old Scotsman Mungo Park, of whom the Association reported:

> A young man of no mean talents, who had been regularly educated in the medical line . . . sufficiently instructed in the use of Hadley's quadrant to make the necessary observations; geographer enough to trace out his path through the wilder-ness; and not unacquainted with natural history.

Mungo Park's two voyages of exploration do not fall within the compass of Saharan travel, since he, like Major Houghton before him, was sent in from the west coast of Africa to 'ascertain the course, and, if possible, the rise and terminus of the Niger

River. That he should use his utmost exertions to visit the principal towns or cities in its neighbourhood, particularly Timbuctoo and Houssa.'

There is the magic name again, Timbuktu (in one of its many variant spellings), the Mecca of all the early African explorers so many of whom, like Mungo Park, died trying to get there. But many of Park's experiences were later to be repeated by the explorers coming from the north across the desert; and, in that regard, the young Scotsman very early in his travels discovered the main clue why the Arabs and Moors had free access to Timbuktu and the other Niger River towns while no Europeans had ever been allowed to explore this country. The reason was simple and is simply stated by an Arab trader: 'The Christians were looked upon there [i.e. in Timbuktu] as the devil's children and enemies to the Prophet. . . .' Consequently Park and many who came after him into Moslem territory were treated with ignominy, sometimes brutality, and often paid with their lives for refusing to conceal their Christian faith. In fact, whether to penetrate these Moslem lands as an undisguised and professing Christian, or a disguised and bogus Moslem, became a highly controversial topic in early Victorian drawing-rooms, and there were bound to be references to the treatment of Mungo Park who was, as he writes, 'obliged to suffer, with an unruffled countenance, the insults of the rudest savages on earth'—including sharing a small hut with a wild hog since the Moors into whose hands Park had fallen at this time believed that there was an implacable enmity between hogs and Christians. The hog, however, seems to have attacked everybody but Mungo Park, who was the only one who did not torment the wretched beast. But the hog was goaded unmercifully and so was the young Scotsman, though he handled himself with superb canniness, as one can see from his account of the visit of the Moorish ladies.

A party of them came into my hut, and gave me plainly to understand that the object of their visit was to ascertain by actual inspection, whether the rite of circumcision extended to the Nazarenes as well as the followers of Mahomet. The reader will easily judge my surprise at this unexpected declaration; and in order to avoid the proposed scrutiny, I thought it best to treat the business jocularly. I observed to them that it was not customary in my country to give ocular demonstrations in such cases before so many beautiful women; but that if all of them would retire, except the young lady to whom I pointed (selecting the youngest and handsomest), I would satisfy her curiosity. The ladies enjoyed the jest and went away laughing heartily; and the young damsel herself to whom I gave the preference (though she did not avail herself of the privilege of inspection) seemed no way displeased at the compliment, for she soon afterwards sent me some meal and milk for my supper.

These 'jocular' interludes in the lives of the explorers, most of whom were to die in their thirties, still struggling to reach their journey's end, are rare, and, when they occur, usually entail a little fun and games with the ladies. We find similar light-hearted moments in the narratives of other travellers of the time, Major Dixon Denham, in particular, appreciating the curiosity of the local damsels. Writing from the oasis of Sockna in the Libyan Desert, he describes the women as

certainly very pretty . . . and a pair of loose white trousers that I wore, into the pockets of which I accidentally put my hands, raised their curiosity to a wonderful degree: my hands were pulled out, and those of three or four of the ladies thrust in, in their stead: these were replaced by others, all demanding their use so loudly and violently, that I had considerable difficulty in extricating myself, and was glad to make my escape. . . .

Major Denham's predecessor in these parts, Captain Lyon, R.N., also has some observations to make concerning the ladies, as he was invited to visit Lilla Fatma, 'the fat wife of Sheikh Barood'.

I must say [the naval officer reports] I never before beheld such a monstrous mass of human flesh. One of her legs, of enormous size, was uncovered as high as the calf, and every one pressed it, admiring its solidity, and praising God for blessing them with such a sight. I was received most graciously and invited to sit close to her when one of the first questions she asked me was if, in my country, the ladies were as fat and handsome as herself?

What the Captain was seeing, of course, was the result of years of deliberately stuffing girl children with milk and meal on the same principle as Strasbourg geese. The children, Mungo Park tells us, were thrashed by their mothers if they cried on being forced to take additional nourishment.

The Captain Lyon, R.N., who reports on the size of Sheik Barood's fat wife, was a member of the expedition which followed in the footsteps of William Lucas, who had started out from Tripoli in 1791 and of Frederick Hornemann who had travelled from Cairo to Murzuk across the Libyan Desert in 1796—one of the greatest journeys of European travellers within the last two centuries.

Frederick Hornemann was born in Hildesheim, Germany, in 1772 and died in Africa in 1801 somewhere on the road to the Coast. He was then twenty-eight and had been three years in the desert.

Hornemann's itinerary which, like Mungo Park's, had been planned by the African Association, required the explorer to cross the Libyan Desert from east to west, a feat that had never been accomplished by a European before and was never accomplished again until the Second World War when motorized caravans, wireless, and the whole resources of military organization made such desert travel relatively easy. But Hornemann had to cross by the immemorial camel routes, and this he set out to do in 1797. First, however, he was 'captured' in Napoleon's occupation of Cairo, but released and sent on his way by the French General who, throughout the wars, allowed scientists and explorers to continue their work and to communicate with their parent societies, whatever their nationality. So we find a Frenchman expediting to London the reports of a German working for the British; and, because of this respect for science, the civilized world was spared the destruction of Frederick Hornemann's *Journal*.

Hornemann was accompanied by a fellow countryman, Joseph Frendenburgh, a convert to Mohammedanism and a man who, in addition to having made the pilgrimage to Mecca three times, spoke both the Arabic and Turkish languages perfectly. 'Without him', Hornemann writes in a letter which General Bonaparte personally forwarded to the African Society, 'I should scarcely be able to pursue my journey without actually embracing and professing Mohammedanism myself . . .' and he adds, in the typically calm and modest tone of the explorers of his time: 'I request the Society the attending to a just remuneration of his services, and specially, if in case of my death, he should faithfully preserve my journals and papers and proceed with them to England.'

The two Germans, then, set out with a West African caravan homeward-bound from Mecca on September 5th, 1798. Six weeks later they reached Murzuk. Hornemann's route passed through the oasis of Siwa in the middle of the Libyan Desert, which he describes in detail, for it was famous from Greek times as the seat of the oracle of Jupiter Ammon which Alexander the Great visited in 325 B.C. We can get some idea of what the young German traveller was up against from this entry in his *Journal*:

When I entered the ruins, I was followed by all the people here, and thus prevented examining the place with any accuracy. On a second visit I was not more successful; and when, after a few days, I returned thither again, some Siwahans directly said to me, 'Thou undoubtedly art yet a Christian in thy heart, else why come so often to visit these works of infidels?' In order to maintain the character I had assumed, I was thus necessitated to abandon any further project of nice examination or admeasurement. . . .

However, Hornemann made an extensive survey of the ruins of the various temples and sent back enough information to the

African Association to keep the armchair archaeologists happy
arguing about his report for months. Sir William Young, the
Secretary of the Association, was particularly scornful of Hornemann's findings, though this was not surprising in view of the
contentiousness of a baronet who opposed the reform of the poor
laws and the abolition of slavery and had a reputation for being
'difficult' since his university days.

Page 15 [begins Sir William]: the extent of the oasis of Siwah
as represented by Mr. Horneman [*sic*] differs widely from that
stated by every other writer ancient or modern. . . .

Page 23: the admeasurements of the Sacred Egyptian building appear to vary in every proportion from those given by a
late traveller of allowed accuracy, Mr. Brown. . . .

Horneman states 1,500 warriors, or *men bearing arms*, as the
data for estimating the population of the country: he must
mean to say, *men capable of bearing arms*, or these are no *data*, and
he means nothing. . . .

The reader today, however, must never lose sight of the fact
that every crumb of information which travellers sent out of
Africa 150 years ago was precious, so great was the craving for
knowledge in this flowering period of learning; and so eager
were scholars to contribute something to the advancement of
science. This is the explanation of why Englishmen who were by
calling professional soldiers, or sailors, or colonial administrators, or aristocrats contributed their time and money to
learned societies; and why a busy parliamentarian and administrator like Sir William Young could spend months writing a
report on Hornemann's 'Antiquities of Siwah'. Similarly, William
Marsden, a clerk in the East India Company for which he spent
eight years in Sumatra, 'amusing his leisure hours by writing
verses and acting female parts in a local theatre', and later becoming first secretary of the Admiralty, found time to write
'Observations on the Language of Siwah as represented by
Frederick Hornemann'.

I directed my attention [says Marsden] to the numerous specimens I possess of the languages spoken by various tribes of Negroes in the Northern part of the continent, but without being able to trace in any of them the slightest similitude. I then pursued my comparison through the Arabic, Hebrew, Syriac, Chaldaic, and the different branches of the Ethiopic. . . .

He finally hits on the solution! The language of Siwah is a variant of Shilba, Berber, or Amazigh. William Marsden strikes one as something of a philological ragbag, but one must admire the sheer exuberance of a senior civil servant who could 'pursue his comparisons through Arabic, Hebrew, Syriac, Chaldaic, and the different branches of Ethiopic. . . .'

What is obvious from Hornemann's *Journal*, though it represents only the beginning of his explorations, is that the young German in his thorough Teutonic way was on the threshold of *Africa Incognita* as no European from the time of the Romans had been before. In fact, to two Germans, Hornemann first, Barth second, goes the crown for Saharan exploration, though it must be added that both men were employed, financed, and encouraged by the British. The last we hear of Frederick Hornemann is his letter to Sir Joseph Banks, dated 'Tripoly, 19th August, 1799'. It is a rather fitting obituary for the young explorer, for it contains in its mixture of myth and fact, hope and resignation, the very spirit of the early African travellers. Hornemann writes:

Christians and tailed men, I suppose, never will be found in the interior of Africa. The Mahometans call *Nazari* (which is properly the name for Christians) not the Christians only, but also every other people who are not of their religion. Of tailed men I heard no accounts, except from one person (but not a *testis fide dignissimus*), who placed them ten days south of Kano; he called them *Yem Yem*, and said they were cannibals. In ten months I shall be near to that direction.

I shall now, Sir, conclude this letter, which I hope will find you in good health. I am, etc., etc.,

Frederick Hornemann

Whether Hornemann ever found his tailed men we shall never know—for he was never seen or heard of again except for a rumour that a white traveller had died in 'Noofy'. If 'Noofy' is Nupe (known today as Bida, a town in south-western Nigeria), then Hornemann had nearly reached the Niger River and the Atlantic Coast. But he never got to his journey's end and died not far in time or place from Major Houghton and Mungo Park and a score of explorers and travellers who followed in his footsteps. Hornemann, it should be remembered, was the first European to cross the Sahara from west to east: that is, from Cairo nearly to Lagos by way of the Libyan, Tibesti, and Central Sahara Deserts, a distance of 2,500 miles across the most desolate wastelands in the world.

So far—that is, by the turn of the century—what the African Association back in London called 'Intelligence Concerning the Interior Part of North Africa' was ominously meagre in view of the cost in time, money, and men's lives. Of five explorers sent out, four had died in the field within a period of some twenty years: John Ledyard in Cairo, 1788; Major Houghton in Nigeria, 1791; Frederick Hornemann at Nupe, 1801; and Mungo Park on the Niger River, 1806 (?). Not only had these explorers lost their lives but they had, in a sense, lost them in vain, since the reports of their discoveries never reached London where the Association with the help of the leading geographers and cartographers of Britain were attempting to draw the map of Africa. Hence, despite the bravery and sufferings of the first explorers, very little was known after twenty years of 'the Interior Part'; and none of the leading questions answered. The direction of the Niger River's current; the final outlet of this great African river; whether it evaporated in the desert as the leading geographers maintained, or flowed as a tributary into the Nile, as Hornemann was told; the location of the various African kingdoms; the size and importance of Timbuktu—these were all questions which European scholars were anxious to get answered, if only the incredible difficulties of trans-Saharan travel could be overcome.

By this time the British Government was beginning to be

interested, for though the exploration of Africa was initiated out of pure scientific curiosity so typical of the age, the big commercial corporations had always had an eye on the potential riches of Central Africa. One says 'potential' because no one knew yet what there was of material value to be got out of Africa, except for slaves, ivory, and gold. Significant are the names of the Atlantic littoral of West Africa: the Slave, Ivory, and Gold Coasts. Merchants and business men, therefore, prodded the British Government through their parliamentary representatives to get on with the exploration of the unknown continent.

The Government's first venture was typical: it failed through the niggardliness of the Treasury in allotting the three explorers engaged for the mission sufficient funds to provide for themselves, let alone the hordes of bashaws, sherrifs, sheiks, marabouts, and so on who had to be bribed and placated with gifts.

However, a mission was arranged, to be led by Joseph Ritchie, a young surgeon and friend of John Keats whom he describes as 'a lad of about 20 who, if I am not mistaken, is to be the great poetical luminary of the age to come'. Ritchie at this time was twenty-five: he was interested in 'the lad of twenty' because of the association between the poet's *Endymion* and the 'Mountains of the Moon' which he intended to discover. He promised to 'fling a copy of the poem into the midst of the Sahara'.

The young Scottish surgeon reached Malta in 1818, and here co-opted the services of Captain G. F. Lyon, R.N., and John Belford, a shipwright. Such was the odd composition of the party which was to cross the Sahara Desert from north to south: a surgeon, a naval officer, and a shipwright. It is not really surprising that the travellers never got much farther than Murzuk, some 700 miles south of Tripoli whence they had set out after the usual frustrating delays. Joseph Ritchie promptly died of fever at Murzuk, 'expiring without a groan or a pang', says his companion, Captain Lyon. He was around thirty years old, which was beginning to be the average age of African explorers when they died. Ritchie, though young and though described as 'a gentleman of great science and ability', was obviously unfitted physically to the rigours and hardships of desert travel for he seems to have been sick most of the time. Captain Lyon was able secretly to read the Protestant burial service over the grave at night and publicly recited the first chapter of the Koran in the morning. For the three Englishmen were travelling as Mamelukes.[1]

Captain Lyon, who now pushed on southwards, is absolutely uncompromising on the necessity for assuming the Moslem disguise. 'I am confident that it would never be possible for any man to pass through Africa unless in every respect he qualified himself to appear as a Mohammedan; and, should I myself return to that country, I would not be accompanied by anyone who would refuse to observe these precautions.' That Captain Lyon knew what he was talking about was to be attested by many future African travellers who were murdered in cold blood merely because they were infidels. Gerald Rohlfs, the German explorer, for instance, owed his life on more than one occasion not to the fact that he claimed to be a Moslem but that he had taken the precaution of having himself circumcised before he set off on his travels. This was as late as 1862, thirty-two years after the French conquest of Algiers.

Captain Lyon had also personally witnessed the fanaticism of the Moslems, even in an international city like Tripoli. It wasn't just the marabouts who ran around with nails driven through their faces, vomiting blood and saliva, which alarmed him; nor even the crazy man who was let out of a dungeon before a religious ceremony to push his hand into a donkey's side from which he tore out and devoured the entrails; it was the Moslem hatred of the Christians whose houses were stoned as the religious processions passed by. In other words, he saw from personal observation what Mungo Park had reported: that Christians were regarded as the devil's children and enemies of the Prophet.

For this reason, he not only disguised himself as a Moslem,

---

1. The Mamelukes were originally soldiers, many of them of European origin, who were converted (in theory) to Islamism. They once had great power in Mohammedan countries.

but 'used all his endeavours to become acquainted with their manners'. The Captain, it seems, kept his eyes and ears open. No detail, however small, escaped his notice:

> I observed a singular custom to be prevalent amongst all Moors and Arabs from the Bashaw down to the poorest camel-driver [he writes], which is that of eructation, and which they perform as often and loudly as possible. Great men go through this ceremony with a solemnity and dignity altogether imposing, stroking their beards and thanking God for the great relief they have obtained. Mukni was quite a professor in this way; and his little son Yussuf (a boy of about eight years of age) promised fair to be equally accomplished. . . .

Dressed as Moors and having familiarized themselves with the customs of the country, Mr. Ritchie, Captain Lyon, and shipwright Belford set off on Sunday, February 7th, 1819 for the interior of Africa. By May 20th Mr. Ritchie was dead, and the other two men so sick with fever that they 'expected in a few days it might be our lot to follow our lamented companion'. Indeed, Ritchie's death on the road and the sickness of his companions were to become a familiar pattern of desert exploration for the next fifty years or more.

Captain Lyon, because of his chronic shortage of funds—he could not even afford to give the alms to beggars at religious festivals, a disgrace for a man in his position—was unable to get farther south than the Fezzan. The fact that he didn't have enough money to feed himself and his horse and thereby push on down to the Kingdom of the Bornu, about which there was so much interest in Europe, was a great disappointment, since he had taken pains to organize his expedition under the protection of the Sultan of Fezzan; and, as he points out for the benefit of future travellers:

> Nothing could have been more fortunate than our travelling with the Sultan; our difficulties must otherwise have been very

great. . . . I was his constant companion, and being of a less sedate disposition than Mr. Ritchie,[1] he always invited me to ride by him. He amused himself by asking questions about my country. . . . He was much astonished that young men did not marry until they had arrived at twenty-five or thirty years of age: this he considered as highly improper: but in some degree reconciled it to his way of thinking by supposing that they must, in that case, have a great number of concubines. . . . He himself had 50 Negresses, which was considered a very moderate allowance for a Sultan of Fezzan. . . . The mother of his little son Yussuf [Lyon continues] had a child about a year since, perfectly black. Mukni being satisfied that it could not be his, sent for the suspected father and made him strangle the infant. . . .

Thus gathering all the odds and ends of information he could, Captain Lyon pushed on south day after day at the expense of appalling physical suffering, since both he and the loyal Belford were racked with malaria and dysentery from the day they left Tripoli. Typical of almost every entry in his journal is some such notation as 'myself much better, Belford very weak'; or, 'I was again very severely attacked with *hemma* [fever] and, as usual, suffered much from pain in the spleen and liver.' But it soon becomes apparent on reading Lyon's fascinating yet modest *Narrative* that this English sailor had all the virtues of the born explorer—courage, resourcefulness, tenacity, physical stamina, a scientific curiosity in all he saw and heard, and, added to these qualifications, the character of a true Christian gentleman and the skill of an artist. His book is illustrated with delightful portraits of tribal types in full costume which he painted en route. This was an achievement in itself as it was forbidden to Moslems (Captain Lyon was supposed to be a convert!) to make likenesses on paper, as the Christians worshipped such images. Moreover, the artist got into trouble for reasons he didn't anticipate.

1. We get several references to Mr. Ritchie's 'sedate disposition'. Quite obviously the two men didn't like each other.

In one instance [he writes] I excited evident jealousy in the Sultan who could not be persuaded that a Negress I had drawn was not one of his favourites. . . .

A worse danger came from the enthusiasts who 'boldly pushed at the drawing with two fingers, one for each eye, to the great risk of its entire destruction, exclaiming "There are his eyes! Look at his eyes! There are two of them! God is merciful! How wonderful! Well! Look! He has a nose and mouth too! Oh! Oh! Oh! Allah! Allah! Allah!" '

On Christmas Day 1819 Lyon and his companion Belford, both almost too sick to stand up, celebrated the holy festival with a small cup of coffee apiece in their tent on the outskirts of a village called Terboo, 'the most wretched mud village I had as yet met with. All the men were mere skeletons, and the women equally miserable in appearance; yet they were obliged, poor and wretched as they were, to feed us and our horses without expecting a reward. I bought, however, a quantity of corn and distributed it among them.' In these surroundings the two Englishmen drank to the health of their friends in England.

A few days later Belford was so weak that he fell from his horse in the desert and was left behind unbeknown to the little caravan. Later, his horse turned up at the camp without its rider; but by this time the shipwright's chances of being found were slim as night had fallen and Belford, being by this time stone-deaf, could not have heard the searchers' shouts. However, he was eventually brought in when Captain Lyon reports, 'Much as he required food and restoration, we had, unhappily, none to give him. . . .'

Nevertheless, the two men pushed on, and in the New Year of 1820 Lyon had the satisfaction of seeing a genuine 'Tibboo'; and though he was obviously unaware of the classical description of these negro people—the 'Ethiopian troglodytes' of Herodotus—who inhabited the undiscovered mountains of the Tibesti, he describes them in almost identical terms—as inhabiting caves, dressing in the skins of wild animals, and still able to run faster than other men! The 'Tibboos' still had need to run, of course, since the slavers were still chasing them in A.D. 1820 as they had been doing in 1820 B.C.

Lyon had now reached their farthest south at Zuila, where he made a cursory examination of the ruins and was puzzled by the inscriptions which the natives claimed were 'Rumi'—that is, Christian. The ruins that he saw and dismissed in a few words were of a Byzantine kingdom called Cellaba which represents one of the most extraordinary chapters in the entire history of the Sahara Desert.

The traveller visiting the site today is almost as greatly puzzled by the ruins as Captain Lyon was, for it seems inconceivable that such massive monuments could have been built this far down in the desert. Merely to reach Zuila means crossing a black stone desert of complete desolation, with not a sign of life, either animal or vegetable. After many weary miles of this lunar wasteland, one suddenly sees the walls and turrets of a castle comparable in size and strength with the great fortresses of medieval Europe. To the west, again, runs a chain of forts and watch towers protecting the oasis from the invasions of the desert tribesmen from the south and west. The danger from the east was negligible, since Zuila is the last oasis before the terrifying wastes of the Great Libyan Desert itself. Yet here, in this inconceivably remote corner of the Sahara, some nation about whom we know precisely nothing built a castle, forts, watch towers, churches, and fortified farms, sufficient to enable some community resembling a city-state to flourish in the middle of nowhere.

One always takes the precaution in these Libyan outposts of calling on the police. I found the gendarmes in the courtyard of the castle. As usual, the thick, sweet tea was brewed and sand-dried dates placed on a piece of sacking. Communication between us was halting, though my card tricks were appreciated, even if spotted at once. In due course, an old soldier who had served with the Italian army of occupation arrived, and I was able to explain what I wanted. I wanted, of course, to visit the ruins.

The main castle, which is still occupied by the poorer families and their animals as well as by the police, must be one of the largest strongpoints in the Sahara Desert. It occupies, in fact, the whole centre of the present settlement and was, like the great medieval fortresses, a complete town in itself. Its immensely thick walls are made of cement blocks covered with stone brought from the mountains. Its four corner towers remain intact, with the long walls in between recessed at intervals so that the defenders above could pin the besiegers into groups under the walls. It must have been the last stronghold of the city after the outlying forts across the desert had been overwhelmed. When this happened, or which invaders overthrew this state, we don't know. We know very little about Zuila. We can only surmise that it was a Byzantine kingdom which sprang up in this oasis at the end of the Roman imperium in Africa when the frontier civilization resisted for a time the invasions of the barbarians from the desert even after the great cities along the Mediterranean littoral had been sacked and destroyed. So either the camel-born armies of the desert tribes finished off Zuila; or, more likely, it fell before the onslaught of the Prophet's armies in the seventh century. The seven large and beautiful domed tombs on the outskirts of the city seem to symbolize the history, and perhaps the fate, of this city-state. Were they the tombs of Byzantine kings? Or were they built for Arab heroes who died in the siege of Zuila—built, of course, by the conquered citizens who alone in the desert had the art and skill to construct monuments in stone? For whatever else they are, these tombs and forts are evidently pure Byzantine; but since they have been looted, the possibility is that they did not commemorate Moslem saints or heroes, but ante-date the Arab invasions of the seventh century.

It is understandable, then, that Captain Lyon was puzzled by the existence of such imposing monuments in this corner of the desert. He made no claims to archaeological knowledge; and he was, in any case, too sick and harassed to do more than glance at the great fort and the inscriptions he appears to have seen. One can get no evidence at all of such inscriptions which would throw the first light on this mysterious Byzantine settlement; and a careful search of the ruins scattered around in the outlying desert revealed nothing which elucidated the mystery. There are

rumours all over this countryside of 'treasure'—meaning gold—
that has been found under the walls and floors of the old city;
but to these people archaeological excavations always means
treasure-hunting. More significant, and needing investigation,
was a report that twenty miles to the north of Zuila, at a gap
through the hills, there are the remains of a paved-road with
'stones' which might be Roman milestones, for this was the
caravan trail which ran north-eastwards across the Libyan Desert
to Siwa and so to Alexandria. Future archaeologists and historians have many years' work ahead of them before we have a
single hard fact on which to base our theories and speculations
about this desert kingdom.

Captain Lyon, however, was more impressed by the people of
this oasis than he was by its lost civilization, and he noted what
is still obvious today: the religious fervour of the priests coupled
with what he describes as the appalling ignorance of the population. The Zuilans today belong to the Senussi sect and they are
exceedingly strict in their religious and social attitudes. They are,
however, also exceedingly hospitable, and saw to it that I ate
couscous for supper, breakfast, and lunch. I wish I could say that
rice and sand dug out of a washbowl with the bare hand is my
favourite food; but I at least appreciate what the cost and pre-
paration of the dish entail. I didn't, then, see the oasis as Captain
Lyon saw it, though he, too, was fortunate in that the holiest man
in town, a congenital idiot called Father Moses, took a fancy to
him. The English officer was henceforth highly regarded in the
town; but though he was liberally provided with what he calls 'a
good mess of sheep skin stewed with onions', he was still too weak
to walk. The marabouts wanted to treat his fever by persuading
him to swallow a draught made of the ink from holy texts; but
Lyon had no great opinion of Arab medicine. He gives us the
following succinct account of the diseases and their treatment:

Diseases	Cures
Liver Complaints	Burning with a hot iron
Asthma	ditto
Consumption	ditto

Blindness	Burning the temples and putting onion between the eyelids
Rupture	Burning
Fever and ague	Charms drunk in water
Venereal	Purges of colocynth and washes of soda. Effectual
Gonorrhoea	Purges and burning
Palsy	Charms

On January 10th, 1820, Lyon and Belford ('Belford was this day a little better') joined a slave caravan and started back on the long homeward journey to Tripoli. Lyon's fortitude and kindness on this trip now became increasingly evident. Scarcely a day passed without his performing some act of mercy to a sick or dying slave. He writes in his diary:

> I had observed a poor slave, of about fifty years of age, belonging to the owner of some of our camels, so fatigued as to be scarcely able to follow us. His frame was quite emaciated, and his feet and legs much swelled. His inhuman master, notwithstanding the deplorable state in which he was, invariably sent him out all night to attend the camels, and he only brought them back to commence another sad day's journey, during which he was frequently beaten. . . . His master, according to custom, beat him severely with a stick, and finding the poor black unable to cry out, actually took stones and beat him on the head with them, another Arab assisting in the cruel task. So much barbarity induced me to endeavour to defend the poor sufferer. . . .

Captain Lyon had the satisfaction of seeing the slave's master get 'a very severe bastinado, as hard as two men could lay it on'; and, he adds, 'while I was in sight, they always caressed the poor slave, who became a kind of pensioner to us'.

On another occasion we find him administering to a fourteen-year-old slave girl who was so weak that she had to be lashed to a camel.

She told me in the morning that the fatigue of the day would kill her; and that I was the only person, with the exception of her companions, who had treated her kindly since she was taken from her mother. She had been ailing for a long time; but her master was a hard man, and she feared to complain. . . . She was buried near the road.

So, letting the weak slaves ride his own camel while he walked and once getting lost in the desert—his most terrifying experience of all, Captain Lyon came back to civilization; and, typical of the man and his generation, 'chanted God Save the King and Rule Britannia as loud as I could roar' on beholding the blue sea again. Even then, within sight of home, he was so ill that he had to fall behind and, 'lying on the ground, I was seized with such a violent trembling that the Arab remaining with me was obliged for some time to sit on and hold me down to prevent my injuring myself'. Left alone in the desert while the Arab went for water, Lyon finally despaired of surviving and was so tortured by thirst that he resolved to drink his camel's urine, for 'I had no alternative but to drink or, as I thought, to expire'.

Despite his fevers and sufferings and near escapes, Captain Lyon got safely back to England. The next we hear of him he is exploring the Arctic region as commander of a British warship. A few years later he is in Mexico as one of the commissioners of a mining company. Next he went to South America, again in the mining business, and returning home in 1832 to seek medical advice for his failing sight, he died at sea on October 8th, 1832. He was thirty-seven years old.

EIGHT

'I suffered much, but complained not'

I

IN THE final analysis the results of the Ritchie-Lyon mission were disappointing to the savants and politicians back in London, since nothing of very great interest or importance seemed to have come out of these explorers' desert travels. Neither the country of the Bornu nor the Niger River had been reached.

But the British Government was now committed to a policy of African exploration, particularly in view of the fact that the French were interesting themselves in the same thing. The nineteenth-century carving up of Africa by the European powers was about to begin. The first step, obviously, was to reconnoitre the vast territory and see what was the most worth 'protecting'.

With this in view the Government decided on another mission to follow up that of Mr. Ritchie and Captain Lyon.

This mission, which was to go in from the north, consisted of Dr. Walter Oudney, a surgeon in the Royal Navy; Lieutenant Hugh Clapperton, a naval lieutenant; and Major Denham Dixon 'of His Majesty's Seventeenth Regiment of Foot'. The title of the publication which resulted from this expedition tells its own story.

Narrative of Travels and Discoveries in Northern and Central Africa, in the years 1822, 1823, and 1824, by Major Denham, Captain Clapperton, and the Late Doctor Oudney, extending across the great Desert to the Tenth Degree of Northern Latitude, and from Kouka in Bornou, to Sackatoo, the Capital of the Fellalah Empire . . . dedicated by Permission to the Right Honourable Earl Bathurst, one of His Majesty's principal Secretaries of State, by Major Denham and Captain Clapperton, the Survivors of the Expedition.

The three men responsible for this enterprise were all, in their way, typical of the early African explorers. All three died young in Africa.

Walter Oudney was born of 'humble parents' in Edinburgh in 1790. It seems that by hanging around the barbers' shops, Oudney picked up enough surgical knowledge to sign on as a surgeon's mate on board a man-of-war. Later he attended the medical school at the University of Edinburgh and acquired an M.D. Described as a small man with a pale grave face, Oudney seemed destined for the university lecture hall, but he was persuaded to undertake the African venture, as a chemist, botanist, and natural historian.

Dixon Denham, Oudney's companion, was in striking contrast to the grave Scottish scientist. Denham was the typical young officer-gentleman of his day, fun-loving, gallant, and extremely popular both with the ladies and his superiors. He distinguished himself at the Battle of Toulouse by carrying his commander, Sir James Douglas, out of the line of fire when that officer had lost a leg. It was in this spirit of devil-may-care gallantry that Major Denham undertook the Tripoli to Timbuktu mission; and we aren't surprised when, after falling into the hands of the Fellalah tribe as a prisoner of war, he escapes, though wounded and stripped literally naked. Nor are we surprised that a man of his type got safely back to England where 'he became the object of public notice and a frequent visitor to the table of Earl Bathurst'. Subsequently appointed Lieutenant-Governor of Sierra Leone, he died in Freetown of the 'African Fever'.

The third member of the mission, Lieutenant (later Captain) Hugh Clapperton, a Scotsman like Oudney, was born in 1788. We are told that he started life as a cabin boy, but showed his independent spirit by refusing to black the captain's shoes. He showed, too, his spirit of adventure in his subsequent career— cook's mate, pirate, lieutenant in the Royal Navy, explorer in Labrador, hunter with an Indian tribe, fiancé of an Indian princess, and finally African explorer. His physical appearance accorded with the kind of life he chose to lead, for he was six feet tall in an age of smaller men, and broad with it. Some idea of his powerful physical magnetism can be gauged from the curious story of how an African *grande dame* chased him back and forth across the Sudan, determined to marry 'the handsome white man'. Clapperton at least knew when this lady was coming because, dressed in scarlet and gold and mounted on a white horse, she was always preceded by a very noisy band. At this point the explorer hastened to move off to the next village. But his adventures, romantic and otherwise, were soon to be over. He gradually collapsed under the strain of dysentery and fever and died on April 13th, 1827, on his second journey in search of the source of the Niger.

The Oudney-Denham-Clapperton expedition was the beginning of the exploration of Africa in depth, for the three explorers crossed the Sahara to Lake Chad, never before seen by a European. They also reached the capital of Bornu and were cordially welcomed by the king. Denham was now able to continue his exploring of the Lake Chad region, while Clapperton and Oudney went on westwards to search for the Niger and the mystery of its source, direction, and final outlet. The explorers found that the African monarchs and Arab merchants welcomed them and were even anxious to enter into trade negotiations with the British Government. In fact, the only obstacles to the success of the mission seemed to be the question of the slave trade (which the British insisted would have to be abolished before friendly relations with the King of England could be initiated) and the fearful 'fevers' which killed Oudney first and reduced the other two men to skeletons with no strength at times to continue farther.

The reception by the African chieftain of the British explorers was immensely encouraging to the Government and scholars back in England whither Denham and Clapperton returned in 1824 to make their report. From this date, with the success of the three-man mission, the exploration and conquest of Africa really begins. The Sahara Desert, of course, had not been conquered, and wasn't to be either conquered, or even surveyed, for the next fifty years. But the ancient and mysterious Africa which lay beyond the belt of sand and rock was finally penetrated.

The information that Denham and Clapperton brought back bears no relation, in a sense, to their experiences, which belong in that realm of never-to-be-repeated adventure typical of nine-teenth-century African exploration. For these first travellers were not only going into the unknown country—as unknown to white men as outer space; but they were going without any proper preparations for the task they were undertaking. They didn't even know enough to use mosquito nets or to boil the scummy water they drew from the wells and ponds in the desert. Mosquitoes to them were like sandflies, ticks, scorpions, and fleas —an annoyance, and nothing else. Their medical knowledge, though superior to that of the Arabs, was still based on cupping and blisters; and they had no special food, machines, equipment, or training, let alone antibiotics. All they had was a consuming desire to reach far-off places with magic names—like Bornu, Kano, Hausa, Niger, and Timbuktu. They went on their own two feet and survived, for a time, on their courage and physical stamina.

This is the story of Oudney, Denham, and Clapperton, as it had been the story of Hornemann, Mungo Park, Ritchie, and Captain Lyon. It is told in the same measured style and was first printed in the same large tomes, on good paper and with a clear type face made for elderly armchair travellers back in Europe.

About sunset, we halted near a well within half a mile of Meshroo [Denham begins]. Round this spot were lying more than one hundred skeletons, some of them with the skin still remaining attached to the bones—not even a little sand thrown over them. The Arabs laughed heartily at my expression of horror and said, 'They are only blacks, *nam boo*!' (Damn their fathers!) and began knocking about the limbs with the butt end of their firelocks, saying, 'This was a woman! This was a youngster!'

Denham's caravan took ninety days to cross the Tibesti from Murzuk to Lake Chad, travelling via Madama, Bilma, and Agadem by a desert route which is infrequently used because of the absence of water. Denham describes it as 'tremendously dreary: as far as the eye can reach, billows of sand bound the prospect'. On one day's march the caravan lost twenty camels from fatigue or straying. The messenger-service by which British explorers remained in touch with the outside world consisted of two couriers (Tiboos) going from Lake Chad to Murzuk, a distance of 800 miles across an almost waterless desert in thirty days with nothing in the way of provisions but a bag of corn, a skin of water, and a bag under the tail of their camels to catch the dung which was used as fuel at night. The couriers travelled by pairs, as only one was expected to survive the journey.

II

On February 5th, 1823, Denham was able to write in his journal:

By sun-rise I was on the borders of the lake [Chad] . . . and very quietly sat down to observe the scene before me. Pelicans, cranes four and five feet in height were scarcely so many yards from my side; immense spoonbills of a snowy whiteness, widgeon, teal, yellow-legged plover, and a hundred species of (to me at least) unknown water fowl. . . .

Shortly afterwards, the British mission was received at a royal levée by the King of Bornu, the first Europeans ever to attend such a function. What His Majesty thought of the three white men, soldier, sailor, and surgeon, we don't know. What Denham thought of the Sultan is not flattering. The royal personage was seated in a sort of wooden cage, surrounded by his courtiers. 'Large bellies and large heads are indispensable for those who serve the court of Bornou,' says Denham, 'and those who do not possess the former make up the deficiency of protuberance by a wadding. . . .' And he adds that his excessive whiteness became a cause of both pity and astonishment, if not of disgust; but not, evidently, to the ladies, to whom he has occasion to refer from time to time with all the gallantry of a Regency beau. There was no doubt that the African women, whom Denham repeatedly describes as gentle creatures, appreciated the English visitors not only for their unusual appearance but, in particular, for their kindness—something these women scarcely expected from a man. To their masters, whether African or Arab, they, as women, were cattle. In some tribes, wives were obliged always to approach their husbands on hands and knees. Richard Lander, the discoverer of the Niger River's estuary, observes (in what must surely be one of the most ironic, or innocent, remarks in Victorian literature):

A mutinous wife, or vixen, sometimes the treasure and delight of an Englishman; the enlivener of his fireside; and his safeguard from *ennui*, is a phenomenon utterly unknown—that noble spirit which animates the happier dames in lands of liberty, being here, alas! extinguished and destroyed.

Major Denham laughed and joked and teased the women (provided they were pretty!) and he seems to have been well rewarded with what he calls 'shampooing' at their hands. Shampooing was massaging the chest, back, and loins with oil if available; otherwise with fat. The major met some delightful shampoo-ers, and observes, after an exceptionally beautiful girl called Funha had shampooed him, 'Verily I began to think that I not only deserved to be a sultan, but that I had really commenced my reign. . . .'

After his three years in the interior of Africa, returning to the comparative civilization of North Africa, he sums up his impressions of negro women in these words:

Though many degrees nearer our own fair and blue-eyed beauties, yet no people ever lost more by comparison than did the white ladies of Mourzouk, with the black ones of Bornou and Soudan. That the latter were 'black, devilish black', there is no denying; but their beautiful forms, expressive eyes, pearly teeth, and excessive cleanliness rendered them far more pleasing than the dirty half-castes we were now amongst. . . .

Next, Denham accompanied the Arabs who had brought him across the desert to Lake Chad on a slave raid; but this was a raid which, for once, didn't come off. The Arabs were routed, their sheik killed, and Denham and his horse wounded. Captured along with others of the raiders, the Englishman had his clothes stripped off him, though he struggled, in vain, to save his trousers. An English officer without his trousers, even in the middle of Africa, was not a state Queen Victoria would have approved of. Left without a stitch of clothing, Denham managed to crawl away while his captors were wrangling over the spoils. Chased through the jungle, wounded, his flesh, as he says, 'miserably torn by the undergrowth', he seized what he thought was the trunk of a tree to lower himself into a stream and found that he was grasping a large boa-constrictor which yielded to the weight of his body so that he fell into the water and managed to get safely across to the other side. Here he met up with a party of fleeing Arabs and travelled forty miles on foot and horseback before he was out of danger.

> I was in a deplorable state the whole night [he reports], and notwithstanding the irritation of the flesh wounds (caused by riding bareback on a lean horse) being augmented by the woollen covering the Arabs had thrown over me, teeming as it was with vermin, it was the evening of the next day before I could get a shirt. . . . I suffered much, both in mind and body, but complained not.

The same spirit of Christian fortitude (for we are dealing with men who believed in their religion) was shown when his companion Clapperton's fever reached an alarming height so that he was continuously delirious; Dr. Oudney was too weak and ill to move, having taken nothing but a little sour milk three times a day for a month; and their handyman, Hillman, was on the verge of madness. 'Still,' says Denham, '*I had much to be thankful for, and I endeavoured to bless God, and ate with cheerfulness.*'

It seems, however, that his forbearance was not always appreciated, for when he refused the gift of three female slaves, all under fifteen years of age, 'explaining in pretty strong terms our abhorrence of such proceedings', he was pronounced a fool 'a hundred times over'. He was not yet proficient enough in the local dialect to explain that he was quite satisfied with the 'shampooing' system, without having to feed three bouncing young girls of fifteen.

Before Denham continued his exploring of Lake Chad and environs while Oudney and Clapperton, though weak with fever, pressed on westwards to Kano, a 'relief' came through from Tripoli in the person of Mr. Toole, an ensign in the Eightieth Regiment. Young Toole—of whom we know nothing except what Denham tells us (which doesn't include the ensign's first name)—had made the 1,500-mile trip from Tripoli to Lake Chad in three months fourteen days. It is interesting to recall that the Maternus expedition in A.D. 70 went south for three months, starting from Germa—suggesting that the Romans also reached Lake Chad. Ensign Toole came through with the loss of only five camels. Denham's caravan, on the other hand, lost as many as twenty camels in one day's march. Alas, the newcomer, though he brought new hope, couldn't bring any change in the three explorers' wretched state of affairs. Within a few days the 'robust, healthy-looking young man' was dangerously sick; and within two months he was dead. Denham's obituary is:

> Mr. Toole had scarcely completed his twenty-second year, and was in every sense a most aimiable and promising young officer.

III

In the meantime, while Major Denham was exploring the eastern shore of Lake Chad, Dr. Oudney and Captain Clapperton had set out for the Sudan, as northern Nigeria was then called. Clapper-

ton writes the journal of this expedition as Dr. Oudney was ill
the whole time with fever and ague. He could take nothing but a
cup of coffee, though he insisted on marching forward with the
caravan and attending to the sick along the line of march. Most
of his patients were either men seeking a remedy against im-
potency or women against sterility. What the Scots doctor gave
them in the way of medicines we are not told, but Clapperton
reports that he was always cupping himself for his perpetual
hacking cough. It did the doctor no good. On the morning of
January 12th, 1824, he tried to mount his camel, but 'there was
the ghastliness of death in his countenance'. He died without a
struggle or a groan and was buried under an old mimosa tree a
little beyond the southern gate of a Nigerian village called
Murmur. The Arabs later destroyed his grave, saying that he was
a 'Kafir', meaning an infidel. Clapperton bade his friend farewell
in these words:

> Thus died at the age of 32 years Walter Oudney, M.D., a
> man of unassuming deportment, pleasing manners, stedfast
> perseverance, and undaunted enterprise; while his mind was
> fraught at once with knowledge, virtue, and religion. . . . To
> me, his friend and fellow-traveller, proceeding through a
> country which had hitherto never been trod by European foot,
> the loss was severe and affecting in the extreme.

Walter Oudney deserves to be remembered for something
other than his 'unassuming deportment, pleasing manners', and
the rest, for he was the first European to have some idea, however
vague, of the depth of the Roman conquest of the desert, and his
monograph *Excursion to Westwards of Mourzuk*, published in 1822,
was, in its quiet way, to change the writing of history.

What had happened was that, while his companions Clapperton
and Dixon Denham were pushing on south from Murzuk,
Oudney had gone westwards along the Wadi el Ajal as far as the
oasis of Germa. It was here that he saw—the first European to
do so in more than twelve centuries—the Roman mausoleum
which has since become a landmark in the history and

archaeology of the Sahara. He reports his discovery in the usual modest style of the old travellers and makes this entry in his diary for June 17th, 1822:

We were conducted today by Sheik Mustapha to examine a building different, he stated, from any in the country. When we arrived we found, to our satisfaction, it was a structure that had been erected by the Romans. There were no inscriptions to be found, although we carefully turned up a number of the stones strewed about, but a few figures and letters rudely hewn out, and evidently of recent date. We imagined we could trace some resemblance to the letters of Europe, and conjectured that they had been hewn out by some European traveller at no very distant period. Our thoughts naturally went back to Hornemann; but again we had no intelligence of his having been here. In short, to confess the truth, we did not know what to make of them, till we afterwards made the discovery of the Targu writing. This building is about 12 feet high, and 8 broad. It is built of sandstone, well finished, and dug from neighbouring hills. Its interior is solid and of small stones, cemented by mortar. It stands about three miles from Germa, and one quarter of a mile from the foot of the mountain. It is either a tomb or an altar; those well acquainted with Roman architecture will easily determine which. The finding of a structure of these people proves, without a doubt, their inter-course here. We were not able to learn from the old sheikh whether any odd coins were ever found, or any building similar to this in the vicinity. Was this the track of the Romans into the interior, or did they come to this valley for dates?

The monument he describes is still there, standing in the shadow of the Djebel Zenkekra. The country round about has not changed in a single feature since Oudney and his successors —Dr. Barth among them—passed this way. To the south runs the high rock escarpment whose flanks for a score of miles are covered with tens of thousands of rock tombs which, surprisingly, the young Scots surgeon never mentioned. To the north lie the

high sand-dunes, hidden away among which are large salt lakes
and two or three villages which are completely shut off from the
outside world. These villagers, called Snake-Eaters, are identified
by Dr. Ayoub, the resident archaeologist, as the descendants of
Herodotus's 'Ethiopian troglodytes' who were chased by the
Garamantes in four-horse chariots. But so far few historians or
anthropologists have visited them to ascertain who they are, where
they came from, and why they live in such incredible isolation.

The valley which Oudney saw 150 years ago is, in fact, probably the richest archaeological zone in the Sahara, and his
'Roman' mausoleum became famous as being the most southerly
classical monument yet found in the Saharan Desert. (Though
this is no longer the case.) And though the Scotsman was puzzled
by the little tomb, seemingly uniquely placed in the rock desert
which flows down from the sides of the cliffs, he did realize that
Germa must have been a Roman stronghold. All the same, he
would be surprised if he could revisit the Wadi el Ajal today with
an archaeologist. For above the mausoleum, on the ledges of the
cliffs, he would see the rock engravings of the first recorded men
to occupy this valley; and nearby the step-pyramid tombs of the
Garamantian kings and queens; and not far away, in the middle
of an abandoned oasis, the actual capital city of the Garamantes
themselves. So Oudney was right. The Romans were here as
conquerors and colonizers; and it was from Germa, or *Garama*,
that they controlled the roads and tracks which went south and
east to the trading posts throughout Central Africa.

IV

After the death of his friend, Clapperton, though sick himself,
pushed on and finally reached Kano, the capital of the kingdom
of Hausa, a city he was much disappointed in, perhaps because
of the house he was given, which he describes as a hovel at the
south end of a morass whose stink was increased by the pools of
stagnant water and open sewers. Here the naval officer was to
spend the next month while preparing the final stage of his journey
westwards. Lying ill in his bed, he listened to the conversation

of a man who obviously knew that the Niger River ran into the Atlantic at the Gulf of Guinea. Clapperton says: 'I place little dependence on such accounts.' He means that he preferred to believe the theories accepted in Europe that the Niger 'evaporated' somewhere in the interior of Africa; or, flowing underground, became a tributary of the Nile. While in Kano he also learnt of the fate of Hornemann. The German explorer had died in Nupe of dysentery and his papers, for which Clapperton offered a reward of 100 dollars, had been burnt in a fire 'set by the rabble from a superstitious dread of his holding intercourse with evil spirits'.

Arriving at Sokoto in western Nigeria, Clapperton again heard, this time from the Sultan, that the Niger ran into the sea. The Sultan also had news of Mungo Park, whose boat, wrecked at the rapids, remained for a long time on the rocks. Park's books and papers were in the hands of the Sultan of Youri whom Clapperton now proposed to visit, partly in order to clear up the mystery of the Niger. But the Arab merchants of Sokoto were now seriously alarmed that Clapperton had come to the Sudan in the role of a commercial agent (they were partly right) and they managed to block him from travelling farther westwards. The Arabs at this time had a very unfriendly argument which they used to influence the African kings: the British had enslaved India which was a long way from their homeland. Why shouldn't they enslave the Africans if they were allowed to come? Both Denham and Clapperton mention this question to which history in a few years was to give the answer.

While Major Denham was exploring the Lake Chad territory and Captain Clapperton was attempting to reach the Niger, the second of the African missions sent out by the British Government was obtaining new triumphs for British enterprise. For in August 1826, fifteen months after setting out from Tripoli, Major Gordon Laing reached Timbuktu, having crossed the Sahara Desert from north to south, a journey of 2,000 miles never before undertaken by a European. One glance at the map of the Great Desert will indicate the fantastic achievement of Major Laing who, unfortunately, never returned alive to tell his tale. His papers and journals, too, were lost, so the expectant world still had to wait for an account of the mysterious city of Timbuktu.

What was this place? Was it all it was claimed to be by Leo Africanus, who himself visited the city, where he found 'great store of doctors, judges, priests, and other learned men that are bountifully maintained at the king's cost', as well as European cloth and horses, a gold currency and a dazzling display of wealth? From Leo Africanus's time onwards, Europeans had been fascinated by the very idea of Timbuktu. So far, not one of them had ever got there.

NINE

'I regret to say the road is a vile one'

I

TIMBUKTU looks very much today as it did when Major Laing arrived there about 150 years ago. Come to that, it looked much the same in the British major's time as it did three centuries before that when Leo Africanus visited it with a Moorish trade delegation. Cities built of mud do not radically change their appearance from one century to another; and Timbuktu is a settlement that has not changed its fundamental style of architecture in 500 years. The two ancient mosques, the Jingereber, built around 1340, and the Sankoré of a somewhat later date, are still the only impressive monuments, as they were in Leo's and Major Laing's time. For the rest, the city must have always given the impression of having been flung down in the dunes between the Tanezrouft Desert to the north and the swamps of the Niger River to the south. By no stretch of the imagination could Timbuktu ever have been either beautiful or imposing by European standards.

Nor is the city any more attractive at close quarters. Because of their long history of wars, violence, bloodshed, and slavery, the citizens have never had the opportunity or incentive to learn more than the rudiments of architecture. The Romans were not this far down to teach them how to dress and build with stone, and the Arabs were never very expert at this type of construction. Consequently the houses, and even the palaces of the native kings, were built of mud which dissolves in the tropical rain storms or is washed away during the seasonal floods of the Niger. It is notable in the desert how the oasis-dwellers dread a downpour of rain which can only result in the collapse of their houses, often with the residents, human and animal, trapped inside.

On the other hand, to the tourist who doesn't mind a week or so of dirt and disorder, the city has many sights and sounds to compensate for the ubiquitous squalor born of disease, poverty, and ignorance. To begin with, there is the extraordinary mixture of races, costumes, customs, and languages—from the black African to the Caucasian Tuareg and the Semitic Arab, with every degree of miscegenation in between. There is, too, the constant spectacle of African street life to divert the tourist: the children running around practically stark-naked; the Arabs hidden in their voluminous white robes; and the veiled Tuareg nobles clinging to their traditional weapons—lance, shield, and sword. All intermingle in the streets and markets. It looks most interesting on the home movie screen.

The houses, in one of which Major Laing lived—it is still there —have not changed in almost a thousand years. The more pretentious have two storeys with wooden doors studded with iron bolts and small high windows latticed over with bars in the Moorish fashion. Inside, the rooms are small and dark and empty, and lead into a central courtyard where the cooking is performed. The whole city, in brief, is typical of north Saharan towns, not of central African villages.

For the visitor who knows the history of this once mythical metropolis Timbuktu represents the quintessence of Saharan trade, travel, and exploration. Situated where one of the three great African rivers and the Great Desert actually conjoin, it was inevitable that it should become not only a great commercial centre, but a crucible of the Arab-African races, religions, and cultures. The net result of this hybridization, however, has not been the flowering of the arts and sciences as it was in Fez and Marrakesh, for instance. The periods of Timbuktu's prestige as a centre of learning and religion were few and brief and invariably interrupted by still another invasion with its attendant massacre of scholars, destruction of manuscripts, and looting of the holy places. This happened so often that though the city survived as a large caravanserai, it never really developed beyond its original collection of mud huts on the edge of a desert, as its population never progressed beyond the stage of medieval Islam. Witchcraft, sorcery, and voodooism are still the basic influences in the everyday life of the population; the traditional diseases are endemic. Those suffering from the guinea worm, for instance, rely on the marabouts and their charms to cure them. Success is considered achieved when the worm, about an eighth of an inch in diameter and many yards in length, finally erupts through the skin, usually between the knee and the ankle. The rest is simple: each day a few inches of the worm is rolled on to a stick of wood, taking care not to break the thread. Other cures follow pretty much the procedures listed by Captain Lyon, though it will not be long now before Mali, together with the other independent African nations, accepts Western medicine which no longer has the stigma of 'colonialism'.

So, in terms of the outer and inner life of the city, Timbuktu looks and lives very much today as it did when Major Laing arrived there in 1826, the first European to do so. On the other hand, there can be no comparison between the modern traveller's impressions and those of the nineteenth-century explorers. These men, from Major Laing, the first, in 1826 to Oskar Lenz, the fourth, in 1881 took over a year to reach their Mecca, walking most of the way across the intervening deserts. And after the desert Timbuktu seems an extensive and populous town, with many of the amenities of urbanized living—inns, shops, markets, public squares, and buildings more than one storey high. To those first travellers, then, Timbuktu offered some of 'the comforts of home'; and even those explorers, like René Caillié, who were deeply disappointed by the contrast between their vision and the reality, were gratified to be numbered among the select few who had entered the confines of this fabulous place. Caillié speaks for all the early African travellers when he says, 'to reach Timbuktu had long been the object of my wishes'.

Well, it is the object of a very few people's wishes today—largely because the gratification of such a wish entails no more effort than buying a ticket. There is no direct flight to Timbuktu, since the place is of no interest to the trans-African air lines, so that getting there involves a tedious journey even today. And the journey itself is only justifiable, as it were, for those who have a good reason for their visit. On the other hand, for a student of nineteenth-century Saharan history, a visit to Timbuktu is in the nature of a pilgrimage, if only to look at two simple plaques over the doors of two mud and plaster houses on opposite sides of the same street: one says, MAJOR GORDON LAING, 1826; the other, RENÉ CAILLIÉ, 1828. The French who occupied the city at the end of the last century posted the plaques with characteristic under-statement and, to their credit, gave precedence to the Englishman whose achievement they once doubted. (Some writers on Timbuktu still ignore Laing's 'discovery' of the city even though Caillié himself generously pays homage to his predecessor and tells us how he 'dropped a tear' at the Englishman's grave.)

So it is the memory of brave men which remains for some visitors the reward of the long, roundabout journey to Timbuktu, and compensation for the disappointment inevitably experienced by those who may still expect to find something resembling the city described by Leo Africanus. For even that former wonder of the central African world, the great mosque of Sankoré, is not architecturally a pleasing monument, while the rest of the settle-ment is much as it has always been, a collection of box-like houses surrounded by tents and hovels. The modern additions to this Niger River trade mart have not improved the appearance of the place, any more than they do the appearance of other African towns. In fact, the probability is that Timbuktu was a much more resplendent city at the beginning of the fourteenth century when, we are told, the Emperor Mansa Musa in the seventeenth year of his reign, accompanied by a host of his followers and preceded by 500 slaves, made his *hadj* to Mecca, arriving in Cairo with 100 camels each carrying 300 pounds of gold.

It was in the expectation of seeing this kind of Eldorado that Major Alexander Gordon Laing set out from Tripoli to cross nearly 2,000 miles of uncharted desert.

II

He was born on December 27th, 1793, in Edinburgh, the son of a Scottish schoolmaster. At the age of fifteen he himself was teaching at 'Bruce's Classical Academy'. At the age of seventeen he joined the army, and it was while in the Royal Africa Corps that he began his explorations of West Africa and, finally, his fantastic journey from Tripoli to Timbuktu where he was murdered by Arabs on the night of September 26th, 1826. He was thirty-three years old.

Major Laing's odyssey started in Tripoli, where he stayed with the consul, Mr. Warrington, fell in love with the daughter, Emma Maria, married her, and set out two days later for Timbuktu. He comforted his new bride by promising to be back in four or five months—that is, home for Christmas.

The first leg of the trans-Saharan journey was from Tripoli to Ghadames, a distance under normal conditions of 500 miles. Sheik Babani led his caravan a roundabout route of 1,000 miles in order to avoid the desert bandits who were very active at this time. The heat was excessive and Major Laing's luck bad, for his baggage arrived at Ghadames in a very sorry condition—most of his instruments rendered useless by damage and even the stock of his rifle broken.

After a month's delay in Ghadames (a city which had not been visited by Europeans since the Romans occupied it), the caravan set out for In Salah, south-westwards along the edge of the Great Eastern Sand Sea of southern Tunisia. They reached In Salah, where there was another delay of a month. Three months had now elapsed since Major Laing had set out, and he was only about a quarter of the way to his destination. However, he interested himself, as did his fellow travellers Denham, Clapperton, Lyon, Mungo Park, Hornemann, etc., in the manners and customs of the people he was visiting—in this case the Tuaregs. He describes himself in a letter to Mr. Warrington, his father-in-law, as 'in excellent health and spirits'.

The caravan now headed south-westward into the Hoggar country and the terrible Tanezrouft Desert, and somewhere along the trail, near the well of Wadi Ahnet, Laing was attacked in his tent around midnight by the Tuareg escort. As he was asleep at the time, these murderous bandits were on him before he had time to reach his weapons, but reach them he did and saved him-

self, though how it is difficult to say. He had received twenty-four
wounds, of which eighteen were serious. He describes them in a
letter to his father-in-law:

All fractures, from which much of the bone has come away.
One cut on my left cheek, which fractured the jaw bone and
has divided the ear, a very unsightly wound; one over the right
temple, and a dreadful gash on the neck, which slightly
scratched the wind-pipe.

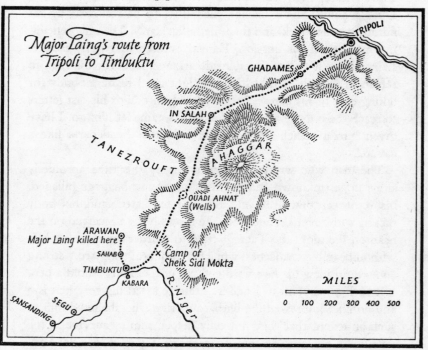

Major Laing's route from Tripoli to Timbuktu

TRIPOLI

GHADAMES

IN SALAH

TANEZROUFT

AHAGGAR

OUADI AHNAT
(Wells)

ARAWAN
Major Laing killed here

SAHAB

TIMBUKTU

KABARA

×Camp of
Sheik Sidi Mokta

R. Niger

SANSANDING

SEGU

MILES

0   100   200   300   400   500

Laing owed his life to the poor quality of the Tuareg weapons,
which gashed without really cutting the flesh. However, the
bandits, having immobilized the traveller, thereupon looted his
baggage and took off. The Major was left dying in the desert.
Sheik Babani (who was later accused of being an accessary to
this banditry) got Laing to a friendly settlement where, after three
months' rest and recuperation, the explorer was ready to continue
his journey. His friend and protector was the father of the sheik

who later befriended Henry Barth and enabled this greatest of German explorers to reach Timbuktu in his turn.

Three months after his arrival at the encampment of Sheik Sidi Moktar, Laing considered himself completely recovered—though his recovery, like his escape from death, was actually a miracle of willpower. It was this force of character which enabled the explorer to set out again across the desert to his still-distant goal, even after another spate of incredible bad luck. This time the entire encampment was smitten with 'fever'—probably typhoid. Laing's guide, Sheik Babani, died first, to be followed by his faithful servant Jack, and then the sailor Harry. The only remaining member of his mission, Hamed, refused to go any farther. Laing, himself full of fever, made arrangements for the man to return to Tripoli. 'I told him he might go. I blame nobody for taking care of his carcass,' writes Laing in one of his last letters to reach the outside world, 'so in God's name let him go. I have given him a camel, provision, etc. So that he departs like a sultan.'

The man who wrote these lines was by this time absolutely alone in an unknown and hostile country, his baggage pillaged, his resources practically nil, his face mutilated, and his body racked with fever. In addition, the blows he had received on the head on the night the Tuaregs tried to murder him had left him with unbearable headaches, while his right arm was hardly strong enough, in view of the sword-cuts, to enable him to hold a pen. Yet such a man still had one inestimable asset: his very heroism and nobility impressed the barbarous tribe who sheltered him to such an extent that they not only helped him to survive in the wilderness but enabled him to reach his objective, for on April 18th, 1826, he saw across the sand-dunes the walls and minarets of Timbuktu, the first European ever to do so. For Major Alexander Gordon Laing more than for any other traveller before or since the sight was worth all the wounds and sufferings of over 200 days in the Sahara Desert.

After so many hazardous and weary months out of contact with any form of civilized life, Laing appears to have found the capital of Negroland all that it was claimed to be—rich, prosperous, thriving, international (in the Arab-Moorish-African sense), lettered, and pleasure-loving—a sort of Paris on the edge of the desert where travellers and merchants from all over North and Central Africa congregated for business and pleasure. The business, of course, was based almost wholly on the slave trade for which Timbuktu was the greatest market in the world; the pleasure was provided by a host of hoteliers, cooks, entertainers, and brothel-keepers, exactly as in any great seaport of the Mediterranean. And Timbuktu was, in 1826, the chief port of the Sahara and the chief city of Negroland.

It seems to have first appeared in history around the twelfth century A.D., the period when the trans-Saharan traffic began to recover from the Arab invasion. Timbuktu was then a small settlement near the Niger River with wells providing good water and pasture. Here came the merchants from Central Africa to meet the traders from Morocco, Algeria, Tunisia, and Libya who had made their way across the desert by the old caravan routes. Here, too, in 1325, came the Emperor of Mali, who made Timbuktu the capital of his empire and built the first great mosque which, of course, gave the city great prestige throughout the African Moslem world. It might have become one of the great cities in the modern world, in fact as well as in fancy, if it had not been for the greed and rapacity of both African and desert tribes who, following the Arab pattern, periodically conquered and destroyed it. But because of the vital need of a meeting place between North and Central Africa, it always arose again; and, because of the flourishing market in slaves, was at its height at the time of Major Laing's visit in 1826.

Actually there seems never to have been a time since its founding that the city was not teeming with life, and the earliest travellers out-do each other in extolling the beauty of the mosques and palaces, the variety of the merchants and their wares, and the splendour of the entertainment which went on far into the night. How much of this was due to the 'Arabian Nights' imagination is not clear. Probably a great deal of it. On the other hand, Timbuktu was always a city of gold in the sense that the Africans readily paid for their cloth or salt or cheap gew-gaws brought in by the Arabs in gold dust or bullion. It was partly this legend of 'cheap' gold that excited the curiosity of Europeans, though during the initial days of Saharan exploration it was rather the mystery of the city which lay near a great river whose direction and source and outlet were still unknown that inspired the first travellers to try and get there.

III

One European, at least, seems to have visited Timbuktu as early as 1660, followed by an American in 1811, both of them ship-wrecked sailors who claimed to have seen the slave capital. The former, Paul Imbert, a Frenchman, was the slave of a Moroccan nobleman called Ammar Pasha whom he accompanied across the Sahara in the role of navigator, as Imbert was familiar with the quadrant and compass. The Frenchman may have visited Tim-buktu, then, and it is claimed that he died there; but the city was probably of no more interest to him than any other African settlement. He left no account of his travels.

The story of the American sailor Robert Adams, *alias* Benjamin Rose, who was shipwrecked off Cape Blanc and taken to Tim-buktu as a slave, was not believed either by his own shipmates or his fellow countrymen. The American claimed to have spent five months in the negro capital, returning to Europe via the Tanezrouft Saharan caravan route to Fez, Tangiers, and so to Cadiz. Here he made his declaration before the American consul, which differed in some respects from the claims he makes in his book. Certainly his description of the site and appearance of Timbuktu is inaccurate, to say the least; and some of his state-ments are very implausible. For instance, he says there are no mosques in Timbuktu; yet the most striking building in the city, and probably the most striking building in Central Africa, was the great Jingereber mosque, with its high tower, not to mention the mosques of Sidi Yahia and Sankoré, both with tall towers. Barth tells us there were, in fact, six mosques. Nobody could be five minutes, let alone five months, in Timbuktu without noting these striking buildings towering over the mud huts and straw cabins of the native population. And since Adams adds other questionable touches to his *Narrative* it isn't surprising that his tale was dismissed by some authorities as rubbish. Dr. Barth, for instance, remarks that 'his narrative does not reveal a single trait which can be identified'.

Even so, there is just a possibility that Adams's errors of fact were more the result of ignorance than of outright falsification, though the circumstances surrounding 'the poor man', as his London editor always calls him, are extremely curious, if not outright mysterious. For according to S. Cock, his editor, Adams was picked up in the streets of London 'in very ill plight both from hunger and nakedness', having begged his way from Holyhead to London in order to get a passage back to America. 'He had already passed several nights in the open streets among many other distressed seamen.'

Mr. Cock now began to question Adams about his travels and 'having furnished him with a trifle for his future subsistence, he desired the poor man to attend him again in the course of a few days'. Evidently when the 'trifle' had been spent the sailor turned up for a second interview one week later, and on this occasion Mr. Cock was able to buy his story in what must have been one of the first journalistic scoops in history. For Cock was now firmly convinced of the veracity of Adams's yarn, though some other 'learned gentlemen' had their doubts, particularly when the sailor described:

. . . a most extraordinary animal named *coùrcoo*, somewhat resembling a very large dog, but having an opening or hollow on its back like a pocket, in which it carries its prey. . . . It will ascend trees with great agility and gather cocoa-nuts . . . but it also devours goats and even young children. Its cry is like that of an owl.

What with his pouched animals and coconuts, Adams seems to have got the Pacific mixed up with Central Africa; but his *Narrative* was none the less published 'as most interesting to the public, and most useful to the poor man himself, for whose benefit it has been committed to the press'. Before it was committed to the press, however, Editor Cock received a letter from Mr. Joseph Dupuis, British vice-consul at Mogador, who had ransomed Adams some years before. It is an extraordinary letter and only serves to deepen the mystery, because according to Dupuis 'Adams' arrived at Mogador only able to speak 'a mixture of Arabic and broken English'. Is it conceivable that a man would forget his mother-tongue in less than a year, and come back to civilization speaking a mixture of two languages? And why did 'Adams' call himself Benjamin Rose in Mogador and Robert Adams in London? One other snippet of information is given by Dupuis regarding Adams *alias* Rose: that 'he had quitted America to avoid a prosecution with which he was threatened for the consequence of an amour, which he was unwilling to make good by marriage'.

Yet the extraordinary thing is that the more one examines the Adams mystery, the more one is puzzled by the American's narrative. For the 'learned gentlemen' of the time who argued the matter back and forth omitted to take into consideration certain very significant facts about the man himself: first, that Adams was a mulatto born in upstate New York which may well have been why M. Dupuis, a Frenchman, thought his English was broken; secondly, Adams had been impressed into the British Navy, which surely accounts for why he changed his name;[1] and thirdly, he was a man without any education whatsoever and therefore liable on the one hand to pick up a great deal of spurious information and incapable on the other of inventing so much that was factual. It is quite possible, then, that the American mulatto from upstate New York, instead of being discredited and forgotten, should have his minor place in the history of African exploration as the first Christian to see Timbuktu and survive.

---

1. The War of 1812 between Great Britain and the United States was imminent, and already being publicly discussed in London and Washington.

IV

After Paul Imbert the Frenchman, Robert Adams the American, and Major Laing the Scotsman came a succession of brave and eager men most of whom were to die on the outward or homeward-bound journey, until the French under Joffre occupied Timbuktu in 1894. The Timbuktu we see today, then, is the remains of a city which ceased to have a reason to exist after the abolition of slavery in the Western world. Indeed, the Timbuktu the French took under their jurisdiction was already little more than a settlement of mud huts rapidly becoming depopulated as the Tuaregs, no longer needed as conveyors of the slave caravans, lived by continuous looting of the oases and urban communities along the Niger.

The French Army now made Timbuktu safe for Europeans and even introduced some semblance of Western law and order; and soon after the Church, which under the leadership of Cardinal Lavigerie had always been eager to establish a mission there, sent the first White Fathers across the desert from Carthage. Naturally these unarmed priests got murdered by the Tuaregs, for if there was anything more abhorrent than a Christian layman to the fanatical Moslems, it was a Christian priest. The Arabs and Berbers, it seemed, had not forgotten the Crusades, particularly the second crusade of St. Louis, King of France, who died of typhus outside Tunis in 1270. True, St. Louis was something of a prophet to the Moslems, and even had his place in their calendar along with Moses and Christ, possibly on the grounds that he 'restrained' the Jews (as persecution was then called); branded blasphemers with hot irons; and rejoiced in war because, as he said, 'he thereby procured the blessings of peace'. The saint also once *fined* a Flemish count who hanged three children who were caught hunting for rabbits in the Count's woods. All these acts were applauded by the Moslems as showing good sense, and, indeed, real religious fervour. On the other hand, the rank and file of the Christian crusaders were far from saintly in their treatment of Moslems, so the feud between the two great religions was aggravated rather than ameliorated with time. The White Fathers of the African order were the victims, until the Hiram S. Maxim recoil-operated machine-gun was able to make the territory safe for Christian missionaries.

Unfortunately, one of the first priests to go into Timbuktu, Auguste Dupuis, or Father Yakouba (Jacob), was in a sense, a convert to the people he was supposed to convert. The Father seems to have adopted the Moslem belief of concubinage being beneficial (contributing, that is, to longevity), though this appears to have made him unpopular with some of the French officers at the fort who claimed to have established priority. However, there were enough pretty women from coffee shades to coal-black to keep the few white men happy, including Father Yakouba, who quietly and efficiently continued his work of proselytizing the heathen.[1] The White Father, in fact, became the most celebrated person not only in Timbuktu, but throughout French Colonial Africa, and later in his life he was pestered unmercifully by journalists and tourists. He lived on the same street as René Caillié who rates a small bronze plaque on the door of the house he occupied for fifteen days in 1828. Père Yakouba put up his own plaque. It said:

> *Oui, ç'est içi. Entrée 2 francs.*
> *50 centimes de supplément pour voir la bête en liberté*
> *sur la Terrasse.*

V

This was the city that Major Laing entered on that April day of 1826. He was fortunate enough to find Sheik Babani's son who procured him a place to live in a two-storeyed mud house which still exists. Laing lived upstairs; and it was on his terrace which overlooked the mysterious city he had come so many thousand

1. William Seabrook gives his version of this story in *The White Monk of Timbuktu*. The children of Father Yakouba deny Seabrook's facts and denounce his methods, as they claim he swindled them out of the royalties he had promised. There is a follow-up to the Seabrook Version by another American journalist, John Skolle, *The Road to Timbuktu*, London, 1956.

miles to see that he wrote with that arm which still gave him so much pain his last letter. The letter ended:

> My dear Emma must excuse my writing. I have begun a hundred letters to her, but have been unable to get through. She is ever uppermost in my thoughts, and I look forward, with delight, to the hour of our meeting, which, please God, is now at no great distance.

Laing only had a few more days to live after writing this letter. He had now been a month in the African city, and at last he seemed to be having some luck. He was accepted by the intellectuals of the place and was shown the many manuscripts which they possessed—manuscripts which gave the history of North and Central Africa from the earliest times—the kind of historical, sociological, and literary material that scholars in Europe were waiting for. He was also able to see for himself which way the River Niger flowed, but his friends, of whom he had many, tried to dissuade him from descending it as too dangerous an undertaking. In any case, he was now ordered by the Governor of the town to leave by the way he had come. He had no intention of re-crossing the Sahara, not because he was afraid to—he was obviously afraid of nothing—but because he felt the cause of exploration could be better served if he followed in the footsteps of Mungo Park and attempted to find the true outlet of the Niger. He planned then to go as far as Sansanding via Arawan and embark on the river at Senu. Fitting out his caravan in a hurry since the populace now, in their fear of the negro raiders who were approaching, were accusing the Christian of befouling their holy city, Laing had to put himself under the protection of an Arab chieftain who hated Christians to the point of fanaticism. Laing himself was uneasy at having to deliver his life into the hands of this bigot, which explains the terse message in his last letter: 'I regret to say the road is a vile one, and my perils are not yet at an end.' He must have finally thought they were insurmountable as he sat, on September 23rd, 1826, under the one tree that grew in a vast and deserted plain, with no one on his side but a black slave he had personally liberated and a young Arab boy he was taking to Sandsanding. And he knew the end had come without the shadow of a doubt when he saw a party of Arabs galloping towards him across the desert.

Orders had been given in Timbuktu to destroy the infidel and every single thing he owned. The task was easy. Laing was unarmed. All that was necessary was for two men to pinion his arms behind his back while the sheik Labeida first insulted him, then plunged his spear into Laing's chest. Another tribesman cut off the explorer's head; another killed the Arab boy and wounded the liberated slave. All that remained was to destroy every particle of the Scotsman's baggage, including his precious journals. For this purpose the assassins made a fire and threw everything they could find into the flames. While the Major's manuscripts were burning—the first street plan ever made of Timbuktu; his scientific observations made during this desert crossing; his itineraries; and copies of the manuscripts he had consulted—the Arabs held their noses to show what they thought of a Christian, congratulating each other on destroying the man's spirit as well as his life. In this they were successful, for, with his life's work ruined, Alexander Gordon Laing could be said to have lived in vain. The other early African explorers had left their memorials in journals and narratives: nothing remained of one of the greatest and perhaps the bravest, except a few letters and his bones, picked clean by vultures, which a passing tribesman buried under the tree, not knowing that he was interring an infidel.

The actual fate of Major Laing remained a mystery for almost a hundred years (so remote and shut off from the outside world was the Sahara and its secret life), until a French explorer, A. Bonnel de Mezières, undertook what was actually a pilgrimage in search of the Scotsman's mortal remains, if any. M. de Mezières's mission met with surprising success, for he not only found what was left of the British explorer,[1] but descendants of his assassins, who were, or said they were, full of remorse for

1. He gives a list of a few oddments taken from Laing's grave in his monograph, *Le Major A. Gordon Laing*, Paris, 1912.

their grandparents' crime. From these men, and from records that were actually made at the time, Bonnel de Mezières was able to reconstruct the crime and to go straight to the spot where Laing was murdered and buried. A nephew of the chief assassin, Labeida, clearly remembered his uncle telling the story of his exploit over and over again. According to this old man, himself then eighty-two years old, but in vigorous health of mind and body, his uncle always finished his account of the murder by saying that the pious among his band held their noses as the explorer's cases of documents went up in smoke.

VI

Two years later a very different type of European reached Timbuktu from the west, stayed there for two weeks, made the crossing of the Sahara from south to north, and lived to tell the tale. He was René Caillié, a Frenchman, the son of a baker, a young man with scarcely any education and no backing from either the learned societies or his government, a wanderer whose *idée fixe* was to see Timbuktu in much the same spirit as less adventurous souls want to see Venice. Without detracting from the courage and tenacity of Caillié, one must recognize that his obsession with Timbuktu and Central Africa was due to a rather boyish love of adventure, not really deepened by any particular scientific interest in what he was doing. He tells us himself that chancing to read Defoe's *Robinson Crusoe* at an impressionable age, he was obsessed with the desire to travel; and at sixteen he set off, as so many boys had done before and so many have done since, 'to see the world', with nothing but his youth, health, and curiosity to help him on his way. He soon learnt that the price of wanderlust in Africa was 'fever'; but though he returned to France, it was only to set off once again in the determination to reach Timbuktu by hook or by crook. He had discovered by this time what was now standard knowledge among the explorers, that a Christian's chances of surviving in the desert, or anywhere else in Moslem Africa, were slim, unless the traveller was strong in gifts or arms. Caillié had neither. He was penniless. But he set

about learning Arabic, getting himself converted to Mohammedanism, and acquiring the manners and habits of the desert
traveller. After a year's study among a Moorish tribe he felt
ready to tackle the dangerous journey disguised as an Arab called
Abdullay, hoping to pass as an Egyptian slave captured by the
French at Alexandria, taken to Senegal, and trying to cross Africa
so as to get back to his own country: a very good story which
saved his life on many occasions.

Caillié entered Timbuktu in 1828 after a year on the road. He
was bitterly disappointed at what he saw, as hundreds of subsequent tourists have been. 'I had formed', he tells us, 'a totally
different idea of the grandeur and wealth of Timbuktu. The city
presented, at first view, nothing but a mass of ill-looking houses
built of earth. . . .' The illustration to the English edition of
Caillié's *Travels* published in 1830 gives quite a different impression of the city, which is depicted like an embryonic New York
in the middle of sand-dunes. It was, in fact, fanciful pictures like
this which caused many observers to be highly sceptical of René
Caillié and his travels.

Once Caillié had reached his goal there was really nothing for
him to do but to start homeward again, since he had no scientific
objectives and nobody back in France eagerly awaiting his reports, as the African Association and the British Government
were awaiting the data collected by their explorers. It is not
surprising that he only stayed fifteen days in this decaying and
stinking slave-market, to reach which, he says, 'had long been the
object of my wishes'. Then, after returning thanks to heaven for
the happy result which attended his enterprise, he looked around
and 'found that the sight before me did not answer my expecta-
tions'. In fact, Caillié in his dry French way completely debunks
the myth of Timbuktu, which he saw and described as it actually
was—a great caravanserai set down in the middle of the desert
with no resources of its own whatsoever, except as a trade mart.
He forced himself to make a cursory survey of the city and collected some information concerning Major Laing who had
lodged two years previously in the house opposite. The account
of the British explorer's murder in the desert agrees in general

with that obtained by Bonnel de Mezières some eighty years later, including the report that Laing refused to embrace the Moslem religion in order to save his life. De Mezières heard that the Major was speared to death by Labeida himself; Caillié was told that he was strangled by negro slaves after the Moors refused to kill him. The Frenchman applauds the Scotsman's decision not to accept Islam and slavery, since if he had he would never have got back to Europe again; and death was preferable to a slave's life in the desert. Caillié adds this little tribute to his predecessor:

In the morning, little before sunrise, the Moors shewed me the spot where Major Laing was murdered. I there observed the site of a camp. I averted my eyes from this scene of horror and secretly dropped a tear—the only tribute of regret I could render to the ill-fated traveller to whose memory no monument will ever be reared on the spot where he perished.

When he wrote this Caillié was heading north with a caravan of 1,400 camels taking slaves, gold, ivory, gum, and ostrich feathers to Tafileft. They were now to march across one of the worst stretches of the Sahara, the Timbuktu–Arawan–Taodini–Taghaza–Marrakesh route, which is not crossed today even in jeeps and trucks. In fact, it was along this trail that caravans of a thousand camels and more had perished, and the same fate seemed likely to overtake Caillié and his train, for they ran out of water and found the wells they were making for dry. But after ten days in the waterless desert they reached the wells of Telig where men and camels fought to get at the first black and muddy liquid which came up from the sand-filled pits.

Not only was the scarcity of water a trial to Caillié, but also the desert 'cuisine', which the caravan guide prepared by the simple method of plunging his unwashed arms up to the elbows in a mess of dirty water mixed with rice and butter. This was hard for a Frenchman to take, even when starving, and it isn't surprising that Caillié mentions this hash a number of times with great distaste. In fact, his squeamishness, which not even months in Africa and the Sahara Desert could overcome, caused him much distress, for when mothers brought him their children covered with sores he couldn't look at them without horror. Something about his innate refinement must have offended the Moors, because they took to insulting and tormenting him, even encouraging their slaves to do likewise. They called him a camel; and when the caravan chief gave him a drink of water he used to imitate the humming noise made to encourage the camels to drink. For the same reason, in order to mock at poor Caillié, the driver, while lifting him on to his camel, 'took every opportunity of playing me a trick which might raise a laugh among his companions at my expense'.

Finally, after weeks of danger, suffering, and sickness, Caillié had crossed the Sahara from south to north, from Timbuktu to Tangiers, a journey of 2,000 miles, every mile of which was made at the expense of body and mind. He was nearly dead when he reached the Mediterranean port and, typical of an African traveller, 'threw himself down under a tree and wrapped up in his old blanket, suffered there a violent attack of fever'. However, he got safely into the French consulate and was successfully smuggled aboard a French sloop bound for Toulon. He tells us that before he left Tangier he was advised by what he calls a 'Jew domestic' of the vice-consul to 'carry the fruits of my travels to England where this nation had offered a reward of twenty-five thousand pounds for the accomplishment of the journey to Timbukto'.

Instead of listening to so contemptible a proposition, I replied that I was a Frenchman and added: 'The recompense to be derived from the French Government would undoubtedly be less considerable; but I should not hesitate a moment to offer to my native country and my king the homage of my modest labours.'

The reference to 'the recompense to be derived from the French Government'—as opposed to what Caillié could have obtained in England—is a nice hint to his compatriots who, so far, had not only contributed nothing towards the expenses of his travels, but had even ignored him as an explorer. When he landed in Toulon the Geographical Society of France had never heard of him, but they send him 500 francs, or nearly twenty pounds, to enable him to get as far as Paris for an interview. The news was eventually published in an official Government paper that 'a Monsieur Auguste [*sic*] Caillié' had discovered Timbuktu. They hadn't even got his name straight, so it was hardly surprising that the British newspapers began publishing articles throwing doubt on this unknown Frenchman's claim, whatever his name might be. The controversy now took on nationalistic, or even jingoistic, proportions, with the French supporting their champion to the tune of several thousand francs prize money; elevating him to a *chevalier* of the Legion of Honour (they got his name correct for this formality); granting an additional award of a huge gold medal; and voting him a substantial pension. Worn out with his travels, Caillié retired to a provincial French town and began the task of writing his narrative, with the encouragement and help of the leading French geographers of the time.

With the publication of his *Travels*, many British observers accepted his claim to be the first European to get to Timbuktu and back (they were particularly impressed by the 'simplicity' of his narration); but by this time Central Africa was beginning to lose much of its mystery and the fame of Caillié himself to be overshadowed by that of other explorers. Doubts continued to be cast upon his achievements. In fact, until Dr. Barth reached Timbuktu in 1854, opinion seems to have turned against Caillié, even on the part of French officialdom which suppressed his pension and left the explorer in obscurity and penury in his provincial town where he died in 1838, aged thirty-nine, his health ruined by one of the great journeys of history, but a journey which he must have thought, in the end, that he had made in vain. Almost twenty years later, however, when René Caillié was not only dead but completely forgotten, Henry Barth sat in his house in Timbuktu and talked to men who had known both Major Laing and Caillié and could show him the houses where the two explorers had lodged, on opposite sides of the same street. Caillié's house, which is still there with its embossed door;

the plaque above the door which reads 'René Caillié, 1828'; and an edition of his *Travels* which has been out of print for well over a hundred years—these are all that remain of a man who made a journey of 4,500 miles through a part of the world which the great nations of Europe, with all their armies and navies, had never penetrated.

In a sense René Caillié wrote his own epitaph at the end of his book. He says:

Some alleged that I never reached Timbuktu; others that I had been shipwrecked on the coast of Barbary and, having obtained possession of some vague intelligence respecting the interior of the country, had imposed it upon the public. I have even been accused of changing my religion *at every station*. To this malevolent imputation I answer: that I externally adopted the forms of Mahometan worship as the only means of penetrating into the countries through which I have travelled.

I must confess that these unjust attacks have affected me more sensibly than all the hardships, fatigues, and privations which I have encountered in the interior of Africa.

TEN

'The secluded African world'

I

Now, from the beginning of Victoria's reign to the end of the century, a constant succession of travellers attempted the desert crossing in this strange obsession to reach either Timbuktu or the cities of the Niger River. It is perhaps the most extraordinary chapter in the history of exploration, if only for the number of deaths and failures. A rough estimate shows that of some 200 Saharan travellers, 165 died of fever or were murdered by the Tuaregs; most were turned back; and only one, Dr. Barth, reached Timbuktu between 1828 and 1880.

A modern observer must repeatedly ask himself why such an assortment of men, ranging from a baker's son to university professors, wanted to subject themselves to the hazards of Saharan travel, already made known by the first explorers from the time of Hornemann; and how so many of them, brought up in the refinements of European capitals, expected to survive a journey which the Arabs themselves fatalistically regarded as their last one every time they took it.

The answer, of course, is in the character of the men who undertook the trip.

Typical of these 'African travellers', for instance, was an English doctor, John Davidson, who was to die in the desert en route to Timbuktu in 1835, aged thirty-nine. The son of a fashionable London tailor, Davidson was one of the first of those rich amateurs who began a sort of quasi-scientific globe-trotting during the nineteenth century. It was these restless wanderers who eventually brought into being the great travel agencies whose success and prosperity derived from their making African travel (i.e. North African and Egyptian tours) less lethal and more comfortable. Thus even elderly ladies were able eventually to see the 'sights'—the pyramids of Egypt, the mosques of Jerusalem, the casbah of Algiers, and the crater of Vesuvius. It was on the slopes of this volcano, for instance, that the agency guides, backbone of the tourist organizations, showed their mettle; for it is reported in one of the brochures of the time how, when Vesuvius rumbled threateningly, 'the intrepid guide packed the luncheon baskets and mounted the ladies with incredible alacrity'.

But this sort of service was not available when John Davidson set out on his travels, first to Eastern Europe; then to Egypt; next to America, north and central; and finally to Africa. This last expedition he paid for himself, which he could at least afford, even though he was robbed every mile of the way by the Moroccans and Arabs. But the more one reads his pathetic letters, published posthumously as a 'Memorial' by his brother, the more one wonders whether such a man as John Davidson was fitted for the undertaking. Even his knowledge as a doctor (he had been a student at St. George's Hospital in London) turned out to be a disadvantage, for his skill caused him to be detained by sultans, bashaws, and sheiks wherever he went. He was always being besieged 'by hordes of patients'. He feels like throwing away his medicine chest. He is worn out examining and treating the sick night and day. He is going mad with frustration. In vain he appeals to the Sultan of Morocco to let him proceed. He wants to be an explorer, not a doctor; he wants to go to Timbuktu, not write charms for barren women. The Sultan, with some reason, finds this hard to understand. By now the monarch has so much faith in the English physician that he asks him to make a check-up on his wives and concubines—all 250 of them, says Davidson; and adds cryptically, 'they were more pleased with the examination than I was'.

In Davidson's case, Davidson's predecessor in these parts, Dr. William Lemprière, who was also summoned by the Sultan to attend one of his sick wives, found the harem a similarly bothersome place from the medical point of view, as he tells us in his *A Tour through the Dominions of the Emperor of Morocco*:

'Seranio Tibib! Christian Doctor!' resounded from one end of the harem to the other [he writes on the occasion of his visit in 1789], and in the course of a few minutes I was so completely surrounded by women and children that I was unable to move a step. Everyone appeared solicitous to find out some complaint on which she might consult me, and those who had not ingenuity to invent one, obliged me to feel their pulse; and were highly displeased if I did not evince my excellence in my profession by the discovery of some ailment or other. All of them seemed so urgent to be attended to at the same time, that while I was feeling the pulse of one, others were pulling behind at my coat, and intreating me to examine their complaints, while a third party were upbraiding me for not paying them the same attention. Their ideas of delicacy did not at all correspond with those of our European ladies, for they exhibited the beauties of their limbs and form with a degree of freedom that in any other country would have been thought indecent; and their conversation was equally unrestrained.

When the Sultan next requested the physician to examine his eunuchs the Englishman refused to prescribe for what he calls 'cold in the ——'; and the number of women who insisted they had carried a dead child around in their womb for years also irritated him to the point of madness.

In fact, it was Davidson's irascibility which, perhaps more than anything, unfitted him for the grandiose and dangerous project he contemplated, for he was in the land of *inshallah*, or 'as God wills', meaning total inefficiency compounded with knavery. But the traveller fumed more and more at the protracted delays while he was obliged to treat hundreds of patients, including the women who wanted love charms.

In addition to his short temper which caused him to cry: 'The grovelling, wretched curs! They came to kiss my knees. Oh that I could get away!', the tenderly reared tailor's son was far too sensitive to stand sights which nauseated all European travellers, but which had to be accepted by a Christian alone among bands of fanatics. But poor Davidson nearly went crazy at the spectacle of the slave purchasers examining the female merchandise before bidding at the auctions. The examination, of course, was a clinical one, but not made according to the best Victorian bedside manner. Davidson prayed that one pretty negress might have a dagger to plunge into the heart of the amateur gynaecologist thus examining her.

In brief, the whole spectacle of slavery and the slave trade sickened Davidson, as it had, indeed, sickened every traveller without exception. And so did the cruelty, the ignorance, the stupidity, the dirt and disease, and the fatalism of the desert inhabitants. But a too great awareness of these defects of the Arab-Moorish-Berber character was an additional hazard to the purely physical dangers and discomforts John Davidson had to face. For his intention was to cross the desert by the Tafileft–Taghaza–Taodeni–Arawan–Timbuktu route, the Mauretanian wasteland in which René Caillié nearly died of thirst. Caillié had taken the precaution to disguise himself as a Moslem. A Christian's chances of getting across and back again were slim, as Major Laing's tragic failure had proved.

Indeed, this region of the Sahara which forms today the independent Islamic Republic of Mauretania is now, and has always been, the most isolated and primitive area of the desert. It has neither roads, railways, nor anything resembling a city. Its area is said to be 725,000 square miles, practically all of it desert. Here live some 630,000 semi-nomads of Berber origin, together with the descendants of negro slaves who were once brought in by the tens of thousands to work the salt mines and the wretched oases. But it is impossible to obtain any reliable figures as to either the area or the population of a sovereign state which exists only as a vast unknown space on the modern maps. In any case, its frontiers are disputed by the neighbouring states of Morocco, Algeria, and Mali, though here again talk of frontiers is illusory since straight lines arbitrarily drawn across 2,000 miles of desert mean absolutely nothing, except to jingoistic politicians, of which

the new African states have more than their share. Fifty years and
more ago, nobody ever went to Mauretania, except those desert
travellers who had to cut across it to reach the Atlantic coast. We
get a very good idea of what life was like in this barbarous and
fanatically Moslem corner of the Sahara from the account of his
enslavement there by Robert Adams, the American sailor; for
even if Adams didn't get to Timbuktu, he was certainly wrecked
on the Mauretanian coast and taken inland to various tent villages
he describes. The country and people hadn't changed when
Caillié crossed, or when John Davidson set out a few years later.
It still hasn't changed today, and one could almost go so far as to
say it wouldn't change within this century were it not for the
known existence of iron and copper deposits unequalled anywhere else in the world. There are mountains of high-grade iron
ore in Mauretania calculated to be worth potentially 150,000,000
tons of metal. Both French and American engineering companies
have their eye on these mineral resources, and somewhere in the
Mauretanian desert geophysicists are exploring the sands for oil.
From the point of view of contact with civilization, they might
as well be on the moon.

This was the country John Davidson chose for his odyssey in
1834, even going so far as to prepare himself for the desert
crossing by subjecting himself to severe bodily privations—the
minimum of food and water, exposure to the sun, and excoriation
of face, hands, arms, legs, and feet. He didn't get even across the
northern fringes of the Great Desert he hoped to traverse. He
was first robbed, then murdered at a place called Swekeza. His
death was a loss not so much to exploration, for which he was not
fitted, as to anthropology, for he was a very keen observer of the
human scene—perhaps the best that European readers had had
so far. Typical of his sharp eye for character and type is this
description of a desert sheik:

> He is an extraordinary person; I have never seen such a
> combination of opposites in any individual: at one time proud,
> arrogant, austere, despotic, and occasionally savage; he then
> changes his character and becomes low and grovelling, or else

full of kindness, frank and open-hearted: now severely punishing his slaves, and now taking the meanest and dirtiest in his arms, passing at once from finery to filth. Although he thinks nothing of cooking three or four sheep a day, yet he will ask for the refuse of my tobacco leaves to fill his pipe. He is much led by others, and in constant fear about his money. He has a numerous family, four wives, forty female slaves, and hosts of children in all the tents, as he is an universal lover. The wretched state of many of his children is beyond belief; they are covered with filth and vermin, and clothed in rags. . . .

The last words civilization received from John Davidson were contained in his final letter:

Before this reaches you, I shall be wending my way over Africa's burning sands to a sort of fame, or the sad 'bourne from which no traveller returns'. . . . Think sometimes of the poor lost wanderer. . . .

This rather pompous, though prophetic, message surely sums up John Davidson's character and helps us understand why a rich young man, born and brought up in the environs of Oxford Street, should be prepared to die somewhere in the Sahara Desert.

II

Though a score or more of individual travellers of the John Davidson type did attempt their private exploration of the still-unknown regions of North and Central Africa, the 'break-through' in true geographic and scientific sense came, as would be expected, from an official British Government mission which left Tripoli for the interior in March 1850, sixty years after the first ill-fated mission of William Lucas and John Ledyard had been sent out by the African Association. This mid-century expedition was well planned and well mounted, and it had as one member of the mission a young German scholar and lecturer at the University of Berlin, Dr. Heinrich (or Henry, as he was later known) Barth, a name which should have the same familiarity as the names of Livingstone and Stanley. Yet far from being a familiar name, Henry Barth has never received even a modicum of the recognition he deserves; and, for that matter, was never fully recognized in his own lifetime. For he emerged from the *terra incognita* of Africa, after five of the most perilous yet fruitful years any man before or since could have spent, to arrive in England almost unnoticed. In fact, the termination of his mission during which three of his fellow explorers had died or were murdered was not even mentioned in the newspapers of the day; and when, two years later, his *Travels in North and Central Africa* were published, the publishers had difficulty in disposing of the first edition of 2,250 copies. His *Travels*, in fact, have never been reprinted since 1890 and are no longer obtainable except in the larger libraries. Yet Barth was the discoverer and cartographer of vast areas of Nigeria; the first European historian of the native African kingdoms; the first reliable anthropologist to study the customs of the negro tribes; the only European to reach Timbukto between 1828 when Caillié left and 1880 when Dr. Oskar Lenz managed to get through; the discoverer of the Upper Benue River and the middle course of the Niger; and the only traveller who had spent five years in the Sahara and the sub-Sahara collecting a vast concordance of scientific data, all minutely and accurately recorded and safely brought back to England. Barth's great venture cost the British taxpayer just a little over £1,000. He was rewarded by being made president of the Royal Geographical Society.

There are a number of reasons why his *Travels* are quite different from and superior to the narratives of his predecessors. The latter were nearly all soldiers, sailors, or adventurers—in the best and original sense of the word. But none of them had that final qualification which needed to be added to the others—courage, fortitude, and physical stamina—so strikingly evinced by the African traveller of 100 years ago. Dr. Barth's additional quality was his immense erudition, his great knowledge of history, archaeology, geography, and languages. This erudition, moreover, was systematized according to the highest criteria of German scholarship: thorough, painstaking, and fundamentally objective. The information that Barth gives us—the history of Timbuktu, for instance—is based on research, not guesswork. He had to spend eight months in this dismal city, wretched in health and personally in the gravest peril as a known Christian among fanatics who had murdered Major Laing less than thirty years before. As usual, religious and political feelings were running high during the German traveller's sojourn, and tribal war for the possession of the caravan centre and its loot was, as usual, threatening. This is how Barth describes his situation:

> Thus I had now reached the object of my arduous undertaking; but it was apparent from the very first that I should not enjoy the triumph of having overcome the difficulties of the journey in quiet and repose. The continuous excitement of the protracted struggle and the uncertainty whether I should succeed in my undertaking had sustained my weakened frame till I actually reached this city; but as soon as I was there, and almost at the very moment that I entered my house, I was seized with a severe attack of fever. Yet never were the presence of mind and bodily energy more required. . . .

Yet despite his sickness and danger Dr. Barth began the very next day his usual methodical and patient exploration of what, up to this time, had certainly been the most romantically mysterious city in the world. The first thing he noted, though without any thought of censure, is that René Caillié's description of the place was inaccurate, due to the fact that the French traveller was (as was Barth) in great danger, courting disaster, in fact, if he had been seen making a plan of the town, or its mosques. But slowly, and with infinite patience, all the time fighting against fever and the machinations of the fanatics who wanted him expelled, Barth collected his facts; made a plan of the city; studied the mosques; obtained news of Laing and Caillié; wrote a history of Timbuktu and the surrounding country; and prepared a long paper on the commercial prospects of the area. In the meantime he had to defend himself, in Arabic, against the charges of being an infidel, which he did so successfully, defending his own Christian faith into the bargain, that he won the respect of the more influential citizens and so was in less danger. Still his work was not finished, for the following year he set out on his 2,000-mile homeward journey, re-crossing the Sahara from Lake Chad to Tripoli, arriving there in August 1855 after five years' absence, during which time he and his original companions, all of whom were dead, had been forgotten. He closes his long narrative with these words:

I have the satisfaction to feel that I have opened to the view of the scientific public of Europe a most extensive tract of the secluded African world, and not only made it tolerably known, but rendered the opening of a regular intercourse between Europeans and those regions possible.

It is a modest claim for a man who discovered more of Africa than any living man before or since.

III

The travellers who now tried to follow in the footsteps of Dr. Henry Barth appear for a moment on the page of Saharan history and are soon gone—usually murdered somewhere in the desert, as the following table can perhaps best show.

A Hundred Years' History of
Saharan Exploration, 1790–1890

Date	Mission	No. lost
1789	Lucas-Ledyard: trans-Sahara. John Ledyard, an American, died in Cairo.	1
1790	Major Daniel Houghton's mission to Timbuktu. Killed in the Sudan.	1
1801	Frederick Hornemann: trans-Sahara. Died in the Sudan.	1

Date	*Mission*	*No. lost*
1806	Mungo Park: the Niger River. Killed (or drowned) in the Niger. Also died— forty-six British soldiers led by Park.	47
1819	Ritchie-Lyon mission: trans-Sahara. Ritchie died in Murzuk.	1
1820	Oudney-Clapperton-Denham: trans-Sahara. Dr. Oudney died in the Sudan.	1
1825	Clapperton: to the Niger with four companions. Four, including Clapperton, died in the Sudan.	4
1826	Major Laing: Tripoli to Timbuktu. Laing murdered near Arawan.	1
1828	René Caillié: Timbuktu to Tangier.	—
1835	Dr. Davidson: Morocco to Timbuktu. Murdered in the desert.	1
1850	Richardson-Overweg-Barth-Vogel: Tripoli to Lake Chad to Timbuktu.	
	1851 Richardson died in the Bornu.	1
	1852 Overweg died at Lake Chad.	1
	1853 Barth reaches Timbuktu.	—
	1856 Vogel murdered in the Sudan.	1
1859–61	Duveyrier's expedition to the Tuaregs.	—
1862	Von Beurmann: Search for Vogel. Murdered north of Lake Chad.	1
1866	Gerhard Rohlfs: the Sahara.	—
1869	Mademoiselle Tinne: Tripoli to Lake Chad. Miss Tinne murdered near Murzuk.	1
1869–74	Dr. Gustav Nachtigal: the Sahara.	—
1873–4	French expedition of Dournaux-Duperre-Joubert: Algeria to Timbuktu. All three murdered near Ghadames.	3
1876	White Fathers' mission to Timbuktu. Three priests murdered near El Golea.	3
1877	Dr. Erwin von Barry: Timbukto via the Hoggar. Murdered in the desert.	1
1880	Dr. Oskar Lenz reaches Timbuktu.	—
1879–81	Project for trans-Saharan railway. Colonel Flatters and company killed in the desert.	90

1885   Second White Fathers' mission to Timbuktu.
        Three priests murdered near Ghadames.   3
1885   Dr. Marcel Palat: Tenus to Timbuktu.
        Murdered in the desert.   1
1889   Camille Douls: Morocco to Timbuktu.
        Strangled by his guides in his sleep.   1
                                                                      ——
        Et cetera.   Total   165
                                                                      ——

Several of these travellers deserve some notice and some
recognition, the three Germans, Rohlfs, Nachtigal, and Lenz
being particularly important names in any history of the exploration and eventual conquest of the Great Desert. Like their predecessor Dr. Barth, these three men were scientists as well as
explorers; and it is almost as though their calm academic view of
the wonders they were seeing for the first time—from the European point of view, at any rate—gave them some extra protection
not only against disease but against the murderous Tuaregs who
killed so many other harmless and helpless desert travellers. At
all events, all three survived their ordeals. Dr. Nachtigal, for
instance, went into one of the wildest regions of the Sahara, the
Tibesti, where no one but an occasional French Foreign Legion
officer, notably Major Jean Tilho in 1917, has been since. Dr.
Lenz managed to reach Timbuktu, the fourth man to do so, if we
omit Robert Adams, the American, as questionable. They were
all first-class explorers who foreshadowed the eventual scientific
surveys of the entire desert.

But two other African travellers are outstanding for other
reasons: one is the young Frenchman, Henri Duveyrier; the other,
the sad and beautiful Dutch girl, Alexandrine Petronella
Francesca Tinne.

Duveyrier had the good fortune to fall under the protection
and guidance of Dr. Barth, who tried to dissuade the young
Frenchman at first from undertaking the arduous labour of
African exploration; but when the great explorer saw that
Duveyrier was neither a globe-trotter nor an adventurer, he gave
him all the encouragement he could, including a letter in Arabic

to all his friends in the Sahara and the Sudan. Barth, by this time, had become practically a 'saint' in the Moslem calendar, and his letter was invaluable.

Duveyrier now set about preparing himself for his African travels and showed his good sense as well as his high purpose in doing so. First, it was useless to 'explore' the desert if the explorer could not produce an accurate map as a result of his travels. 'Ten days' march south from the oasis of El Golea' was an excellent description of a location to a caravan leader, but it meant nothing to the cartographers in the capitals of Europe. Duveyrier, then, began by learning to use navigational aids and to fix latitude, longitude, and altitude.

He therefore studied astronomy and meteorology under the leading professors of his day; also geology, mineralogy, botany, ethnography, and epigraphy. The results of all his hard work are seen in his classic study *Les Touareg du Nord*, in which all the skill he had so conscientiously studied are shown to have borne fruit in a book of genuine scholarship.

For those interested in the more human side of Saharan travel a hundred years ago, Duveyrier's *Journal* makes delightful reading; for here, for almost the first time in the narratives of the African travellers, we have the viewpoint of a lively young Frenchman who was able actually to enjoy his adventures without that overriding feeling of doom so common to—in fact, so inseparable from—the early travellers' accounts. Of course, the reason was largely due to the gradual lessening of lawlessness throughout North Africa where the French Army was now pretty well in control as far as the fringe of the true desert; but the fact that Duveyrier found the Tuaregs sympathetic—and they him— was even more important. It signifies, indeed, almost a new phase in African exploration.

He was seventeen when he began his travels, and nineteen when he set out to make his classic study of the North African tribes, notably the Tuaregs. He was to spend three years in the desert, travelling on foot and by camel throughout southern Algeria and Tunisia, where he was the first to examine with fair scientific knowledge and skill the remains of the Roman frontier system, the investigation of which, apart from Baradez's aerial survey, has still hardly even begun.[1]

Here Duveyrier's knowledge of epigraphy was invaluable, since he was able to make good copies of the inscriptions he found on the stones of Roman buildings which were half buried in the sand. In this way he recorded the evidences of Roman occupation which have since been lost. Archaeologists today will find scarcely a vestige of the sizable Roman settlements which were still visible in Duveyrier's time in the palmeries around the Chott Djerid in southern Tunisia. The sand and the concretion of a hundred years have since covered up whole Roman villages, which were more populous than the present cases, since more land surrounding the settlement was cultivated, thanks to the superior Roman irrigation system. Duveyrier was also the first traveller to see some of the typical farm-fortresses built deep in the desert; and though he identified oil mills and storehouses, he was naturally unable to believe that there was once a thriving agricultural settlement in the midst of this vast and empty waste. Later archaeologists, of course, were able to show that the type of fortified farm Duveyrier had seen was just one small point along a frontier system which crossed the entire western half of North Africa.

For three years, then, he continued wandering through the Sahara, conscientiously recording everything he saw, not omitting temperature readings. In his *Les Touareg du Nord* he gives nearly twenty pages to temperatures taken in different places. If anyone wants to know the degree of heat in Haoudh-el-hadj-Said at 4.30 on the afternoon of August 9th, 1860, they have only to consult Chapter V of Duveyrier's book. They will also get the barometic pressure at the same place (733.43) and learn that the 'state of the sky' on that day was 'clear'. But in his *Journal de Route*, published posthumously from his notes and diaries, we come, for the first time in the narratives of the African travellers, to a more modern view of travel—the view that was to be expressed in thousands of books by late Victorian and Edwardian tourists to new and exotic places. But Duveyrier's *Journal* has the

1. See Chapter Four.

inestimable advantage of sparkle and freshness, as the nineteen-year-old boy, calling himself in Arabic 'The Happy One', rides cheerfully through the desert to arrive at forgotten cities like Ghadames, where instead of dying of fever, or getting his throat slit, he proceeds to enjoy himself greatly, thanks, as he tells us, to the ladies.

Ghadames, where Duveyrier now made his headquarters, lies on the western edge of the Hamada el Hamra, the 'Red Rock Desert' which extends for 300 miles east to west and over a hundred north to south, some 35,000 square miles of wasteland inhabited by a few hundred nomads. The hamada is beautiful or terrifying according to the circumstances. To come charging up a long dune only to be faced at the top with a 300-foot precipice usually means that your guide is lost or has gone too deep into the sand sea. The traveller is not then interested in the awe-inspiring scenery but is taking precautions not to slide over the top into the crater below, where his chances of being found will be slim; for these cliffs of sand, their edges sliced off as with a razor, signify a region of shifting dunes in which a vehicle would be quickly swallowed up in a sand-storm. In the Hamada el Hamra, however, the main obstacles are the salt lakes, which can suddenly turn into vast seas of shallow water surrounded by quagmires. Not a blade of grass, tree, or shrub grows around the perimeter of these *chotts*, one of which must be negotiated on approaching Ghadames from the east.

To the Third Augusta Legion, however, neither the sand seas nor the salt lakes seem to have presented any obstacle, for the legion built a desert fort here around which a Romanized provincial town soon sprang up under the protection of the eagles. The ruins of this fort, whose dedicatory stone was set in place by a centurion of the Third Augusta Legion in A.D. 230, even now dominate the surrounding desert. A very grim desert it is, too, and the modern traveller with any imagination at all must ask himself what life could have been like to the legionnaires who manned this outpost seventeen centuries ago. Not all that comfortless, judging by the artifacts that have been found in haphazard excavations over the last fifty years. The countless bits of pottery still lying about suggest that the garrison at least had enough kitchen utensils! And the exhibits now displayed in the museum at Tripoli show that they had, too, some of the amenities of city life—probably a small temple, baths, and a few more imposing houses from which came a statue or two, carvings, and friezes depicting rural scenes—a camel pulling a plough, ostriches, tigers, and horses—all of them very rustic in comparison with the treasures unearthed in the big cities of the coast. The Ghadames sculptures are undoubtedly the work of local stonemasons, judging by the carving of a child's tombstone that has survived. The portraiture is African; the inscription is Roman. What remains of it reads:

TIB V
DEBUI
M. VI. D. XX
IE. COND

The Roman fort, then, stood outside the actual oasis which is situated around the fresh-water spring which bubbles up where the Arab conqueror's horse is supposed to have pawed the ground with its hoof. Knowing the Romans' obsession with water, we know better than that. But a spring there is, and it is tempting to hang over the reservoir wall and pass the time watching the upflow of air bubbles which bring the water from deep underground. And there is enough water, and always must have been, to support a thousand or two inhabitants, their date palms, and their miniature vegetable gardens.

This was where Duveyrier lived a hundred years ago, and it would be gratifying to know which was his house. Like Major Laing's and René Caillié's houses in Timbuktu, it deserves a plaque. But nobody in Ghadames has heard of Henri Duveyrier, of course. They don't seem to have heard even of the Romans, and have no idea that their town played a small role in the history of Western civilization. The Byzantine columns in their mosque is visible proof of this, but they don't mention the fact, for they live a strangely secret life. It is to be expected in a community

where men live in a different section of the town from women.
For the whole of Ghadames is divided into two levels, the women
living in the upper storeys of the houses, the men in the lower.
The town, in fact, is like a single large house, honeycombed with
tunnels at street-level. Mothers, wives, and sisters can occasionally come downstairs to visit the men; the men never go upstairs
to the women's quarters. The battle between the sexes has finally
been resolved in Ghadames.

This curious troglodytic existence is, of course, confined to the
Berber population of the town. The Tuaregs, whom Duveyrier
was studying, have quite different customs, else the young
Frenchman would not have left the oasis alive. Merely to have
spoken to one of the Berber women could have got him murdered. Luckily for him—and for his researches—the Tuareg
girls were not only permitted but expected to flirt, a practice
which has a curious resemblance to the medieval 'courts of love'.
It is well known, of course, that much in the Tuareg way of life
is medieval, including their weapons, which are said to have been
copied from the Crusaders'; their love songs and the lute-like
fiddle that accompanies them; and, above all, their division of
society into nobles, serfs, and slaves.

At all events it was the Tuareg ladies who made life tolerable
for Duveyrier in Ghadames, as it was nearly always women who
brought rare moments of fun and relaxation into the grim
routine of those explorers who pushed on down farther into the
desert. As for the nineteen-year-old Frenchman, he was by no
means averse to the flirtations and teasings. The austerity of
desert life had had its effects on him, sharpening his perceptions
among other things, whence this description of two girls at a
well who covered their faces at his approach:

> Despite this, I could see they weren't bad-looking. One of
> them, while bending to pick up her pot, gave us a few moments'
> glimpse of her pretty little well-rounded breasts which she
> didn't mind us seeing, though she took good care to hide her
> face. . . .

Duveyrier was very popular in Ghadames with the Tuareg ladies who used every possible excuse to come and see him—unfortunately, he says, always in twos or threes. When a pretty girl asked him if he had any tobacco he said no, but if she would come back alone the next day he would be richer. Next day this *belle* did return, though with her girl friend. Her name, she said, was Telengui; she was married; but her husband was leaving on the morrow. Duveyrier at this point, not having any tobacco, gave her the money to buy some. He also gave Telengui and her pretty friend a scarf and a mirror. The former promised to return in order to teach the visitor how to write Tifinagh, the written language of the Tuaregs. 'She disturbs me greatly,' he adds; 'I have made her promise to return.' She did return several times, until the inevitable message came that her husband was home and he was a very jealous man. It appears that the Tuareg women had to be careful not to go beyond a certain point. Up to this point they knew how to tantalize the handsome young Frenchman unmercifully, for one pretty girl called Chaddy informed him that she had a sickness of which only he could cure her. She proceeded to write down what it was, and her remarks, says Duveyrier, 'were not altogether orthodox'. Having teased him thus, Chaddy ran off and left him. However, a very pretty negress —and 'quite crazy'—decided to move in with him, and after her arrival we hear no more of girls' breasts or the teasing of the Tuareg women. Duveyrier now settles down to his archaeological and ethnological studies, only pausing to remark that the pretty negress has made his house completely topsy-turvy, but 'she amuses me greatly'.

IV

A few years later a very different type of explorer was to try to reach Ghadames and to die in the attempt. Alexandrine Petronella Francesca Tinne was the first European woman to travel in the Sahara Desert. She was also the first of a succession of adventurous women who were fascinated by deserts, by desert people, and, it seems by danger itself. Yet Alexandrine Tinne was the antithesis of the female dragon who later was to march through the African jungles armed with an umbrella and an autocratic manner. She was a born romanticist and her short life was quintessentially poetic. It was almost inevitable that such a beautiful person should die young. The biographer of Alexandrine in Lavousse's *Grand Dictionnaire* justly says of her:

Of all the victims who have died on the soil of Africa, none appears under such a poetic aspect as this young woman who, cruelly deceived in the dawn of her life, said farewell for ever to the civilized world and sought to forget her disappointment in that inhospitable land where a cruel death awaited her.

Miss Tinne was born in 1839 at The Hague, the daughter of an English merchant and his second wife, the Baroness Steengracht-Capellen. Her father died when she was a baby, leaving her with an immense fortune. What with her wealth, beauty, and charm, she became a favourite at the Dutch court where she met a young Englishman from the British Embassy. She fell violently in love with this diplomat and was on the point of marrying him when he confessed that he was already married. Alexandrine was seventeen at the time.

She now did what generations of Victorian girls disappointed in love had done before and since: she travelled, first to see the glaciers of Norway; then up towards the North Pole; then right in the opposite direction down to Smyrna, Palestine, and Cairo. She was accompanied on these travels by her mother and her aunt, both of them baronesses. The three ladies, all of them greatly impressed by Pharaonic Egypt, organized a trip up the Nile as far as the First Cataract. Delighted with this adventure, Alexandrine and her relations now discussed going up the Blue Nile into Ethiopia. Eventually they decided to take the White Nile as far as the great marshes which separated Egypt from Africa proper.

Notwithstanding warnings that the country was malarial and

the tribes at war with each other along the slave-caravan routes,
the three Dutch ladies went ahead with their preparations and,
on January 9th, 1862, set off with an enormous suite, on three
large boats en route for Nubia and the Sudan. Suffice it to say
that the pessimists in Cairo and all over Europe—for the Tinnes
were well known in society everywhere—were wrong about the
dangers of such a journey: the three ladies were received like
royalty. The fame of Alexandrine, exaggerated reports of her
wealth, beauty, and prowess, had long preceded her and were, in
fact, passed by travellers as far south as Khartoum and as far west
as Timbuktu—in fact all along the caravan routes which served
as the main lines of newspaper correspondence. Somewhere along
the way some amateur gossip columnist regaling the caravan
company with the latest news of the outside world started the
rumour that Alexandrine was the daughter of the Sultan of
Turkey. Many years after she had been murdered in the Libyan
Desert explorers visiting oases where no Europeans had ever set
foot heard the story of the Sultan's daughter, *alias* Alexandrine
Tinne. The fact is the Mohammedans, who normally despise
women, and put them on the level of animals (though not as
high as a beautiful horse or white racing camel), occasionally
deify a woman who appeals to their deepest instincts. Beauty, of
course, is not the first requisite of such apotheosis: there are
plenty of beautiful women in the harems. Great wealth is a
definite asset. But the greatest asset of all is a free, noble, and
masculine spirit which refuses to allow such a heroine to accept
the slavish role which men have forced upon women and women
are slavish enough to accept.

Alexandrine Tinne had all the virtues which Moslems, and
particularly the desert nomads, looked for in a true heroine. She
was not only beautiful and rich, she was not only good and
generous, but she rode a horse better than a man; and, best of
all, she was afraid of no man. This was truly a woman of royal
lineage!

For a while this aura of semi-divinity that surrounded her
protected Alexandrine from all the dangers of the desert except
disease. Her enormous wealth enabled her, in fact, to remove one

other disagreeable aspect of African travel: namely, discomfort. She spent 150,000 francs, for instance, on her first Nile voyage. Even more was spent on the second, which was intended to be a scientific expedition in the grand manner, with two German scholars brought from Europe for the purpose. The destination of the mission was the unknown country 500 miles above Khartoum where the Bahrel Ghazal, or River of the Gazelles, joins the White Nile from the west. Nothing was known of this region, or the people who inhabited it, but Alexandrine Tinne was determined to find out. This time, however, neither her aura nor her wealth could help her: the expedition proved disastrous. First the liberated negro slaves who were always in her retinue died of 'fever'; then one of the two German scientists; then an Italian secretary and her two Italian maids; and finally her mother and aunt.

Far from being discouraged by this catastrophe, Alexandrine was more determined than ever to 'conquer' Africa. By now, at twenty-three, the Dutch girl had renounced Europe for ever; and if she had not been so rich that she lived like a sultana, the Western world would have called her a beachcomber. For she now dressed like an Arab woman; ate Arab food Arab-style, sitting on the floor; surrounded herself with Arab men and maid-servants; cleared out everything from her palatial villa but her African trophies; and banished everything European from her life. When her brother-in-law arrived from Holland begging her to come home, she replied that she would never leave Africa. She never did. In fact, she planned to build a great palace on one of the Nile islands, but she was outwitted in this plan by the Khedive, who privately wished that Mlle Tinne would take her beauty, money, and aura back to Europe. He wanted no part of this remarkable girl. She was a thorn in his side, and it seemed to him and his political cronies that every time they stepped out-side their front doors there was Mlle Tinne ready to talk their ear off on the subject of the slave trade. Indeed, it was Miss Tinne's adamant refusal to admit that God had created black men for the express purpose of being slaves and eunuchs that made her *persona non grata* among the Egyptian officials, however much the poor and hungry blessed her. But, of course, nobody could touch her: she was inviolate.

For four years after the disastrous second Nile expedition the world saw and heard little of Alexandrine Tinne. Most of the time she was aboard her steam-yacht visiting the North African ports; and it was no doubt that while anchored at Tripoli she saw and became fascinated by the great slave caravans that had just crossed the Sahara from the country of the Bornu by way of Bilma and Murzuk—the route first traversed by Oudney, Clapperton and Denham over forty years before.

She lost no time in organizing an immense caravan. As usual no expense was spared. Her private entourage alone consisted of fifty people and seventy camels: the personnel included two Dutch sailors from her steam-yacht, her dogs, and her German kennelman, and the usual liberated negro slaves, who were, of course, a smack in the eye to the Arab slave-owners, as Alexandrine meant them to be. This vast private caravan, the like of which no one in Tripolitania had ever seen before, set off in 1868, led by the twenty-nine-year-old Dutchwoman. The first objective was Murzuk whence so many expeditions had started in the past; and here she was met by Dr. Gustav Nachtigal, the great explorer of the Tibesti, who was to accompany her across this vast mountainous desert to Lake Chad. That was not all. From Lake Chad the Tinne expedition was to try what no other European traveller, and very few Arabs, had successfully accomplished: a trek eastwards from Chad to the Nile via Darfur and Kordofan to Khartoum. Every single explorer who had attempted this journey so far had either been murdered or turned back. It was this that made Alexandrine all the more determined to accomplish it.

Arriving at Murzuk, however, she appears to have changed her plans, perhaps after a sobering talk with Dr. Nachtigal, for she now decided to head in the opposite direction—that is, going *westward* from Lake Chad to Timbuktu; and for this purpose she needed to secure the protection of the Tuaregs across whose territory she would be travelling. In the meantime, like every other explorer before her, she fell sick of the 'fever' in Murzuk,

and her sickness may well have clouded her usually clear judge-
ment, because she was soon to make a fatal mistake. She entrusted
her safety to *two* feuding Tuareg tribes, those of the Air and those
of the Hoggar.

In the meantime, what with her sickness and the delay in the
arrival of a whole cargo of sumptuous presents for the Sultan of
Bornu and others, the expedition was not advancing very far.
What was advancing at a great rate was the rumour of Alexandrine's immense wealth. Her camels, it was said, were loaded
with metal boxes packed with gold: there were hundreds of such
camels and boxes.

All this wealth and gold of the 'king's daughter', as she was
called, was now the main topic of conversation in the camps of
the Tuareg from Murzuk to Timbuktu: it was almost as though
the poor woman was asking to be murdered, for she was in the
country of the world's worst bandits—the robbers and pillagers
of travellers from time immemorial. Alexandrine must have forgotten what Major Laing and a score of others had suffered at
the hands of the Tuaregs; or, alternatively, her trust of the desert
nomad—'simple child of nature'—was unshakeable.

In the midsummer of 1869 Alexandrine, with a smaller retinue
than usual, set out for Ghat, some 300 miles due west of Murzuk
by way of Germa, the old Roman outpost. It was hard going,
even in terms of desert travel, but she was used to hard going;
and, like all African travellers, she was glad to get away from the
fever-ridden Saharan towns to the open desert. Her armed escort
were Hoggar Tuareg, though she had made a pact of friendship
with their worst enemies, the Air Tuareg. The veiled men of the
two rival tribes looked and spoke alike to Alexandrine, but that
impression was, again, a serious mistake. For she was now en
route to a stronghold of the Air Tuareg in the company of the
Hoggar tribesmen who probably assumed that if they themselves
didn't kill and plunder the white woman their enemies would,
since such was the way of the Tuaregs.

Alexandrine died in the way she had lived for the last ten years
of her life—surrounded by a bunch of quarrelling Arabs whom
she was trying to pacify. She had had to do this a hundred times

in her desert travels—march up to these filthy and ragged nomads and overawe them by the sheer force of her spirit. But this time the quarrelling of the camel-drivers seems to have been the signal to the Tuareg warriors standing nearby watching the scene from behind the slit in their veils. For when she raised her right arm to command obedience this was an automatic invitation to a Tuareg to strike. One of them struck. With the blow of his sword he hacked off her arm and with another struck her on the nape of the neck. Leaving her to bleed to death on the sand, the murderers then finished off her companions, looted the baggage, and disappeared into the desert. Such is one version. Another, given by a local sheik, varies in some minor details, for it has the Tuareg cutting off her hand instead of her arm, while a comrade shot her in the breast with his rifle. The result was the same. The twenty-nine-year-old Alexandrine was murdered for loot.

They went on talking about the 'king's daughter' for a long time in the Saharan oases, and travellers who went through Murzuk fifty years later could still hear the story of her death. Everybody knew what had happened and where she died. But today Murzuk, once the centre of Libyan exploration as it was of the Lake Chad–Tripoli slave trade, is a mouldering oasis of just over 2,000 inhabitants, most of them descendants of Arab slave-dealers and their black concubines. Now that the caravans no longer pass through, there is nothing to do in the town but gather and ship dates to the north. Nobody now remembers or cares who Alexandrine Petronella Francesca Tinne was, or where she died. Yet the place is full of her presence, and of the ghosts of those other fabulous African travellers who stopped here—Hornemann and his companion Frendenburgh who died here, 1799; Joseph Ritchie who was buried under the walls of Murzuk—Ritchie for whom his friend, Captain Lyon, read the two burial services, the Protestant by night and the Moslem by day; Denham and his *belles*, thrusting their hands into his trouser pockets; Oudney and Clapperton, both of whom were to die somewhere in Africa; the great Dr. Barth who, of course, drew a plan of the town; Henri Duveyrier, Gerhardt Rohlfs, Gustav Nachtigal, and Alexandrine Tinne. . . .

For a miserable settlement somewhere in the Libyan Sahara, Murzuk is strangely bound up with the fate of the European empires; for it was from here that the explorers who passed through on the way south opened the road for the new conquest of Africa.

ELEVEN

The fly-whisk that changed history

I

By one of those freaks of history the vast territory which the British had done most to explore from the formation of the African Association in 1788 was ultimately conquered and occupied by their strongest competitors in the great land grab called empire-building. So characteristic of the nineteenth century was this process that by 1911 almost every yard of the black continent —over 11,000,000 square miles of it—had been occupied by the great powers. Only Morocco and Abyssinia remained 'independent', and both of these states were to be stuffed into the European grab-bag before the partitioning was over.

If one looks at a map of 1911 one can see the division of the African continent into a score or more of colonies differentiated by splotches of colour to represent ownership. In point of actual area, the French came off best, with practically the whole north-western quarter of the continent falling to their share of the loot: that is, Tunisia, Algeria, the Sahara, the Sudan, and the French Congo. The British, on the other hand, were content with Nigeria, South Africa, Rhodesia, East Africa, and the Anglo-Egyptian Sudan—not as large an area as the French North and West Africa, but a potentially much richer one. In other words, the French were welcome to the Sahara Desert even though British explorers and their German associates had really done the spade work in the exploration of this vast area of the earth's surface. The French, then, had an enormous new empire to keep them happy; the British had the commercial and strategic colonies they wanted; and there was still enough left over to appease the

Germans, Spanish, Belgians, Italians, Portuguese, Egyptians, and even the Turks.

The partition of Africa by the end of the nineteenth century, after fifty years or more of jockeying for position in the fields of exploration, commerce, diplomacy, and missionary work, was as follows:

	Square miles
French Africa	3,866,950
British Africa	2,101,411
Egyptian Africa	1,600,000
German Africa	910,150
Belgian Africa	900,000
Portuguese Africa	787,500
Independent Africa	613,000
Turkish Africa	400,000
Italian Africa	200,000
Spanish Africa	79,800
	11,458,811

From these figures it can be seen that the French actually acquired one-third of the entire land mass, and almost twice as many square miles as the British who had been nibbling away at the coastline since Elizabethan times. But of their 4,000,000 square miles, over 2,000,000 were within the area of the Sahara Desert, and no nation could be bothered with developing and exploiting a wasteland in an age which was steadily moving towards the 1914–18 climax of European rivalries. The resources and energies of the imperialist powers were directed towards an armed showdown inside Europe itself. In any case, the empire-builders were not interested in colonization in the Roman sense: they were interested in trade, as were the Phoenicians 2,500 years before them. Thus, gew-gaws, shoddy textiles, antiquated armaments, and cheap booze were again shipped into Africa in return for the ivory, gold, diamonds, and the fabulous wealth of a world not yet stripped by civilized looters. The modern European merchant, moreover, proved an even better business man than his Carthaginian counterpart, whose methods, on the whole, were relatively honest. The Carthaginians at least left their goods on the shore for the Africans to come and make their selection at their leisure and on a basis of mutual trust. The Europeans instituted a system of serfdom based on fear. It proved to be much more profitable.

II

How and why, then, did the French acquire control of the Sahara Desert, once the almost exclusive domain of the British explorers?

The answer one gets will depend to a great extent on the nationality of the historian. So, of course, with every great event in history. To British historians the naval forays of Sir Francis Drake and his kind were glorious deeds of patriotism; to the Spanish they were brutal acts of piracy. So, too, the conquest of Algeria and Tunisia by the French between 1830 and 1880 was described by their own statesmen (and later their historians) as undertaken 'for the benefit of all Christendom'. This justification was acceptable to all those states who were busy establishing 'Christendom' elsewhere; but it certainly didn't appeal to the British Government, which was still, at this time, sending in scientific-commercial expeditions obviously with a view to extending their influence throughout the area. The British, with some justification, could and, naturally, did make references to the 'morality' of the French conduct (the French were always considered immoral in international politics as in national behaviour, in any case), since they, the British, had been penetrating Africa peacefully with such expeditions as those of Mungo Park, Ritchie, Lyon, Oudney, Clapperton, and Denham, while the French were suddenly penetrating with full-scale armies and navies.

A great deal of diplomatic huffing and puffing now ensued, accompanied by distinct growlings and rumblings on either side, particularly when a French deputy suggested using Algiers as a port for preying on British ships. This was too much only eighteen years after Waterloo. However, the prime movers behind the scenes were able to find a *modus operandi*, particularly when the French Minister Polignac admitted that the Algiers campaign was only intended as 'a diversion to distract attention from the national sadness and an opportunity to restore something of the national pride through military activity'. Finally, the French venture in Algeria was accepted by the British on the grounds that the territory itself, being largely desert, was worthless and the conquest of such an inhospitable part of the world would be a 'safety-valve' for the colonial ambitions of France. British statesmen were to use the same 'safety-valve' argument a hundred years later *vis-à-vis* the colonial ambitions of Hitler.

To the other interested nations, including the United States, the French assault on Algiers was presented as a lofty enterprise to end piracy in the Mediterranean. By 1830, of course, the Christian nations had forgotten that piracy on the high seas for at least 300 years had been practised by their own seamen.

So respectable and, indeed, commendable was privateering, that Robert Cecil, the chief minister of King James the First, had sent his ship *True Love* to engage in piracy off Morocco in 1597. It was British pirates who helped keep Tunis prosperous by bringing in their prizes, selling them at the auctions, and spending the entire proceeds in the bars and brothels of the North African port. In fact, English pirates in the Mediterranean were described as 'more barbarous and sanguinary than the Barbaresques'.

But the English, though they were certainly the most notorious and active pirates, were not the only ones. As late as 1815 we find the British Governor of Malta protesting to the Bashaw of Tripoli about an American privateer using that port to bring in two British prizes. In short, every nation practised piracy ostensibly as part of naval warfare, much as guerilla tactics, which are basically contrary to the laws of formal warfare, are admired and encouraged in modern war. In fact, piracy was always legalized in one form or another; for we find it defined in naval law as 'the operation of vessels owned and manned by private persons, but furnished with the authority of their Government to carry on hostilities'. The authorization to equip and man a privateer is called a Letter of Marque; and armed with this document, pirates from the time of Sir Francis Drake have boarded and seized merchant ships with the tacit blessing of their home government.

As might be expected, the governments of the seized ships, especially when they were not at war, objected violently to this practice. This is why to foreign historians national heroes like Drake, Sir Henry Morgan, Richard Giffard, Sir John Pennington, and other British sea-dogs are nothing more or less than criminals, belonging to exactly the same class of enemies to law and order in which the British chose to place the Barbary pirates. In fact, the whole of Europe united during the reign of Queen Elizabeth I to condemn the English pirates as 'the disturbers of the world', not without reason when Spanish seamen and their ships were sold at a public auction in Dover in 1570; the Venetian ambassador was robbed by English pirates on his journey to London in 1603; and King James's own brother-in-law, the King of Denmark, was attacked by English pirates just off Yarmouth as late as 1614.

But all the recriminations hurled by one nation at another were only pots calling kettles black, since every maritime nation in the world from the middle of the sixteenth to the middle of the nineteenth century engaged in piracy which became, in fact, 'big business' organized by private investors and taxed by the Government like any other lawful enterprise. The proceeds were divided in a legally fixed proportion between the company (i.e. the private owners of the privateer), the captain, the crew, and the Government. No business venture could have been more respectably run than piracy.

But, of course, there were always these damned foreign pirates —the pests who preyed on English ships and the monsters who carried off British subjects into slavery—the men to the galleys and the women to the seraglios. Great indignation was felt throughout the civilized world at this intolerable interference with the peaceful use of the sea-lanes by the Barbary pirates who dared to defy the kings and navies of Europe to the extent of raiding the coasts of Italy, France, Spain, England, Ireland, and

Denmark. The Corsairs liked Southern Ireland, in particular, as it provided, among other facilities, 'a good store of wenches', some of whom finished up as favourites in the harems of the deys, beys, sultans, and bashaws of the Ottoman Empire and played a small, if unrecorded, role in international affairs. One such may have been the Irish girl the French historian Father Dan saw in the Algiers slave market in 1631.

Father Dan, born in 1580 in Paris, was a representative of the Redemptionist Order of Our Lady of Mercy, founded in 1218 with the express purpose of ransoming Christian captives in the time of the Crusades. A brisk business in the buying and selling of Christians had been going on for centuries, with Catholic priests acting as brokers in the international market, one of whose main emporia was Algiers. Thither, for instance, went St. Raymund Nonnatus in 1234, only to be bastinadoed at the street corners by order of the Dey for preaching Christianity to his Moslem subjects instead of keeping strictly to business. The fact that the populace didn't understand a word the good friar said didn't prevent the Dey from having the priest's lips bored with a red-hot iron and his mouth locked up with a padlock, the key of which the Algiers governor kept himself and only gave to Raymund's gaoler when the prisoner was to eat. Such was the state of affairs in the thirteenth century.

By the middle of the seventeenth century, when Father Dan made his business trip to Algiers, the number of Christian captives in that North African port alone was said to be at least 20,000.[1] These unfortunates were not prisoners of war but civilians seized by pirates either on the high seas or from coastal villages as far north as Britain and Denmark. And typical of the merchandise offered on the Algiers slave market was 'a very affable English girl captured at the age of fifteen' who was to become the second favourite of the Moroccan tyrant Mulay

1. It should be pointed out that the reverend father spins some pretty tall stories, and it isn't surprising that his editor remarks, rather peevishly: 'Father Dan's manuscript is very interesting, but it is made exceedingly difficult by the terrible handwriting, the absolute absence of punctuation, the enormous number of spelling mistakes, the diffuse style, and the plentiful naïvetés.'

Ismail, whose harem contained a minimum of 500 women, many of them Europeans. One would like to have the memoirs of this 'affable girl' if she survived the sadism of this bloody monarch whose black eunuchs killed thirty women a day.

Such was the extent of piracy in the Mediterranean from the eleventh to the nineteenth century, the high point being reached in the seventeenth, eighteenth, and early nineteenth centuries. Now while the European governments allowed the pirates of their own countries to flourish in ports like Dover, Plymouth, Torbay, Brest, Naples, Amalfi, Leghorn, Marseilles, and hundreds of other bays and inlets, they all agreed that the North African ports of Salee, Tangiers, Algiers, Tunis, and Tripoli were 'nests of sea devils' and 'lairs of robbers' and that non-Christian pirates were 'a wicked and cruel people, without faith, without humanity'. The conviction that the corsairs were devils incarnate was, of course, largely due to the activites of the Barbarossa brothers, always called 'pirates' by European historians, but actually properly appointed and constituted admirals of the Turkish fleet. The fact was that Khair-ed-din, or Barbarossa, beat the Genoese and Spaniards in sea battles and turned the Mediterranean into a Turkish sea by his superb seamanship. Undoubtedly both officers and men of Barbarossa's great fleet behaved like soldiers and sailors of any other nation when it came to looting a fallen city like Nice, or landing along the coast of Italy in search of supplies and women. At any rate, Barbarossa's name became synonymous with a specially terrifying form of piracy, namely Moslem raids on the shipping and coasts of Christendom. It isn't surprising that he was, and still is, regarded in Europe as a monster, which is precisely what he was—only a monster in an age of celebrated cut-throats and bandits like Sir John Hawkins and Sir Francis Drake. All three men were regularly appointed admirals of fleets; and all three left a trail of death and desolation in various corners of the globe. Barbarossa's special contribution was visible until a hundred years ago on the island of Djerba off the south Tunisian coast: the so-called Tower of Skulls, consisting of the thousands of crania of Spanish sailors and soldiers killed and captured in a great sea and land

battle between the Turks and Spaniards in 1560. Tourists of
Victorian days who thought they were visiting the celebrated
island of the Lotus Eaters, described by Homer as the scene of a
perpetual binge (some of Odysseus's companions had to be
carried back to the ships, obviously dead drunk), must have been
surprised, to put it mildly, to see on the beach at Houmt-Souk, a
hundred yards or so from their hotel window, a mound of grinning human skulls almost eighty feet high—a pyramid of some
6,000 quasi-fossilized human heads, in fact: the evidence that
Barbarossa had passed that way three centuries before. The skulls
have since been removed and a modest stone monument pro-
claims this event in history. Tourists to Djerba today—most of
them Germans—lie happily on the marvellous beaches in the
winter sunshine, oblivious of Barbarossa, who is remembered, if
remembered at all, as the sort of monster who was to die as a
result of excesses in the harem, a fitting end to a Turkish pasha.
To his own countrymen, on the other hand, and indeed throughout the Moslem world, he is a great hero of Islam in its endless
and irreconcilable struggle with Christendom.

That struggle reached a new phase which was to affect the
whole of North Africa and the whole of the Sahara Desert when
the French decided in 1830 to wipe out the Barbary pirates by
seizing one of their strongholds. From this moment the Ottoman
Empire and the Turkish regencies were doomed; and the power
of Islam about to be ended throughout a continent which the
Arabs and their co-religionists had controlled for a thousand
years. Europe and Christendom had finally decided on a showdown with the Middle East and Mohammedanism.

Moral justification having been found for attacking Algiers,
the French had next to look for a pretext, or provocation, for in
those days it was still considered necessary to have a tangible
reason for attacking another state—other, that is, than not liking
its way of life. The 'provocation' was, of course, obvious: the
Barbary states were far too weak *vis-à-vis* European naval strength
to justify their piratical activities. We have a number of modern
parallels to this situation—notably that of Cuba which was not
powerful enough to threaten its giant American neighbour, but

which had the temerity to make a show of doing so. In other words, might always making right in international affairs; the French attack on Algiers is merely another instance of this law. All the civilized states recognized the 'rightness' of the French policy, which was particularly gratifying to the United States, still too young to have a powerful army and navy. The lack of the 'big stick' which was later to become an essential part of American foreign policy was a grave disadvantage to the new nation; and since no European power would give American ships naval escorts, the United States had to do what other weak states were doing: namely, bribe the pirates to leave their ships alone— a system of paying 'protection money' which, a hundred years later, was widely adopted as an efficient method for the conduct of internal business in the States. Adams, Franklin, and Thomas Jefferson successfully negotiated a 'treaty' with Morocco by which the Americans paid the Sultan, Mulay Sulaiman, $10,000 a year for 'protection'.

The American negotiators, however, were not so successful in their dealings with Algiers, Tunis, and Tripoli: they just couldn't afford the premium demanded by the pirate bosses of these three city-states. But no premium, no 'protection'. American ships began to be seized in the Mediterranean and several hundred U.S. citizens joined the ranks of those Christian 'slaves' who were being held for ransom. It cost the American Government $542,500 in cash and the promise of an annual delivery of $21,600 worth of goods to ransom their citizens. There was no doubt that piracy, though on its last legs and rapidly losing the respectability which it had in the great days of Drake and Hawkins, was still a lucrative business; only those who weren't getting rich on it considered it highly improper.

This reasonable attitude is well summed up by the first United States consul to Tripoli, William Eaton, sometimes called 'General', a title which was conferred on him by one Hamed, a pretender to the throne of Tripoli. It was Eaton who, in 1805, led a motley force of Hamed's 300-odd supporters, stiffened by a few U.S. marines, on a march from Alexandria to Derna, 1,000 miles east of Tripoli, which was the General's objective. 'From the halls of Montezuma to the shore of Tripoli'—that is, to within two months' marching distance thereof, since Eaton got no further than Derna where he holed up until the end of the war between the United States and Tripoli.[1] William Eaton was the diplomat who was enraged at having to take off his shoes when he entered the Moslem house of the bey of Algiers. 'Is it not unbelievable,' he cries, 'that this elevated brute has seven kings of Europe, two republics, and a continent [*sic*] tributary to him, when his naval force is not equal to two line-of-battle ships?'

Naturally, then, the ignominy of having to pay this heathen protection money infuriated a patriot and business man like William Eaton. 'God,' he told his Arab friends, 'has promised a separate heaven to Americans.' He added that his compatriots would be free, if they wished, to make up parties to visit the paradise of Mohammed, for the same purpose, one surmises, that a group of butter and egg salesmen from the midwest visit the hotspots of Paris. His Arab listeners appear to have been dubious about Christians, even American Christians, being allowed into the Abode of the Houris, the delights of which were reserved for 'sincere Moslems'.

If Eaton had been alive in 1830 he would certainly have applauded the French response to the insult of the Bey of Algiers daring to strike their consul (and hence every Frenchman) with his fly-whisk. It was bad enough having to kiss this 'elevated brute's' hand. But to be struck with a fly-whisk! A strong nation seldom had a better excuse to declare war on a weak one. Thus the angry old Turk's peevish gesture provided the French Government with the 'diplomatic incident' they needed, and the French Press with the ammunition to whip up the righteous in-dignation necessary to the successful prosecution of war. In short, furious that the Bey had not given them preferential treatment in the matter of trade-cum-piracy; mindful that the British had received special privileges after their naval bombard-ment of Algiers in 1815; aware that even the Americans had been

1. This war began when Yusuf, King of Tripoli, cut down the flagpole in the American Consulate, May 14th, 1801. It lasted for four years and one month.

able to intimidate the Bey with their infant navy and thus secure themselves more favourable treaties with the Algiers regency; and recalling that they themselves had bombarded the port five times in the seventeenth century with good effect—the French argued it was about time they repeated the chastisement of 'an enemy of Christendom'. All sections of national opinion— political, religious, and popular—were now convinced, thanks to an old man's moment of irritability, that war was not only necessary but morally right. And even if everybody but the historians had forgotten previous insults on the part of Barbary potentates to French *amour propre*—during the 1683 French bombardment of Algiers by their navy the Bey had loaded their consul into a cannon and used him as ammunition against the offending ships—there was enough public indignation to make the declaration of war a popular, as well as a political, cause.

The old stories of Moslem atrocities, most of them essentially true, were resuscitated, and the world's attention drawn to the number of European slaves still held in the dungeons and especially the harems of the North African monarchs. People shivered with a sort of indignant thrill at the thought of some fat old Turk sitting amidst a bevy of French, English, Italian, and Spanish beauties. It was enough to drive monogamists mad! Such a monster was too wicked to live! And this was indeed true in the case of a tyrant like Ahmed, the Bey of Constantine, whose huge seraglio was regularly weeded out by taking the women who displeased him, sewing up their lips, tying them in a sack, and throwing them off the cliff into the Rummel below. This was taking venery a bit too far.

So while there was nothing unusual in a bey striking a consul —they had been maltreating these commercial agents for decades, the British consul at Algiers in 1716 having been shoved into the sea by a bystander—the gesture, as Alan Houghton Brodrick remarks, was out of date. In the nineteenth century this meant war, if such a policy was expedient.

To justify the ways of a Christian God to Moslem men, therefore, an invasion army of 37,000 soldiers crossed the Mediterranean under escort of the French Fleet, landed without resistance at Sidi Ferruch, twenty miles to the west of Algiers, marched against the Bey's headquarters, bombarded it point-blank for five hours, and accepted the surrender of Hussein, the reigning monarch. The whole campaign was over in about three weeks, for a total loss, on both sides, of 415 dead. The victorious French general announced the results of the expedition in this order of the day:

> Twenty-three days were sufficient for the destruction of a state which has annoyed Europe for three centuries.

He might have added that in return for twenty-three days' fighting and a score or so of soldiers killed in action France had acquired undisputed access to nearly 4,000,000 square miles of territory. The Franco-Algiers War must be the shortest and cheapest campaign in history, for the 55,000,000 francs of treasure taken from the Bey's palace nicely covered the expenses of the expedition. There was, in fact, something left over—making a clear profit to the French Government of 7,000,000 francs.

III

But the French were to pay for their easy victory during the next hundred years, during no decade of which were they really psychologically as well as physically secure. They were hated from the day they drove out the so-called Turkish tyrants until they were driven out themselves. It is not hard to see why. This description of the 'pacification' process, by the French historian Louis de Baudicour in his *Histoire de la Conquête de l' Algerie*, is almost sufficient to explain the revolt a hundred years later of a people so seemingly easy to conquer at the time:

> Our soldiers returning from the expedition [against the Kabyles] were themselves ashamed of the vandalism, and atrocities they had been required to commit. About 18,000 trees [i.e. olive trees on which the Kabyles depended] had been

cut down; houses had been burnt; women, children, and old men had been killed. The unfortunate women in particular excited cupidity by their habit of wearing silver ear-rings, arm-rings, and leg-rings. These rings have no catch like French bracelets. Fastened in youth to the limbs of girls, they cannot be removed when the girls grow up. To get them off, our soldiers used to cut off their four limbs, and leave them alive in this mutilated condition. The unfortunate women, armed with rifles and knives, defended themselves like lionesses. . . .

This war of frightfulness, which Europeans were to object strongly to in 1939–45, was carried on against the native Al-gerians for the next fifty years: 300 villages in the Kabyle country alone were burnt; trees and plantations were systematically des-troyed; oases were laid waste, with tens of thousands of palms cut down by the French soldiers; animals and land were seized; enormous fines were slapped on villages; all weapons of self-protection were confiscated; and men and women were executed, gaoled, and deported by thousands. The struggle ceased at the end of the nineteenth century with the exhaustion and apathy of Arabs and Berbers alike. The Christian French had finally knocked it into the Moslem heads that they, the Berbers, were an inferior breed—to such an extent that it was a simple matter to prohibit Moslems even to market at the same time as Europeans.

But before the French Army could demonstrate to the natives that Algeria was to enjoy the benefits of a European Christian culture many hard campaigns had to be fought in mountain and desert. As so often has been the case in French military history, the politicians and generals didn't have a synchronized policy. Announcing one day that the whole province must be reduced to submission, and the next that the occupation of Algeria would be limited to the principal ports, the French Government had, ad-mittedly, to be cautious in view of the jaundiced eye the British were now casting on the North African scene. A succession of French generals left over from the First Empire went to Algeria to try their hand at a little more 'pacification'—meaning, of course, the occupation of more and more cities and strongpoints in the interior and the building of a chain of forts connecting them with Algiers. Like the Romans before them, the invaders met their match in a native patriot who was to harass them for many years to come: what Tacfarinas was to the Romans, Abd-el-Kader was to the French. Both 'rebels' had to be liquidated not merely as the leaders of guerilla bands, but as the symbols of freedom and independence.

The job of crushing the Moslem revolt led by Abd-el-Kader fell to old Marshal Bugeaud in 1840, ten years after the twenty-three-day conquest of Algiers with 37,000 men. The French Army in North Africa now numbered 108,000, and was fighting most of the time against Abd-el-Kader and his allies. The Romans used detachments of one legion of 12,000 men to dispose of Tacfarinas, though it took them about ten years to do so. Abd-el-Kader evaded fifteen legions of French troops for over fifteen years. The careers of the two rebel leaders who defied, in each case, an empire, are remarkably parallel. So was their end which was, of course, inevitable: they were not powerful enough militarily to prove themselves right.

With the last resistance in the person of Abd-el-Kader crushed, the French were now on the threshold of the Great Desert itself, which lonely travellers like Dr. Barth were still crossing with no other protection than their personal courage and no other object than peaceful scientific inquiry. But, in a sense, these explorers belonged rather to the eighteenth than to the nineteenth century, for the European nations were now far more interested in conquering than in exploring Africa. Exploration was, then, to become part of military strategy; the day of the lone scientist like Dr. Oudney reporting back to the savants and scholars of learned societies back in London was over. The day of the soldier was to begin.

IV

Whatever the methods and practices of the French Army in North Africa, the junior officers who stayed to serve in the desert were a brave, dedicated, and even intelligent corps of men, superior, probably, to their counterparts in any other army. The trait common to so many of them, from the rank of colonel down, a certain 'inwardness' which could almost be called spirituality, was a result, one supposes, of the ascetic life they had to live. What a contrast that life was to the regimen they had known before! For nearly all French officers at this time—the mid-nineteenth century—were of aristocratic or near-aristocratic origin, and for them military service had largely consisted of parading in very tight uniforms and ogling the pretty ladies in the drawing-rooms and parks of the big cities.

These young soldiers, refined, mannered, and educated in the classical French style, underwent a profound change after a few months in the field—when the field, that is, was the Sahara Desert. It was as though the pitiless sun burnt out of them the mannerisms and memories of the Champs Élyseés on a Sunday morning. There were no longer any pretty ladies to ogle. There were no more parades, or military balls, or Strauss waltzes, or flirtations on flower-banked balconies. There was usually a mud-brick fort in an empty and hostile desert. The officers in command of these Saharan outposts soon lost the mannerisms of the picture-postcard soldier. They became, of course, much tougher physically: one would have found very few fat soldiers in the African army. But they also underwent a special kind of spiritual metamorphosis which seems to be typical of all those Europeans who become identified with the desert.

At least, this is the impression one gets from the writings of those officers who served in the North African army and went into the desert either on punitive or reconnaissance expeditions. There is both a melancholy and cynical sound to their words which is strangely 'un-Victorian', as though a few weeks in the Sahara were enough to disillusion them.

'An expedition in the Sahara', writes Captain Trumelet in 1860, 'offers neither the attractions nor the excitement of the wars in Europe; and I readily agree that any well-known writer would be wasting his time to come here and exchange his comfortable life for the life I am talking about.'

Captain Trumelet is writing from the oasis of Ouargla, a

French Army outpost on the edge of the Great Eastern Sand Sea.
He has been in the desert for several weeks now, and he knows
what he is talking about. He is listening to the muezzin call the
faithful to prayer from the minaret of the mosque. Romantic?
No. A very nasal sound; and the Captain remarks that he doesn't
know whether praying or singing through the nose is agreeable
to God, but it certainly isn't agreeable to him. A marabout and
his wife come in on foot from the desert. They are not hurrying
—not like us Westerners. And my God! exclaims the Captain,
where are we going so fast? The Moslem, he says, can teach us a
great deal about life on earth and in heaven; and he spots in this
respect what other observers have since noted: that Mahomet's
concept of Paradise is the reason for the enormous success of
Islam in all hot and waterless regions of the world. For, according
to the Koran, in that garden of Allah to which the faithful will go,

> the water of the brooks is never bad; the rivers of milk are
> always fresh; the rivers of wine are a delight; the rivers of
> honey are pure, the faithful lie on carpets of brocaded richness,
> and they are shaded by trees which let down their fruits of
> themselves. The just shall be served in silver goblets and
> served by boys eternally young; at their feet will run streams
> of limpid water; they will have as wives dedicated virgins with
> round breasts, big black eyes, and complexions like ostrich
> eggs hidden with care in the sand; and concubines specially
> created for them, having been touched neither by man nor
> genie.

Captain Trumelet's comment on the Moslem heaven is terse
and to the point: what better paradise could there be, he asks, in
countries where both the women and the water are mediocre?

In this comment the Frenchman is echoing, though in a more
subtle manner, the contention of Sheik El Nefzawi who points
out in his *Perfumed Garden* that 'reading the *Koran* predisposes to
intercourse'. It was this theory, perhaps, which caused Victorian
critics to condemn the Mohammedan bible as 'unfit for the
perusal of a modest female'.

What we are getting for the first time in Captain Trumelet's memoirs, then, is an account of life in the Sahara as seen by Europeans who were neither explorers nor travellers, but administrators who had to share the conditions they describe. Hitherto, as we can see at once from the illustrations which adorn the narratives of the early travellers, the desert was always seen through the eyes of wonder and astonishment: a haze of glamour lay over even the terrible sufferings of a Major Laing, sabred in his tent by the blue-veiled Tuaregs. Tuaregs and Timbuktu! Sheiks and sultans and bashaws and slave caravans and eunuchs and harems and concubines! It was a good old feast for the minds and the imaginations of Victorian readers sitting before a nice coal fire on a cold winter's evening in foggy London; and none of it seemed very real. The reason was, perhaps, that certain details of life in the desert had been omitted by the travellers who, of course, had other things to think of. The French officers who came to live in and administer the oasis towns were very aware of these details, which, in fact, were the reality of everyday life.

Listen to Captain Trumelet on the subject of the interior of a well-to-do Arab's house:

A smell of mildew, airlessness, sickness, and dirty clothes gripped us by the throat and made us start back. We returned, however, to the fray. Once our eyes had got used to the darkness, we saw that we were in the master-bedroom. Strips of old carpet hung from the walls. Some filthy rags, which hadn't been removed in a long time, seemed to have been thrown into a corner to serve as a bed. In another corner of the room sat a woman that one knew must still be young, holding on her knees—her gaze fixed in silent grief—a three- or four-year-old child who seemed dead and whose terribly emaciated body was partly covered with a piece of rag. The child's poor little limbs, puny and stunted, were wrinkled like burnt leather. . . .

Trumelet is seeing this room and these people not as a traveller and passer-by, but as a man who must live among them. He is

going to see these sights every day of his life in the African
service, so it is natural that he sees the Arabs as they are, in their
homes and on the streets, not as they appear in books, mounted
on thoroughbred horses or racing camels.

The population of Ouargla [he writes] is even more wretched
than that of the other oases we passed through. All we see in
the streets are dying men, wrapped up in their ragged and
filthy bernousses. They don't walk; they drag themselves painfully along, pausing every moment to lean on the wall. Their
skin is flabby and loose; their eyes are red with ophthalmia;
their arms and legs carry the marks of wounds received on the
battlefields of vice, corruption, and poverty. Some of these
miserable creatures propped up against the walls watch our
approach with heavy eyes and murmur God knows what sort
of malediction between their rotten teeth. Others, perhaps
more fortunate since they can't see the foreigner in their city,
cock their heads on one side and present us with their sightless
orbs. The children, hung along the walls like dirty washing,
are abandoned to the flies. These ferocious insects continue
their work of destruction avidly: standing in layers, the flies
eat the eyes of the children who, without the strength to brush
them aside, seem actually to co-operate with them with typical
Moslem fatalism. . . .

The French captain, it will be seen, is an acute observer,
though the traveller to remote parts of the desert had no need of
a sharp or inquisitive eye to see what life was like. An almost
unmitigated squalor was, and still is for that matter, the chief
characteristic. Moreover, a few weeks living in an oasis which is
not on the tourists' circuit are enough to convince the Western
observer of the impossibility of any radical improvement, certainly for a long time to come. Nor is this a criticism of the
central governments who can't be blamed, in any case, for all
the poverty and problems of desert communities. Perhaps this
incident will illustrate why.

On one occasion, spotting what was obviously an ancient fort (a rough-and-ready guide to desert antiquities is the height and brickwork of buildings), I turned off the track to investigate and found myself in a recently abandoned village. The date palms were still there, bearing their clusters of orange fruit; the scaffolding of the wells was still in place; the houses hadn't yet crumbled back into the sand from which they were constructed. But the oasis was utterly deserted. The explanation? A plague of scorpions of unprecedented proportions had driven the distracted people away. The Central Government couldn't be held responsible for this catastrophe, since nobody has yet found a ready and easy way of stopping scorpions from stinging a child playing in the sand. The best the inhabitants of such places can do is to keep a few hens, for the miniature Saharan chicken will eat scorpions, probably for lack of anything more attractive in the insect line. (Even the desert fowl draw the line at ants, however.) So scorpions, snakes, mosquitoes, and flies are still the everyday concomitants of life in an oasis such as Captain Trumelet described for us just a hundred years ago.

One of the solutions to the world's problems is said to be education. Well then, schools have now been built all over the Sahara, and the most remote village usually has an elementary education system—at least for those boy children who can be spared from field work in the palmery. Only a very few girl children, if any, attend. See, then, the scholars issue from the mud hut where they have been having their lessons. They march out in the late afternoon, a line of incredibly ragged little boys, their faces covered with flies. They raise their right foot high and stamp it down at every fourth step. They are to receive a piece of dough with a dob of jam on it for their tea, and they enter the kitchen by fours, receive their cake, and walk off with solemn faces to eat it somewhere in the sand. They are as disciplined as soldiers, as quiet as mice, and as patient as donkeys. What makes the spectacle pathetic is the certainty that they have little hope of escaping from this fly-blown world into which they were born; or of ever seeing it changed.

Of course, Moslem fatalism helps. It helps the scholars and the schoolteachers who are similarly condemned to this squalid and monotonous existence. Anybody with the fortitude to travel by desert bus at night will have seen these young teachers, fresh from the training colleges in the big cities of the coast, drop off at some collection of huts, distantly glimmering in the moon-light, and walk off at midnight into the emptiness where they are to spend the next three years of their life. These teachers, one feels, are the real victims of the desert, for they have been chosen to do the impossible. They try; they do their best. They have clean water to make their tea, and clean floors on which to sleep, even if there is nothing but matting on the sand. You will also often find one of them in the most remote village reading some book in English by the light of a hurricane lamp, since the luxury of electricity is unknown in such places. It seems like a flicker of hope in the surrounding night of ignorance.

The teachers, then, with their odds and ends of textbooks and paper and pencils, are doing what they can to improve conditions in the oases, but it is a Herculean task. The older generation show no inclination to change; and they, together with the priests, determine both the present and the future. The women know this now; the children will realize it by the time they leave school at ten or eleven years of age. Nothing is going to change the basic pattern of life. It is difficult to see how it can when the fruits of continuous labour are two crops of dates a year, a little grain, a handful of onions, an occasional egg, and, on feast days, the meat of a work-worn camel butchered in the sand.

In the first place, change is impossible so long as custom and religion sanctify the serfdom of women; for though women in the oases are at least better off than women in the cities in so far as the former can work out of doors as field labourers, they are still serfs living in a society which accord them no real human rights. An old man can marry a girl if he can afford it, and will do so if he has a plot of land that needs an additional farmhand. Girls are good with the donkeys that draw up the goatskin bags from the wells. It is cheaper to marry than to pay wages.

In the second place the tradition of indifference to suffering, animal and human, precludes any radical changes in the system. It has always seemed more practical to desert people to beat an

animal to make him work than to feed him. Thus the blows inflicted on the donkey who carries almost the entire economy of
the desert on his back may strike the Western observer as completely senseless; to the donkey-owner it is merely habit. One
watches a native load his two pack-donkeys with dirt for his
plantation. He puts so much soil in one of the donkey's two
panniers that after a hundred yards the saddle-bags slip off the
animal's back and the contents are back on the ground again. It
is the signal for the native to wield his club and beat the donkey
over the head. The donkey moves in a slow circle, stands still, is
loaded up, and trots off delicately across the desert. One can be
reasonably sure the scene will be repeated a couple more times
before the load reaches its destination. It is the system hallowed
by tradition.

This is what appears to have impressed Captain Trumelet who
had plenty of time to record his impressions: the ugliness of
Saharan life is inescapable, largely because of the universal dirt
and disease. He is a Frenchman; and neither of these characteristics of nomadic life is attractive or romantic to him. He is also
a cavalry officer, and the sufferings of beasts of burden are particularly disagreeable to him. A man is responsible for the animal
that serves him so well—often saves his life, in fact. Yet the
camel, which carried the entire commerce of the Sahara on its
back in Trumelet's time, is an animal in constant torment because
of the neglect of its masters.

The signal to load up is also a signal for a prolonged groan
along the whole line of the camels. To load these animals is to
renew their sufferings. The pack-saddle, which is put on from
the moment that they can carry loads and is scarcely ever taken
off until they die, covers a multitude of miseries. Let us copy
the camel-drivers and not remove the pack-saddle in case the
horrible spectacle underneath is not to our taste. We would
see there the running sores in which an army of white worms
is crawling and writhing about. During the summer, the flies
also take up their quarters there and go about their small affairs
unmolested: there they are born, there they live, and there they

die. The only remedy and the only palliative used by the Arabs is a handful of dust scattered over the sores. . . .

The camel, of course, is not the only one to suffer from this indifference to pain and discomfort so typical of the Arab. The camels live in constant pain from their sores; the horses are starved; and the poor little donkeys, always the object of an obsessive antipathy among Moslem as among pagan peoples,[1] come in for the lion's share of abuse. These unfortunate burros, Trumelet informs us, are 'rectified' by their owners on the grounds that Allah made a mistake when he created them, omitting to give them an adequate breathing apparatus. The Arabs, therefore, slit their nostrils right up to their eyes to enable them to breathe better.

> Trotting along almost under the belly of the horse they invariably accompany [says Trumelet] these tiny animals await, with true Moslem resignation, the crumbs left over from a meal to which they are never invited. . . .

So Allah wills it that the animals, including Man himself, must suffer—not necessarily from unavoidable scourges, but even from those that can be avoided. Hence the Arab tolerates quite patiently his fleas and bed bugs. True, there arrives a moment when he has so many of them that something has to be done. He then lights a fire, holds his bernous over it, and gets a friend to bang the cloak with a stick. Quite a lot of the fleas and bugs, unused to this rough treatment, drop into the flames. But normally the host does not trouble his parasites unless one of them is biting him in a private place, in which case he removes it delicately between forefinger and thumb and flicks it disdainfully to the ground. In brief, in the vent of reincarnation, the wise man will choose to be a flea if he is returning to a Moslem world, not a horse, camel, or donkey.

Or, of course, a woman. The woman, naturally, ranks higher than the ass, but not necessarily as high as a thoroughbred horse

1. Compare the treatment of the ass in Apuleius's novel *The Golden Ass.*

or a white trotting camel. The shrewd eye of the French captain quickly noted what every traveller, from the day of Captain Lyon tramping across the desert with a slave caravan, had noted:

For the Arab, woman is only an instrument of pleasure and reproduction. . . . He doesn't look for qualities in her either of the heart or the mind . . . for him, in a word, beauty in a woman is simply a matter of weight. . . .

Let us see what Mahomet has said on the subject:

'God has created two things for the pleasure of man: woman and perfumes.'

'Your women are your field. Go to your field and plough it as often as you like.'

'How can one attribute to God, as his offspring, woman who, because of her lack of reason, is always ready to quarrel without motive?'

'A man who has two wives and shows great preference for one of them will appear on the day of the Resurrection with unequal cheeks to his behind. . . .'

The last dictum puzzled Captain Trumelet since he noticed that all the rows in the Moslem households were caused by men's preferences for certain of their wives. 'Needless to say it was never the youngest and prettiest who complained,' he adds. In short, a great many Arabs were going to be resurrected with unbalanced buttocks. . . .

V

One thing that the French officer did not notice, or failed to discover due to the relative impossibility of frank communication between himself as a usurper and the Arabs as a conquered people, was the dissatisfaction of Moslem men with the Koranic system. Today the student who gains their confidence will be left in no doubt as to their attitude: they are sick and tired of the matrimonial and sexual conventions laid down by the Prophet thirteen centuries ago—though one should qualify this statement by limiting it to young men of modern education and outlook. You see these 'new Moslems' by the hundreds in the streets and cafés of Tripoli, Tunis, and Algiers, or, for that matter, in any capital city of the Islamic world. You see them, too, on holidays, roaming the parks or attending the football matches in packs— thousands upon thousands of them, and not a woman among them. In brief, a young Moslem must live a womanless life, apart from his association with his own blood relatives and his visits to the brothels. Otherwise he never speaks to a girl, never takes one out alone, never dances with one, or even meets one at a social gathering. If the Western observer, then, is in the confidence of a young urbanized Moslem he will soon hear of the boredom and sterility of life in this austere masculine world, in which there are no other amusements for him than football matches, the cinema, and endless hours spent in cafés drinking beer and smoking with other similarly bored male companions. In addition, the requirements of Koranic law make marriage extremely expensive in all levels of Moslem society above that of the peasants who, as has been remarked, marry three or four wives as labourers. But for an educated young man, working as a clerk, for instance, in a big city, the choice of suitable girls is limited to his *milieu*; and the cost of 'buying' a wife prohibitive. The result is thousands of unmarried youths and men, bored, cynical, and embittered.

It is not (as one learns from talking with young Moslems) basically a sexual problem. The privations caused by the system are social and human. A young man wants to be with a girl not simply in the expectation of sleeping with her, or flirting, or marrying; but merely to see a different face and to hear a different voice—in other words, to discover and enjoy a whole new world at present hermetically closed to him.

There is another fundamental cause of the intelligent Moslem's dissatisfaction: he is no longer willing to marry a woman whose face he has never seen and whose mind and character he knows nothing about. He considers this—the *marriage de convenance à l'arabe*—an unnatural and even distasteful custom; and what with the expense involved in 'buying' a wife via family negotiations, a whole generation of young Moslems refuses to get married at all. Those with the minimum of opportunity—meaning contacts with Western acquaintances—hope for a meeting with a European or American girl whom they proceed to court, under enormous difficulties, with a view to marriage. In the meantime they sit by the hundreds in the cafés, drinking beer, smoking endless cigarettes, and watching the semi-Westernized street scenes with chronic lassitude.

TWELVE

'We go to lift the veil . . .'

I

WHAT, then, were the motives, and what the rewards, which took so many of France's 'best' young men first to fight and later to administer a land as austere and disagreeable as North Africa and its contingent desert? Sitting in his tent at night, Captain Trumelet reflects on these matters and gives us his answer. The motives were based on that grandiose patriotism which was one of the most distinctive characteristics of the nineteenth century—without which, in fact, the great European empires in Africa could never have been founded. This patriotism in the mouths of young soldiers like Captain Trumelet of the First Regiment of the Algerian Rifles was not the mere jingoism which twentieth-century cynics interpret it as—for the simple reason that men like Trumelet were ready to live and die for their country. The very thought of it sets off a flow of poetic hyperbole which is extraordinary coming from the pen of a soldier—not merely the high-flown language, but the fact that the military mind was able to see the job in this light. Imagine the soldier of a modern army writing in these terms about a forthcoming campaign!

We go to lift a veil which has hidden these mysterious and poetic countries from us—many of them still virgin to European footprints; we go to penetrate the Sahara, traverse its vast wastes, navigate its seas of sand, endure its tempests and its angers; we go to journey side by side with its intrepid caravans, camp with nomads whose life is all powder, blood, and love; we go, as our fathers went in Egypt, to surrender ourselves when dying with thirst to the fairy seductions of the mirage; we go to show the flag of France to people who, hitherto, have never even heard our name.

And the rewards? Eventually elevation in the army hierarchy with, as it so happened, an excellent chance of dying as a general officer in a century of almost continuous wars. The immediate rewards which Captain Trumelet describes for us are the stuff of poetry and romance—the very basis of all adventure stories ever written from the time of Homer. For he speaks of the evening, the day's journey done, the tents pitched and the fires lit. It is the best moment of the day, the moment which makes it all worth while, when life becomes really beautiful. The enormous desert stars shine overhead; one is snug and warm inside one's burnous; one squats by the fire, a cup of delicious coffee in one's hand, listening to the interminable Arab stories of love and war. Or one lets one's imagination or memories run whither they wish, back into the past or into the future, back home to some shuttered house in a Paris street or out into the empty desert. It is a time of great happiness for no particular reason—and perhaps the desert is the only place where one has such moments of pure joy. . . .

It is in vain that one tries to get back a taste for European life on one's return to civilization [writes Conrad Kilian, who was to die in the desert]. How can one forget those wonderful evenings when one relaxed under the world's clearest moon-light, listening to some enchanting song and occasionally the warlike sound of swords struck in time to the rhythm of dancing slaves? Or again, the shy voices of the choirs of young girls. . . .

These moments of 'pure joy', however, were often followed by days and nights of 'pure terror', as many French officers and their men were to discover before Bidon Cinq could be placed on the Tanezrouft trail midway between the Atlantic

Ocean and Central Africa, in one of the most desolate places on earth.[1]

The French, once they had established themselves in Algeria and Tunisia, in the north and in Senegal in the south, were almost obsessed with the grandiose idea of joining the two colonies by means of a railway across the Sahara Desert. This trans-Saharan railway—the famous *transsaharien* of the 1870s–1890s—was to the French Government and people almost what getting to the moon is to the Americans. It was, that is, comparable for the dangers, difficulties, and expense involved; and, for the more sceptical, about as illusory. But to French patriots of the imperialistic school all the obstacles to this fantastic enterprise were worth surmounting for the simple reason that a railway would, *ipso facto*, justify French claims to the entire western Sahara; help subjugate and civilize the still untamed Tuaregs who controlled the desert and the caravan trails; establish a French monopoly on trans-Saharan trade; and, above all, demonstrate French enterprise and engineering skill to the entire world.

'Paris to Timbuktu in eight days' became the battle-cry of French imperialism. Especially interested were the French African military and colonists; the big engineering firms; the construction engineers; and the politicians in favour, or in the pay, of these pressure groups. Disinterested were the taxpayer, big business apart from steel, and the African people. More than interested—in fact, fanatical on the subject—were a number of retired generals, colonels, and what not who had served in North Africa and for whom *le transsaharien* was more important than Suez or Panama. As one of the fervent supporters of the scheme writes:

> It would be shameful for France not to accomplish an undertaking less considerable and less difficult than that which has just been executed by the orders of the Emperor of Russia—

1. Bidon Cinq, or 'Petrol Can Number Five', is a famous 'station' on the trans-Saharan caravan trail. There is no water in either direction for a hundred miles. The story is told of a negro attendant at Bidon Cinq who sold his supply of water at an enormous price, then died of thirst when his relief failed to get through.

in three years!—and to hesitate just when this same sovereign has ordered—or so say the newspapers—the construction of a new line—the Siberian line of 5,000 miles across country!

But it wasn't just the Czar of Russia's railway which fired the zeal of the *transsaharien* faction in France, nor, for that matter, the new American trans-continental railroad joining New York and San Francisco; what was obviously behind the clamour for a nice long railway across the desert was French eagerness to grab a huge chunk of Africa before it was too late. In fact, with that political naïveté which is almost charming in an age of cynical slogans (occidental and oriental), highly placed Frenchmen came right out with their demands—reserved, one had always thought, for the British inventors of 'jingoism'.

> More than ever before France needs colonies [cries General Philebert] if she doesn't want to become a Greece or a Rumania in a hundred years. . . . And more than any other nation, France knows how to colonize; and only she has known, thanks to her generous nature, how to make herself loved by the natives and how to concern herself sincerely in the work of civilizing them.

This chauvinistic rubbish sounds like a joke today in view of what happened to French colonization in Algeria and elsewhere, but it was extremely persuasive at the time it was uttered in 1890, only a generation after the shameful defeat of the Franco-Prussian War. Yet, oddly enough, it wasn't the Germans who inspired French aspirations to become a great empire, but 'perfidious Albion', roundly hated by all foreign nations at this particular juncture of history. What the Americans say today about the Russians, and vice versa, has an almost perfect parallel in the abuse exchanged between France and Great Britain at the end of the last century. Both nations accused the other, directly or by implication, of being international gangsters, while each assumed a pious and highly moral tone about its own foreign policy. The French went so far as to accuse the British of trying to swallow the entire African continent—'from the delta of the Nile to the Cape of Good Hope'. Shall we see them accomplish this truly colossal plan? asks General Philebert, the typical French Army anglophobe. Fortunately, he concludes, they are finding obstacles in their way—including Portugal, 'showing how a little country sometimes knows how to defend its rights against a big one'. But the best antagonist of all, says the French general, and therefore the best friend of France, is Germany which is firmly and skilfully blocking Britain's expansion. A curious alliance in view of the fact that France and Germany had been at war twenty years previously; but a switch in love and friendship to which we have since become accustomed.

While outrightly accusing the British of robbery on a continental scale, the French piously claim that they were *simples spectateurs* of the dastardly business: all they want in Africa, they say through their mouthpieces, is to do their Christian duty of combating slavery. Envy is not a fault of the French nation. Still, wouldn't it be better to divide Africa up among us by common agreement—for there is enough for everybody—and to unite for the struggle against barbarism?

All such talk, of course, was a sort of verbal smoke-screen which hid the true motives of politicians and business men. The problem for the politicians was then, as now, to manipulate the inert mass of the public, indifferent to such projects as trans-Saharan railways, or colonies on the moon—indifferent, that is, except in so far as such enterprises make sensational and romantic reading. For this purpose, the anglophobes and trans-saharan-philes stressed specific examples of British intransigence in what should have been, according to the patriots, French Africa.

The following is the kind of incident which caused all good Frenchmen to seethe with hatred for the British. It was reported by Colonel Eugène Hennebert in his book *De Paris à Timbouctou*, published in 1889 at the height of the *transsaharien* fever.

A French steam packet called the *Joliette* decided to challenge the British monopoly of navigation on the Niger River. The elegant little craft of 400 tons, pride of the Marseilles shipyards, was built expressly for the West African trade. She could burn either coal or wood. She was armed with four rapid-fire cannons of the Hotchkiss type and a Maxim machine-gun.

Arriving in the Gulf of Guinea, the captain of the *Joliette* asked for a native pilot to take him up the main channel of the Niger. The pilot, 'under the orders and out of fear of the British', asked a £20,000 pilotage fee!

The French captain decided to find his own way up the river, only to be blockaded by a British ship which pretended to have run aground in the channel. By-passing the English vessel, the *Joliette* was next attacked by pirates—'brave pirates in the pay of Her Majesty the Queen of the United Kingdom'. Still farther up the river, a British gunboat pretended to take the *Joliette* for a slaver and removed all her coloured crew. The English missionary at Oritsha wouldn't let them get supplies on shore.

Eventually the French boat got as far upstream as the confluence of the Niger and its great tributary, the Benue, at a place called Loukodja, a kind of internal port for the whole of the western Sudan. Here the captain called on the British consul who is described in these terms:

> The consul's appearance could hardly be said to be top-drawer. He was a tall man, with green eyes which occasionally lit up, but were for the most part dead. He wore no hat, he was practically bald, and grey-bearded. His face revealed an extremely tenacious character, a sort of knowing cynicism, and a watchful manner. This gentleman prided himself, above all else, in being absolutely correct. He received the French travellers in official costume with a smile on his lips, and offered them a small fête in honour of such distinguished foreigners.
>
> Our French sailors were next invited to meet the charming ladies who made up the official court of Her Grace, the consul's better half. Some of the black venuses had everything on but stockings; others everything but the upper part of a dress. *Honi soit qui mal y pense.*
>
> From the enormous number of Anglo-Saxons who have elected to reside permanently at Loukodja, the consul presented the representative of the African Exploration Society,

the African Exploration Fund, and the heads of the different missionary societies.

It was a splendid reception; and the next day the consul appointed an excellent pilot to take the *Joliette* up the Benue—a man who had got slightly bottled at the party the night before. He put the ship fair and square on the first sand bank; and there she remained.

The procedure was not lacking in elegance. . . .

What is droll about this story, of course, is the classic French suspicion of the smiling British diplomat—an officer who, from the sound of it, was probably genuinely pleased to have visitors from the outside world, with news and newspapers and a few of the comforts of home for sale. But 'he received the French travellers with a smile on his lips and offered them a small fête in honour of such distinguished foreigners'. Ha ha! Obviously that smile was Machiavellian! And the party was put on simply to get the river pilot tight in order to run the French ship aground 'with a certain elegance!'

Colonel Hennebert who reports this horrendous story of British perfidy himself adds the moral in case anyone was too obtuse to see it for himself.

From which it appears that while the English didn't invent the art of delusion, they are born deceitful; and every attempt on our part to use the Lower Niger will take the grave risk of being a miserable failure. We must, then, find another way to reach the Sudan. Which way shall we take?

The answer, of course, *Le transsaharien!*

II

Agitation among retired generals, the directors of steel and rolling-stock companies, and railway engineers eventually pushed a reluctant government into doing something about building a railroad across nearly two thousand miles of desert '*pour la patrie*'.

Despite the palpably ridiculous claim of some of the enthusiasts that such a railroad would give France 100,000,000 new customers, not even the most ardent supporters of the project could prove that such a line would ever be economically sound, since there was nothing to be brought out of the regions served by the railway but a few carloads of dates and maybe a box or two of ostrich feathers then in great demand for ladies' hats. Otherwise there was no more commerce across the Sahara Desert than there had been in Carthaginian times—not as much, since negro slaves were no longer in demand in the European colonies.

Even so, the *transsaharien* supporters were sufficiently highly placed—or made enough clamour in the Press—to get something done; for inasmuch as their whole argument was based on 'patriotism', no minister or public official could afford to ignore them. The arguments were summed up by M. Adolphe Duponchel, a powerful figure in the Department of Civil Engineering.

(1) By means of her travellers, merchants and diplomats, England has established herself on over half of the African shores;

(2) From Tunis and Morocco, English and German explorers are travelling continuously southwards. They will end by barring us altogether from Central Africa;

(3) In the meantime, the Turkish rulers of Tripoli are trying to gain the allegiance of the Tuaregs; and the emperor of Morocco claims sovereignty over the oasis of Tuat. If we are not careful, Algeria will soon be a colony shut off in the south by Morocco and Tripoli.

(4) While we do nothing, trade is escaping us. The caravans are going either towards Tripoli by way of Ghadames; or towards Morocco by way of In Salah.

(5) We had better bestir ourselves to face the dangers that menace us.

This was enough to make the French Government of 1879 act —in the characteristic manner of governments: i.e. a 'preparatory commission' was set up with the idea of keeping everybody happy until the pressure was dissipated in a mass of documents that few could be bothered to read. The Preparatory Commission was followed by a General Commission to which almost every retired general of the French Army was appointed, together with all those engineers, like Alphonse Duponchel, who had an iron in the fire. This commission voted a further study of the project *in situ*, which became, a year later, the famous and disastrous 'Flatters Mission', which was to put an end to the grandiose design apparently for ever. Like so many other missions into the Sahara Desert, that of Colonel Flatters was never to return. The Trans-Saharan Railway remained a mirage.

But it was much more than that to Frenchmen in the last decades of the nineteenth century. In the bars and cafés and salons of every city and hamlet in France, as well as in the government ministries, the very mention of the name Flatters would cause a silence to fall, and a gloom comparable to the announcement of a national disaster in wartime.

The failure of the Flatters Mission, in short, and the horrible tale that was eventually whispered all over Europe, seemed almost like the end of French aspirations in Africa.

III

Colonel Paul François Xavier Flatters was the son of an impecunious German sculptor who chose to live in Paris where his son was born in 1832. Paul, a graduate of Saint Cyr, became a professional soldier, serving in Algeria, at the desert outpost of Laghouat. Though only a lieutenant-colonel, he was considered the ideal man for the job of surveying the Sahara with a view to tracing out the route for the railway which was to link Paris and Timbuktu.

In March 1880 he assembled his expeditionary party at Ouargla, the pestilential oasis which Captain Trumelet had visited and described almost twenty years previously. Colonel Flatters set out south into the open desert with a sizable force consisting of ten French military and civil engineers; twelve regular soldiers of a

North African regiment; thirty native troops; fifty camel-drivers; and 300 camels carrying six months' supplies. Crossing the 300 miles of the Great Eastern Sand Desert, they arrived without incident at the oasis of Temassinin, today called Fort Flatters, until recently an outpost of the Foreign Legion. This miserable oasis with its one well yielding little, though good, water and inhabited by a few serfs in bondage to the Tuaregs seems to have been first seen by Colonel Flatters and his party, though we can be reasonably sure that flying columns of the Roman Third Augusta Legion passed through either from their command post at Ghadames (Cydamus) to the north-east, or Ghat (Rhapsa) to the south-east.

Colonel Flatters pushed on southwards again, but now it seemed to him that he was being shadowed by the Tuaregs who appeared and disappeared over the dunes and rocks of the vast desert; and by the time the expedition had camped on the shores of a dry lake in the mountains, Colonel Flatters had the feeling that he was being surrounded by the tribesmen as so many travellers had been surrounded and annihilated before. The French officer now began parleying with the Tuareg chieftains, and finally decided to bribe them to leave at night while he withdrew his party from their exposed position on the lake. The ruse worked, because when the Tuaregs awoke next morning to find the Frenchmen gone, they were without leaders and were thrown into a state of confusion. Either they were bewildered at losing their prey, or they were disappointed that the Frenchmen would not treat them as friends, it has never been clear which. There has been a certain amount of criticism of Colonel Flatters's precipitate withdrawal by his fellow officers, though no one could doubt this soldier's bravery and devotion to duty after what happened on his second, and last, mission.

The second Flatters Mission was much larger than the first and consisted of ninety-seven men, of whom eleven were French soldiers and engineers; ninety-seven riding and 118 transport camels; and three horses. This sizable force left Ouargla on December 4th, 1880. On April 4th, 1881, twelve survivors were found by a relief force south of Ouargla, all of them dying of hunger and thirst. These twelve had kept themselves alive by eating their dead comrades. Neither Colonel Flatters nor any of the French officers were among them. The Colonel had died a thousand miles to the south, sabred to death by the Tuaregs; the others along the line of retreat.

The story of the Flatters Mission is really the story of the ordeals, hazards, and dangers experienced by the French in their conquest of the desert—or certainly the first chapter in that long epic. For it is the beginning of almost a hundred years' military campaign against two of the most implacable enemies of civilization in North Africa: the Central Saharan Desert and the Tuareg tribesmen. So powerful were, and are, these two enemies of European progress that still no railway spans the desert.

We have Colonel Flatters's diary from Saturday, December 4th, 1880, when his caravan left Ouargla, until Thursday, January 29th, 1881, the date of the last entry. It is, unfortunately, very much of a soldier's diary, entirely devoid of personalities, emotion, or colour, restricting itself, rather, to distances, times, and the kind of data the railway engineers would require when the time came for them to begin work. His letters, even those to his wife, don't tell us very much more. The last one to reach the outside world is to Henri Duveyrier, the explorer and historian of the Tuareg.[1] It is written on January 29th, nineteen days before he was to be murdered and his expedition wiped out. It says:

All goes well for the moment . . . and it may be that we shall go from Asiou to Agades by Dr. Barth's route. I shall be sorry if so, because this will be the first part of our journey already visited before us. But if I get to Asiou, the problem of the *transsaharien* can perhaps be considered solved. . . . All this doesn't mean that we shall get through easily. So we go then to our fate. As God wills! And let come what may. . . .

What came was what had come to so many travellers at the hands of the Tuaregs, from Major Laing to Mlle Tinne: treachery, cold-blooded murder, and robbery. Despite the calmness of his

1. See Chapter Ten, III.

diary entries and last letters, Colonel Flatters could sense the atmosphere of danger all round him. First the terrain itself was the most formidable in the whole of the Sahara, not on account of the usual sand-dunes which those ignorant of this vast waste-land associate with the desert, but because of the bare and eroded mountains devoid of water and pasture for men and beasts. This was the terrible Tassili-n-ajjer country. To the west was the Hoggar *massif*, inhabited—or controlled rather—by the Hoggar Tuareg who were the bitterest enemies of the French. Terrain and natives, then, were hostile to the expedition: the former showed it by first weakening, then killing, many of the camels; the latter by shadowing the caravan along a parallel route to the west.

The plot to wipe out Flatters and his mission—whether it was hatched up among the merchants of Tripoli or Ghadames, or by the fanatical Senussi as far away as the oasis of Kufra in the Libyan Desert—the plot was now about to be put into effect: the time and place were just right for bandits like the Tuaregs.

The first phase of the trap was for the guides to tell Colonel Flatters that they had missed the well, though actually they had deliberately by-passed it. They persuaded him to make camp there and then and to return with them to the well to water the camels. This seemed reasonable enough, and the need for water being now desperate, Colonel Flatters with four of his French lieutenants followed the Tuaregs back to the well. After a march of two hours through a ravine so narrow that only one camel could pass at a time, the five Frenchmen and the ten native soldiers who were with them arrived at the well only to discover that they had been ambushed. A band of Tuareg warriors, armed to the teeth, rode full pelt down the slopes yelling their war cries. At this moment one of the guides killed Beringer, the chief engineer of the expedition; and the native camel-men fled to leave the warriors to finish off the Frenchmen. Colonel Flatters and his second-in-command, Captain Masson, tried to hold off the attackers with their pistols to give the others time to get back to the main camp and raise the alarm. But first Flatters was sabred to death, then Masson, and finally Corporal Dennery.

Only eight of the fifteen managed to get back to the camp where Lieutenant Dianous had been left in command.

What happened next is, in some respects, puzzling. As soon as Lieutenant Dianous got the report of what had occurred at the well, his first thought, as a soldier, was to fight it out with the Tuaregs and, if possible, revenge the murder of his fellow officers. His men, too, were prepared to fight since they numbered fifty-nine well-armed and well-trained professionals against an unknown number of tribesmen armed, for the most part, with swords, lances, and shields. In other words, prudence as well as duty pointed to a bold policy of carrying the war to the Tuaregs, not of running away at this particular moment. But, for some reason we shall never know, Lieutenant Dianous was talked into an immediate withdrawal by the *mokkadam*, or headman of the Algerian troops. Even more strange, the lieutenant agreed to abandoning the camels to the Tuaregs, which meant making the thousand-mile journey back to Ouargla *on foot*—a fantastically difficult and dangerous undertaking. But at the insistence of the *mokkadam* he finally decided to leave the camp at midnight; and to this end he ordered the caravan supplies to be divided up among the fifty-nine survivors of the expedition, including the food, water, money, and effects—as much as, and more than, each man could carry.

It is clear that from the moment Lieutenant Dianous took the decision to retreat in this fashion—every man more or less for himself—his leadership was ended and the military discipline which might have saved the column was destroyed. The consequences of his decision were soon to become obvious. The marchers began to be picked off one by one, or in groups of two or three, while some simply deserted with the idea of making their way back alone. The Tuaregs shadowed the column the whole way; and before long men began to go mad with thirst or hunger or fear. The veiled tribesmen appeared and disappeared like phantoms; and choosing their moment when the French force had neither food nor water, they offered an armistice and, as a sign of friendship, gave the starving travellers a gift of dates. The dates were poisoned.

.

Still the column stumbled across the bare and waterless Hoggar Mountains, united to some extent in their hatred of the Tuaregs and their longing for revenge. Lieutenant Dianous improvised a flag which was carried at the head of the company, and he ordered his men to chant their Arab hymns in defiance of the enemy. This brave gesture didn't last long; for soon the party fell into two groups: the stronger who pushed on ahead; and the weaker who were left to follow.

The vanguard led by Lieutenant Dianous finally got close to the oasis of Amguid where the Tuaregs decided to fight in order to prevent the French party from getting water and supplies. The two sides battled continuously for eight hours, and at the end all the Frenchmen were dead with the exception of Sergeant Pobéguin, who was wounded in the foot and unable to walk. Pobéguin now commanded what was left of the force. But there was no longer any pretence of discipline. The men began straggling along in groups or by themselves. They had three camels which had been captured during the battle with the Tuaregs. The sick and wounded, including Sergeant Pobéguin, took turns at being carried on the back of these beasts. But as their hunger became worse, the Algerians demanded that the camels should be killed for food, and Sergeant Pobéguin was now too sick to prevent this final breach of group discipline. The sick were left behind with a canteen of water. The others continued their march northwards. They had three days' supply of camel meat and nothing else left.

When that was gone, they began to eat their dead. Sergeant Pobéguin, too sick to resist, was murdered by one of the Algerian riflemen, and he, too, was eaten.

On April 4th, 1881, after forty-eight days' march across the desert, twelve survivors more like skeletons than men stumbled into the oasis of El-Meseggem in the Great Eastern Sand Desert. They were what was left of the biggest, best-equipped, and best-organized force yet to cross the Sahara—nearly a hundred professional fighting men and a caravan of 215 camels.

This disaster was not, however, the last the world was to hear of Colonel Flatters. To the contrary, the mission and the men who took part in it lived on for more than twenty years—in fact, right up to the outbreak of World War I which swept them away along with many other nineteenth-century legends: they lived on in Frenchmen's hearts and minds as a heroic myth, comparable to certain episodes in classical or medieval romances. E-F. Gautier, himself an explorer of the desert and one of those writers whom modern realists call a 'Saharan mystic', sums up the Flatters legend for us:

From the moment that it was known, the death of Flatters has taken on a special significance and has instantaneously become a myth. It has become the Death of Siegfried or Achilles. . . . Everything about it excites the imagination. It happened in the Desert, the country of mirages. The extent of the disaster was exceptional, since the Mission was wiped out almost to the last man: there suddenly arrived at the southern Algerian outposts the few survivors—several exhausted and half-mad natives. It is from their contradictory and suspect babblings that one must reconstruct the drama, and this reconstruction has for the public something strange and mysterious, through which we glimpse certain weird details, like the story of the poisoned dates and the scenes of cannibalism. . . .

'Sunday, 27 March. A piece of human flesh was offered to Pobéguin who at first refused it with horror, then ate it with the others. . . .'

The result was a false image of Flatters throughout the nineteenth century. In 1895 a certain Mr. Djebari, an ex-military interpreter, announced to the world that the members of the Flatters Mission were still alive, prisoners of the Tuaregs. Mr. Djebari had seen them; he had spoken to them; he described them. Flatters himself had become a naturalized Tuareg called Labran: he was alive in the oasis of Tagaïss with his adopted daughter Ismaou whom he adores.

Actually, those twelve survivors who stumbled into the oasis of El-Meseggem were all that was left of the dream of a Trans-Saharan Railway. For almost ten years, no responsible French official dared mention this project: there were only solemn references to the 'frightful catastrophe'. Then towards the end of the century the old soldiers returned to their theme.

> The Trans-Saharan Railway! [writes General Philebert in 1890]. What hasn't been said about it? What criticisms, what ironies haven't been levelled at this project for an iron road across the desert? Isn't the idea utopian? Uneconomic? It doesn't matter what they say, it remains one of the great conceptions of our age, and we shall one day realize it perhaps too late. . . .
>
> But for some ten years, since the frightful massacre of the Flatters Mission, one has scarcely dared to pronounce the word '*transsaharien*'—so impressionable and so easily discouraged are our countrymen. . . . But if we wish to safeguard the future security of Algeria, we must be prepared to build the trans-Saharan railway. . . .

So once again the old arguments were heard in the clubs and army messes of Paris and Algiers; and once again there were those who argued for the *tracé central*, or *occidental*, or *oriental*; for termini at Timbuktu, or Lake Chad; with figures and maps to prove how easily the railway could be built and what enormous benefits would result from it. But all these proposals and plans seemed somehow more and more like old soldiers' pipe dreams; for, as usual, patriotism had to be tempered with economics. Statesmen, politicians, and business men alike believed in annexing the Sahara to the French African empire; but only if the conquest of this wasteland could be paid for in men's lives, not in hard cash.

At the beginning of the twentieth century the arguments, with a few insults or vituperations thrown in, were still flying back and forth, the protagonists for or against solidly lined up behind two explorers who knew the affair from firsthand experiences. One of them, Robert Chudeau, clearly stated that the project for such a railway wasn't even worth discussing; the other, E-F. Gautier, championed it as an excellent and necessary enterprise.

Since the two men had been colleagues on another trans-Saharan expedition, it was difficult to know who was right.

By 1910 the idea was practically dead and forgotten, and it might never have been heard of again except among a few die-hards if it had not been for the collapse of France in 1940 and the renewed importance in the eyes of the dishonoured French of their African empire. Not having any other outlet for its national aspirations and energies, the Vichy Government actually trotted out the *transsaharien*, with, incidentally, the approval of their German masters who were interested (1) in trans-African communications; and (2) a pipe-line to bring peanut oil from Central Africa to Europe to overcome the chronic shortage of fats in Germany and occupied Europe. Once they had decided to build their railway, the Vichy Government drew up an ambitious programme for laying 1,000 kilometres of line a year, thus completing the link between Algiers and Gao in three years. They laid a total of eighty kilometres. The *transsaharien* stops about forty miles south of Colomb-Bechar at a whistle-stop called Abadla, population a few hundred. The line peters out, as it were, on the banks of a ravine. No one has yet quite figured out how the railroad is to cross it, because, perhaps, the desert proper begins on the other side, and nobody any longer cares whether there is a Trans-Saharan Railway or not.

The mausoleum at Germa—once considered the most southerly monument of the Roman Empire. It was discovered in 1822

A seventeenth-century map of North Africa—a fairy-tale landscape drawn from imagination

Top Left: The castle at Zuila, the last outpost of a Byzantine kingdom which marks the end of the Roman imperium in Africa. *Top Right:* A Roman mosaic of horses, immortalized by their names. *Bottom Left:* Tombs on the outskirts of Zuila. Were they the mausoleums of kings? *Bottom Right:* Archaeology is only just beginning to reveal something about the Garamantians....An offering table taken from a royal tomb

THE TUAREG

Left: Tuareg children.
The boy's upswept hair-do
and plump face will shortly
be covered with the blue
veil of his race

Right: A Tuareg wedding
group. The bridegroom is
the worried-looking man
on the left

Left: A Tuareg warrior in
ceremonial dress

Right: An old blind
pipe-player turns up with
his all-women Tuareg
orchestra of drummers
and timpanists

Alexandrine Petronella
Francesca Tinne, the first
European woman explorer
of the Great Desert

Captain G. F. Lyon, R.N., leader of the expedition of 1818

Mungo Park

Major Dixon Denham, member of the Tripoli–Lake Chad expedition of 1822

THE EXPLORERS

Captain Hugh Clapperton, R.N.

Major Alexander Gordon Laing, discoverer of Timbuktu

Cardinal Charles-Martial
Allemand-Lavigerie,
primate of Africa

Spahis: a group of junior French officers commanding a regiment of native
troops

THIRTEEN

Laperrine

I

FOR almost the next hundred years after the easy capture of Algiers in 1830 France hazarded little in the conquest of the Sahara except the lives of her professional soldiers. A comparison, for instance, of the methods and results of colonization between the Roman and the French conquerors of this territory is revealing. We have seen in the early chapters of this book what the Romans accomplished and how they accomplished it. We have seen that they conquered, controlled, and civilized their vast North African empire practically with a single legion. They completely changed both the people and the land itself: they metamorphosed barbarians into recognizable human beings, as they did all over the Roman world. The decorated African tribesmen, like the painted British warrior, both of them scarcely out of the neolithic age, were brought to a very high stage of culture within a comparatively few years.

The results in Roman Africa were impressive and have endured in the form of tens of thousands of towns, villages, farms, forts, baths, roads, wells, reservoirs, dams, and the rest of it. The results of the French colonization are, in comparison, less imposing with the exception of the army's magnificent contribution in exploring, mapping, and finally pacifying the Sahara Desert.

The most objective of the French historians of North Africa point out this failure of their nation to exploit the vast territory which fell into their hands almost by accident. They observe that only a few of the more conscientious of their countrymen saw that it was necessary to do something more than to raise the tricolour over the ruined Berber villages or to preside paternally

over the palavers of the local chieftains. As early as 1880 the first
Flatters Mission had noted that certain areas of the Sahara could
be irrigated and cultivated without any great expense to the home
government. In fact, the army officers on their continuous expeditions to explore, map, and administer the desert zones frequently reported the evidence of extensive Roman exploitation
and suggested ways and means of repeating the process. Some
of these schemes, like that of a Trans-Saharan Railway, were
obviously motivated by the imperialistic, or personal, ambitions
of professional patriots. Others were still rather grandiose, but
none the less worth consideration—if the economic wellbeing of
the native inhabitants was regarded as any sort of criterion. Such
a scheme—and one still vaguely talked about—was the plan to
join the vast and useless salt lakes of southern Tunisia with the
Mediterranean in order to help irrigate the surrounding desert
and to increase the humidity of the atmosphere—an important
factor in land reclamation.

Towards the end of their dominion in Africa, the French—and
this was also true of the other colonial nations—made an effort
to administer and develop their colonies not only along economic
and technological lines, but in the social and humanitarian spirit
resulting from a guilty national conscience and the lessons of
various wars and revolutions. The education, health, and wellbeing of the native populations now became an urgent aspect of
colonial policy. Schools, hospitals, roads, land reclamation, and
social benefits of one sort and another were hurried along, and
full citizenship offered to the hitherto subject people. As a result,
what we see that is progressive and efficient in the now-inde-
pendent African states is nearly all the result of the final ten years
or so of enlightened colonial administration. Unfortunately for
the European powers, the change of heart and policy had come
too late. Nationalism, the cardinal political creed of the late
nineteenth and early twentieth century, had taken hold among
the African peoples, even though the vast majority of them have
no concept of 'nationhood'. They are still basically tribal people,
as a visit to any part of Africa will show. But 'nationalism' meant
to the native politicians and business men the eviction of rich and

powerful Europeans and their replacement by rich and powerful Africans. And this is what has happened in the former colonies; and where there is a semblance in these new states of modernization, it is due to what the colonizers left behind in the form of universities, schools, hospitals, roads, bridges, farms, and even factories. What the conquerors—again in contrast with the Romans—did not bequeath to their subjects, however, was a corps of trained administrators, scientists, and technicians capable of keeping the machine of a modern society functioning efficiently. This is the key problem of the new African nations.

Because most of them are rich in their own right, however— or can certainly lay their hands on tidy sums of money merely by playing a simple game of international politics—they can afford to meet this problem by hiring European and American technicians to run their countries for them. While the politicians frequent the capitals where they can play the tricky game of local politics, Western (and increasingly Soviet) engineers, doctors, educators, and other professional men keep the wheels of an antiquated and inefficient economic and social machine turning. Thus it is that far down in the desert itself one will find in some small town (by definition, an oasis with one paved road, flickering electric light, and a half-made airport), English engineers, French doctors, Italian masons, and German technicians. These men are struggling to erect government buildings, radio masts, telephone systems, and the other paraphernalia of a modern community. One finds them lodged in the local 'hotel', a broken-down caravanserai in which there is, of course, a bar, but no bathrooms. Loud are the complaints and criticisms of these men who have been away from home for a year or more; and their censure of the country and people for whom they are working can be summed up in a sentence or two: the native workmen don't know how even to screw a nut on to a bolt; from the engineers' point of view, they are 'hopeless'. Schedules are not kept; promised materials don't arrive; new machines are abused and then wrecked; age-old phrases implying indifference are constantly on the natives' lips; nobody from the top to the bottom has any sense of responsibility or pride in his work.

It is interesting and instructive to talk to these men who are trying (for well-earned salaries) to 'modernize' the African countries—and to compare what they have to say about the practice with what we hear concerning the theory. For the Western politicians who sit in conference rooms discussing ways and means of helping the undeveloped nations have very little idea of what it is like to be in the field trying to implement their theories. From the viewpoint of the practical engineer on the spot, for instance, the spectacle of a native driver hitting the carburettor of a brand-new car with a rock in order to start an engine which has no fuel is not likely to endear him to the man who will have to repair the damage.

I could appreciate this impatience with the 'hopelessness'—or indifference would be a more accurate description—of the Saharan when I was waiting to leave an oasis to return to 'civilization'—namely one of these towns with a paved road, electric light, and an airport from which the weekly plane made contact with the outside world. We were due to leave at one o'clock in the afternoon. At three o'clock the Land Rover arrived. I observed that it had a flat tyre and no cap to the petrol tank (this is standard). As I was due to cross a sand sea, I looked under the canvas flaps at the back of the car to see if there were spare cans of fuel and a spare tyre. There was a spare tyre. It had no air in it at all. There were also about nine passengers of all shapes and sizes, and one large sheep. This was no way to try to cross sand-dunes with a desert wind blowing. I therefore requested the hitch-hikers and the sheep to dismount, and the driver to put some air into the tyres. At four o'clock this was done, and off we went, pausing to pick up a couple of the more artful passengers some way out of the oasis. You have to give people a lift in the desert. We also stopped for eggs along the way and spent a long and animated time with the driver of a truck who had been stuck on the road for two days and wanted messages carried to the next town. Then we set off across the sand sea. The sun was getting uncomfortably low in the heavens.

It next became apparent that the driver neither knew how to operate the four-wheel drive nor the route we were supposed to take. Instead, we headed for the deepest of the dunes, and there eventually we came to rest, buried practically up to the bonnet of the car. *Inshallah* was now the operative word: it was as God willed. But as the sun was fast descending and nobody knew we were in this corner of the desert, I felt God's will was not enough. We had to do something ourselves. The driver agreed and placed the jack on the sand under the front bumper and pumped away. The jack rapidly disappeared. At this point I looked around at the towering cliffs of sand, breaking like frozen waves over the precipices, and reminded myself of the first rule of desert travel— never to leave your vehicle. I also recalled how cold the desert was at night. To work, then. The sand was cleared from under the car; the car itself put into four-wheel drive; the driver and the two passengers pushed; we moved slowly backwards away from the precipice and back down the long slope of the dune up which we should never have come. Navigation was now stricter, and with the sun on the western horizon, we could at least recognize the north which was our general direction. It was an interminable and hazardous ride, but at last the red light on the hill near the airport was spotted, and we were able to spend the night in a bed.

The engineers and others who were in residence at the hotel which I finally reached were cynical. They had all had similar experiences, and the more disillusioned of them maintained that the desert people invariably got lost and the best thing was to ignore all their 'lore' and rely on a compass. There is some truth to it, or there is from the Westerner's point of view. We are not accustomed to travelling by camel; we don't have the camel-driver's mentality. We travel by car; and to do that we must know how to drive and maintain it. And, above all, we don't accept it as Allah's will that we should sleep and freeze and possibly die in the desert. These ideas and attitudes are funda-mental, and they indicate, in a rough and ready way, the difference between Africans and Europeans-cum-Americans.

However, these reflections are in no way intended to be con-clusive: they are only suggestive of the nature of the problem that the African nations themselves face in this Western-instigated fervour to modernize and industrialize at all costs—to the end of setting up a European-American society in this continent. One could just as well argue that when we had the chance to create such a society—over a hundred years or more—we meticulously avoided doing any such thing. For all the projects to 'civilize' the African territories came up against the same obstacles, or were met with the same arguments. What was there in it for the colonialists?

As far as the French were concerned, the excellent ports and the rich agricultural lands of the Mediterranean littoral were well worth 'modernization'. Consequently the navy and the steamship companies took over the ports of Oran, Algiers, and Bizerta; and the *colons* took over the farms. Apart from exploiting these two profitable resources, hardly anything was done from the Atlas Mountains in the north to the Niger River in the south. Why? Well, what did southern Algeria and Tunisia (once the granary of Roman Italy) produce other than dates? What precious metals or farmlands could the Sahara Desert offer? None. (Or so it was thought before the discovery of oil all over the desert.) The whole territory, in brief, was a financial liability and the only reason France undertook to administer it was for the sake of prestige. Prestige, however, didn't mean raising the standards of life for the natives of the country. That seemed to be a Roman idea and had no place in nineteenth-century imperial policy. The results are, of course, being felt today. And where the Romans stayed for some five centuries in relative peace and prosperity, the French remained for just over a hundred years, with scarcely a decade of real tranquillity.

II

The French, of course, had a much greater area to contend with than the Romans. The latter had scant interest in either the desert proper or Negroland to the south of it. They could have invaded and conquered these territories if they had wanted to, but they seldom occupied regions they couldn't colonize and civilize. The French, on the other hand, found themselves the possessors of some 3,000,000 square miles of the Sahara Desert by sheer accident of history: they didn't even have to fight another Christian nation to acquire them. But once having done so, they had to go through the motions of what imperialistic powers have always dignified with the term 'pacification'. This, of course, was a job for the army.

The generals began pacifying Algeria and Tunisia by the usual means: namely the use of French soldiers fighting in the European manner, pretty much as the British later were to pacify Egypt and the Sudan by using Redcoats in the same formations as they had used during the Napoleonic Wars. At the same time the French tactics in 1840 anticipated those employed a hundred years later in the Second World War: namely, victory by pulverization. Thus the Allies pulverized the Germans in their foxholes during the Normandy campaign by dropping from the air a thousand tons or more of high explosive per each enemy infantryman. Even if the necessary numbers of Germans weren't annihilated by this process, due to errors in navigation and the like, the countryside for miles around was; and this implies a victory in warfare. So with the French destruction of the Berber and Kabyle villages in central and southern Algeria: the pulverization and firing of the natives' shacks could be reported in the official communiqués as another victory for French arms.

Unfortunately the natives themselves didn't concur with this conclusion, and they never really did consider themselves conquered by the invaders. Defeated, yes; and, after a time, subjugated. But never conquered. The victories were all to the French. Here is a typical communiqué of the period:

> Our losses were two officers killed, two wounded, 48 soldiers killed or disappeared, 26 wounded. A part of the convoy was carried off when the Arab camel-drivers fled with their animals.
> The losses to the enemy were considerable. They are estimated at several hundred killed. The Arab women fought with the men and showed an unimaginable fierceness. . . . The few

prisoners we took, before they were shot, apprised us that our column had fought against the army of Bou-Amama.

There are several significant items in this terse official report— the number of soldiers who took the opportunity to 'disappear', i.e. desert; the unreliability of the native camel-drivers impressed into service by the French; the heavy losses of the natives who were armed with sticks, stones, and a few antiquated muskets; the presence of the native women who preferred to be killed fighting rather than in their homes; and the classic remark casually slipped into the communiqué, 'the few prisoners we took, *before they were shot . . .*'

After fifty years of these tactics, it is not surprising that the French had no more control over their Saharan possessions than they had over the desert tribes. Wherever they went, they had to go as an army; i.e. as a sizable force, European style, cannons and all the rest of it. Thus, as late as 1901, in order to occupy the Tuat region in southern Algeria,[1] several thousand heavily armed infantrymen were marched into the desert, where their only enemy, of course, was hunger, thirst, disease, and boredom. Having got this ridiculous army into the region, the French High Command had to feed them—a colossal task under those conditions. Practically the entire camel population of Algeria was impressed into the supply service; and within a month thousands upon thousands of these beasts were dead from exhaustion.

The desert trails for thousands of kilometers [writes E-F. Gautier] were strewn with carcasses thicker than telegraph poles along a European main highway. During the first months, a blind man could have found his way without diculty by the smell. The complete skeletons, and, indeed, the entire cadavers mummified by the desert, existed for years, and there are still places where they are found. Even the jackals and the vultures were overwhelmed with the immensity of their job.

1. Today the site of the French atomic testing grounds at Reggan.

In short, half the camels in Algeria, Gautier tells us, were wiped out in a month as a result of some stupid general's decision to occupy an empty desert according to the best Napoleonic Wars tactics.

However, luckily for France, there were a number of intelligent army officers in the lower echelons, and it was these men who ultimately 'conquered' the Sahara with a few score native troops as contrasted with the ponderous 'missions' sent out by the old-line generals in Algiers. The native troops under French officers became, in fact, the best trained and certainly the most useful units in the French Army. Mobilized towards the end of the nineteenth century, they were still fighting the French wars for them fifty years later. Their names, uniforms, and deeds of prowess belong to the romance of war. They ceased to exist with the last of the gunpowder wars; and only those who witnessed the North African campaign during the 1939–45 war have seen such units as the *Chasseurs d'Afrique* and the *Méharistes* in action under wartime conditions. The *Méharistes*, or Desert Camel Corps, were operating down around the Chott Djerid in 1942. They were responsible for the southernmost section of the Allies' Tunisian line, though what these camel-mounted tribesmen under the command of their French officers were supposed to do in the event of a German tank thrust across or around the Chott was not clear then, and has never been clear since. But they were a romantic group down there in the desert, and it was in its way a touchingly nostalgic experience to share a couscous with these beautifully cloaked French officers, lying under a palm tree which sloped at exactly the right angle for a motion-picture shot, while looking out across the clean sand-dunes or up to the enormous stars of the Sahara at night.

The native troops, then, were organized into specific regiments which rapidly brought the vast territory under control. They were:

    (1) *Tirailleurs d'Afrique* (infantrymen)
    (2) *Chasseurs d'Afrique* (light cavalry)

(3) *Spahis*   (troopers)

(4) *Méharistes*   (camel corps)

(5) *Régiments Étrangers* (Foreign Legion)

Of these five it is the Camel Corps which, almost without help, and certainly without the usual military tactics, quickly and silently conquered the Sahara Desert for the French.

The realization that the desert and its inhabitants could neither be conquered nor even properly explored by European-type armies seems to have occurred first to a young soldier who was typical of the French officers who did their stint in the colonies before finishing up, as many of them did, generals, and even marshals, of France. Marie Joseph François Henri Laperrine was the youngest son of an aristocratic and impoverished family, who, like so many of his contemporaries from the same social milieu, had no alternative but the army. He left Saint-Cyr a second lieutenant and went straight to North Africa where he was eventually posted, in 1901, to the command of the Saharan Oasis Territory, at that time a region of the desert which had neither been explored nor brought under French control. It was still the country of the 'terrible Tuaregs', the Veiled Men of the Desert who had wiped out the second Flatters Mission twenty years before, a ghastly tragedy wrapped in horror and mystery, which the French had never forgotten. Laperrine's job was to patrol the Saharan oases. No one expected him to subdue the Tuaregs, for the total force available to him was less than 200 men.

A couple of years before Laperrine took command of his three companies of *spahis*, the Algerian High Command, hypnotized by the Flatters disaster, had sent a mission across the Sahara consisting of a highly trained infantry regiment complete with armaments for a full-scale war, or series of battles, with the Tuaregs. This was the Foureau-Lamy expedition of 1898–9 which actually marched on foot the 1,500 miles from Ouargla in southern Algeria to Zinder in Bornu. This mission, like that of Flatters, was nearly another catastrophe; and, considering the effort and expense in money and lives, it achieved almost nothing. The Tuaregs, still armed for the most part with spears, swords, and shields, were not so foolhardy as to attack an infantry regiment armed with rifles, machine-guns, and light cannon. All the Tuaregs had to do was to refuse to supply the column with food and transport. The French mission lost all their camels in the Air; they had to burn their baggage; and then continued their journey almost simply as a test of endurance, like swimming the Channel. Swimming the Channel, from west to east, or vice versa, is a splendid physical achievement; but one would hardly say it has any other significance. So with the Foureau-Lamy walk across the desert: it had no result other than showing that it could be done. As for taming the Tuaregs, it had no effect whatsoever.

Laperrine, quietly and efficiently, without consulting the elderly generals back in Algiers, went about creating a force which, within ten years, was crossing and re-crossing the desert in all directions, meeting the Tuaregs, fraternizing with them, receiving their collaboration and submission to French rule, and actually, by way of a test, travelling without an escort to the remotest oases of the Sudanese Desert. What neither an 'army' nor projects for a Trans-Saharan Railway could do, Laperrine with a few hundred *méharistes* travelling in small groups of twenty or less accomplished almost without firing a shot and with the loss of scarcely a man or animal. In less than ten years this one major had really joined the French Sudanese colonies with Algeria to such an extent that a regular postal service now crossed the Sahara from Timbuktu via the Hoggar, In Salah, and El Golea to Algiers; it was expedient and safe (though not exactly comfortable!) for French officials serving in Senegal to return home by the land route; and the Tuareg terror had ceased to exist. Naturally nobody could believe it. In fact, the army command went on planning to conquer just one small region of the desert—the Tuat—with an army of 4,000 men. Major Laperrine, with 200 native tribesmen and half a dozen French officers, had already done it for them.

How had he accomplished this swift, efficient, and bloodless conquest of a desert that had defied powerful and civilized states since Carthaginian times?

The answer is that, like the Englishman Colonel Lawrence, Laperrine surrendered himself to the desert, its people, and its way of life. He was one of those for whom the limitless expanse of sand, the movement of a caravan across it, the arrival at a green oasis, the curious timeless rhythm of desert life became a completely satisfying and even hypnotic experience. He wanted no other. He served forty years in the Sahara Desert and died there, sitting in an aeroplane, his shoulder broken. He died during a sandstorm.

But this was at the end of his life—he was sixty and a general—and his work began twenty years before when, as a major in the French cavalry, he realized that the desert would never be conquered with traditional armies; or, if it were, the conquest would have no meaning. Rather, the outsider would have to surrender to the desert, not vice versa. The Sahara, then (we are speaking of the end of the nineteenth century: all this has changed since), had certain definite and unbreakable rules of procedure. Those who flouted these rules, as most of the military expeditions had done up to that time, achieved nothing. Those who recognized them might achieve much. Major Laperrine didn't know how much; but he intended to find out.

The first rule of the desert was to travel light and to travel fast. Speed was absolutely essential, which explains why even the largest and slowest-moving of the caravans travel an average of twenty miles a day, and usually more. A military force must travel twice as fast as this. The second rule was never to seek a quarrel, but always to try, through normal contacts and normal familiarity, to accustom a hostile people to the idea of friendship.

Laperrine first set about transforming his native troops into expert *méharistes*, or camel cavalrymen who, together with their French officers, lived exactly the same life as the desert nomads—notably the Tuaregs. The native trooper, instead of being regarded, and regarding himself, as a military peon, was encouraged to think of himself as a free and independent warrior. He could come and go pretty much as he wished; he was bound to his commander and troop only by ties of loyalty and prestige.

Laperrine's *méharistes* had no headquarters, no barracks, and no administration. They lived with their camels—several to each trooper—in the desert, wherever there was pasture. They never went near the cities, and they continued to live the nomadic life they had always known. The only difference was they were the toughest and most specialized soldiers in the French, or any other European, Army. If proof were needed of that, we have the evidence of Major Laperrine's patrols during the years 1901–10. In the summer of 1905, for instance, one of his officers, Captain Dinaux, crossed the Sahara *four times in the hottest season of the year* without losing a single man or animal. It was really quite incredible when one thinks of what these journeys had been like for the hundreds of explorers and soldiers who had died in the desert. Now, a handful of French officers, mounted on trotting camels and accompanied by a score of *méharistes*, patrolled the entire Sahara from southern Algeria and Tunisia to the Niger River and Lake Chad. They never encountered any resistance; they never had to fire their rifles except for game; and the Tuareg chieftains welcomed them whenever they wished to visit their camps.

If one looks over the enormous number of monographs written on aspects of the Sahara Desert—from such topics as *Trade between Beni-Ounif and the Tafifelt* to *Some observations on Camel Breeding Among the Chaamba*—one will find almost half of them have been written by French Army officers, because these were the lucky explorers who, at last, could go in safety into the dreaded country of the Air and the Hoggar Tuareg. When one remembers what had happened less than a hundred years before to Major Laing and Miss Tinne—and only twenty years before to Colonel Flatters—the change is incredible. But change there was. In brief, the Sahara had finally been conquered, and was, with reasonable precautions, safer to travel than a city street.

Even so, men were still to die in this pitiless wasteland, as they had always died; and their number was to include the man who had gone so far as to wed himself to the desert which finally betrayed him.

III

The story of General Laperrine's death is best told by the men who were with him at the time. These were Major Vuillemin, the pilot of one of the planes, and his observer, Lieutenant Chalus; and Sergeant-Major Bernard, the pilot of the second plane, and the mechanic Vaslin. General Laperrine was a passenger in the second plane which, like the other, was a two-seater. The General, therefore, had to sit on the mechanic's lap. The two aeroplanes were World War I biplanes—300 h.p. Bréguets. Their mission was to fly from Algiers to Dakar down the entire depth of the Sahara Desert. Such a mission was, perhaps, the most important event in all Saharan history, for once a regular air route was established, with stopping places at all the important towns, oases, and military posts throughout the desert, this remote region of the world—a world apart, in a sense—would not only be conquered by Europeans, but would become part of Europe. In other words, a traveller could now reach Timbuktu from Tripoli in a day, without even a minute's danger or discomfort. It took Major Laing a year and a month of indescribable danger and hardship to cover the same distance.

General Laperrine, despite the fact that he belonged to the pre-automobile, pre-aviation generation of explorers, was none the less forward-looking enough to see that the day of the camel was almost ended. He had already supervised the first motor convoys which had reached as far as Tamanrasset. These early cars and trucks, Renaults and Fiats, had only relative success; and the first aeroplanes didn't have much more. A joint expedition of cars and planes set out from Colomb-Bechar in the west to Ouargla in the east, a distance of 500 miles, as the crow flies, across the Great Western Sand Desert—a route, incidentally, for which there are still no roads or caravan trails. Cars and planes went round the Western Desert by way of Beni-Abbes, Adrar, Aoulef, In Salah, and El Golea—the route which is today paved in places and regularly marked and serviced all the way along. It represents a journey of 1,200 miles which the 1919 cars covered in twenty-seven days, travelling, that is, at just under fifty miles a day. Of the five 80 h.p. Farman aeroplanes which set off with the cars, only two arrived at Ouargla one day ahead of the automobiles. It wasn't very impressive, but it was a portent of what was to come.

What was to come, then, was a regular airline between Algiers and Dakar via the French Sahara—a military airline, of course, flown and supervised by the army. Somebody had to make the first complete crossing of the desert, and that extremely dangerous task fell to Major Vuillemin and his three fellow aviators in their two 300 h.p. biplanes. There wasn't even a seat for a fifth man, so that when General Laperrine decided to go with them, Major Vuillemin must have had his doubts. In the first place the General was a very distinguished old soldier of sixty; in the second he was not an aviator; and in the third he was stealing the Major's thunder. But a major is in no position to argue with a general; so on February 18th, 1920, two fragile and wobbly aeroplanes left the makeshift runway at Tamanrasset with Major Vuillemin piloting the first and Sergeant-Major Bernard the second, in which rode General Laperrine perched on the lap of the mechanic Vaslin. The cockpits of both planes, of course, were open.

Major Vuillemin tells his part of the flight in his report.

18 February.—We leave Tamanrasset at 7 o'clock, accompanied by Sergeant-Major Bernard's plane (passengers: General Laperrine and the mechanic Vaslin). Our flight plan was as follows:

My plane being slower than Bernard's, I should go ahead flying by compass. Should I miss the route, Bernard, directed by General Laperrine, will overtake me and indicate the correct course by the line of his flight. We have to fly over Tin Regho (recognizable from the characteristic faults in the land formation as shown in the general's photographs) and land at Tin Zaouaten. This landing is obligatory for Bernard's plane which has only five hours' petrol. I took off with nine hours' supply because there are no means of refuelling in this region.

We have placed all our confidence as regards the direction

to follow in the knowledge of General Laperrine who has crossed the Sahara eleven times on foot or by camel; we think that his air training is adequate since he has just flown over a thousand miles without once losing himself.

I learnt subsequently, from his pilot, that he was lost one hour after we took off.[1]

First following the Wadi Tamanrasset, then flying by compass, we think we recognized the characteristic formation of the Tin Regho region. We next fly over a mountain resembling Tin Zaouaten and I supposed that Bernard's plane, which had overtaken us, is going to lead us to the landing ground. (Actually we were 75 miles E.S.E. of it.)

The fog, which was light when we left, is now more and more thick. Bernard is losing height rapidly; I am able to follow him for a moment, but I lose him in the fog. After searching for him vainly for half-an-hour (as well as for the landing ground which I thought was nearby), I decide to go on by compass towards the Niger. I gain altitude while flying south-west; but I note that my compass, very exact up to then, doesn't tally any longer with the sun's position. Not being sure of the time, I made a guess, which caused me to make an error of around 20° to the east, without my knowing it.

In addition, I can see from time to time the landmarks set out along the route (the occasional tree and the white circles).

Towards four o'clock, the vegetation increases; I follow a wadi running from the north-west to the south-east until it joined another, very large and green, which went towards the south. This latter wadi was followed until five o'clock. Having only about 20 gallons of petrol left, I decide to land in a place where I think I detect a camp. I make a normal landing, but there is nobody there. We eat a cold meal and spend the night in the aeroplane, our rifles at hand, woken every minute by the cries of wild animals.

19 February.—At daybreak we start the motor and take off

1. Despite Major Vuillemin's cautious and relatively objective account of the event, one surely detects a querulous note in this short, simple statement.

with the intention of following the wadi south as far as the Niger.

Around eight o'clock, we make a normal landing at the French post of Menaka, 160 miles east of Gao, whither we send some *goumiers* to get petrol and to apprise the authorities. . . .

In the meantime, what had happened to the other aeroplane? We hear this part of the story from the two survivors of the forced landing, Sergeant-Major Bernard, the pilot, and Vaslin, the mechanic.

According to them, General Laperrine decided soon after take-off to follow the lead plane. The implication is, as Vuillemin states, that he was lost, despite the landmarks which marked the route they were supposed to follow from Tamanrasset to their next stop, Tin Zaouaten. It was very natural, in fact perhaps almost inevitable, that an elderly soldier used to navigating on land from a few feet off the ground atop a camel should quickly lose his bearings at 10,000 feet, which was the altitude Vuillemin was flying. At all events, the general advised Bernard, his pilot, to follow the lead plane, though he was uneasy about the direction they were taking.

At 10.30 Bernard advised him that he only had enough petrol for another hour. At 11.30 the landing place at Tin Zaouaten was still not visible, but they had to land all the same. They now had no alternative.

The flight orders were specific. They said that if for any reason whatsoever one of the planes had to land, and if it made a normal landing on good ground, the other plane should also land. If, however, the ground was bad, the second plane should fly over, mark exactly the place, and reconnoitre the best means of bringing rescue teams overland.

At 11.30, then, Bernard began his descent, sending out a radio message to Major Vuillemin who was now flying nearly a mile ahead and to the left. Bernard radioed: 'We are lost. We think we are east of the trail. We are landing to the south among the dunes.' There was no reply. The pilot sent the message a second time. Still no reply. He now began radioing repeatedly S O S, at the same time searching for a landing place as he only had twenty minutes of flying time left. He found what seemed a suitable spot and made his approach, but fifteen yards off the ground he was caught in a violent turbulence which practically overturned the plane. Fighting to keep control of his bucking machine, Bernard was still unable to make a three-point landing. The right wing touched down first, then the right wheel, then the left wheel; the wheels jammed in the sand; and the machine capsized. General Laperrine, who was not strapped in, was helpless, wedged between the windshield and the body of Vaslin, whose head had furrowed the sand when the plane turned turtle. Sergeant-Major Bernard got out unhurt. The General had broken his left shoulder; he had a crushed rib and internal injuries. But he only mentioned his shoulder. Vaslin complained of injuries to his back and his right leg.

Bernard now collected the vital articles that had fallen from the plane and were scattered all over the sand—the water-bottles, food, equipment, and so on and gave the General a few drops of brandy. The temperature was almost 100°F. in the shade of the aeroplane's wings.

'My children,' said Laperrine (who always addressed soldiers as *mes enfants*), 'we will try to eat and rest until tomorrow morning; and then we will see. . . .'

The next day the three men set out for the north-west towards the mountains of Adrar which the General thought he recognized. They marched for two days in this direction, suffering more and more from thirst and fatigue. At the end of the second day, standing on a rock and scanning the terrain for a long time through his field-glasses, General Laperrine, who had crossed the desert eleven times, had to admit that he was lost. There was no point in going on farther; he advised returning to the plane.

They started the return journey at dawn on the third day. Occasionally the General would stop to write a note in Arabic and Targui (the language of the Tuareg) explaining the situation. These notes were placed between large stones so that they would not be blown away. They were an indication of this sixty-year-old soldier's courage and desert training and will to survive, something the Sahara had certainly taught him. For it is incredible that a man so injured could undertake the journey he was making and still have the mind and energy left to write notes in two foreign languages. He was so weak, in fact, that when they at last sighted the wrecked aeroplane in the evening of the fourth day, he stopped, worn out, and murmured: 'My children, go to the plane. Drop your gear, and come back for me when you're rested.'

On March 1st Vaslin wrote: 'It is now twelve days since we saw anybody, friend or enemy. We are beginning to despair and show it.'

On March 3rd Bernard informed the General that he had decided to go with Vaslin towards Tin Zaouaten.

'I agree to it, my children,' he said. 'But if you go there you certainly won't come back.'

But the two men felt there was nothing else they could do. They therefore prepared two water-bottles for the General, attaching a tube to each so that he wouldn't have to move to reach them and drink. In any case, he was now incapable of moving. They left on the morning of March 4th, but in three hours were back at the aeroplane. Sergeant-Major Bernard had decided they couldn't leave the old General to die alone.

He died on March 5th in the afternoon without saying anything. Earlier he had whispered to them when they brought him water, 'My children, I have been a trial to you.' Then he seems to have crawled a little way away from the aeroplane and to have died alone in the sand.

Ten days later a search party of *méharistes*, camel-corps cavalrymen trained by General Laperrine, accidentally stumbled across the half-buried aeroplane. Bernard and Vaslin were still alive. During the final days they had drunk everything liquid that remained, including eau-de-Cologne, glycerine, and the liquid from their compasses. They had tried to drink their own urine. Before they decided that they were going to die they had managed to scoop a shallow grave in the sand in which they interred their general. And so that this small tomb would one day be found they marked it with the spare wheel taken from the aeroplane;

and in the centre of the wheel they placed the General's *kepi*, the high-peaked cap of the *méhariste* officer.

General Marie Joseph François Henri Laperrine d'Hautpoul, usually referred to as Laperrine, is now buried in a little cemetery almost in the exact geographic centre of the Sahara, at the desert town of Tamanrasset. He lies next to Father de Foucauld, the saintly monk who sacrificed his life for his beliefs as Laperrine may be said to have sacrificed his.

FOURTEEN

The Foreign Legion—non-Hollywood version

THE *méharistes*, or *compagnies sahariennes*, which General Laperrine created and exploited so brilliantly, did not, for obvious reasons, ever catch the public imagination like another force of North African troops—namely, the Foreign Legion, without which Hollywood would never have been able to make films of the Sahara Desert at all. In point of fact, the desert was not the territory of the Legion, who were either confined to their barracks in Sidi-Bel-Abès just south of Oran; or sent anywhere in the world wherever there was some particularly tough and unpleasant fighting. In other words, the foreign legionnaire from the point of view of the French High Command was expendable, as commandos and parachutists are expendable in wartime. This 'expendability'—called in romances or film epics 'courage'—is the essential characteristic of the Foreign Legion, making it a little different from most other military units.

The Foreign Legion as we know it today was officially formed in 1831—'*une légion composée d'étrangers*', said the order of Louis-Philippe, King of the French at the time. The idea, of course, was to attract to the French Army the mercenaries, revolutionaries, and adventurers of the period in the belief that such men would be enthusiastic and experienced soldiers, grateful, when their service was done, for the reward of French citizenship. The theory was based on the Roman system of enlistment under the Empire. What the French Army got, however, and continued to get, was an assortment of thieves, cut-throats, deserters, criminals, vagabonds, and unemployed, varied on rare occasions by some immature and misguided romantic who believed what he had seen in a motion picture or what he had read in a popular novel. In addition, there was an occasional recruit suffering from a broken heart.

Typical of the Legion was the very first battalion, formed in September 1831. The first day that this unit of 200 men came ashore in Algiers thirty-five deserted. The next day the entire company got roaring drunk and beat up their officers. The regular army had to be called out to round up this mob, who were thrown into gaol, except for the ringleaders who were shot.

The French High Command now turned over the organization of the Legion to German and Swiss commanders; and the fact is that from its origin the force has been a quasi-Prussian outfit, both in numbers, training, methods, and outlook. It has always attracted Germans of the blond Nordic type so beloved of Hitler, who instinctively divined their 'killer' qualities; and, after the Germans, the dregs of the Mediterranean seaports. The few English and Americans who joined the Legion—and eventually wrote a book about it—were, on the whole, the 'romantics' who upheld the myth that a foreign legionnaire was a broken-hearted lover, an unsuccessful poet, or a religious mystic. As with all other books extolling military units, very few accounts of the Foreign Legion tell the truth about the organization. Conversely, there is a mountain of monographs, memoirs, histories, rolls of honour, and the like which glorify the deeds of these highly trained killers who were used by the French for 130 years to try to hold together their crumbling empire.

All went well in the beginning during the early days of the conquest of North Africa, for the various battalions of the Legion, constituted at that time by nationalities—as the Second Battalion, Germans; the Seventh, Poles, and so on—were used largely as labourers to build roads and forts in the mountains of Algeria. The tougher battalions were sent on the *razzias*—that is, terror raids—against the Kabyle villages; and it was these soldiers who burnt the olive groves as well as the houses of the tribesmen, and cut off women's arms and legs to get at their bracelets and ankle-rings. In other words, they soon acquired a splendid reputation for ruthlessness, and were used by the aristocratic and more squeamish regular army commanders to do the necessary burning, pillaging, and terrorization of the native population. Moreover, they *had* to fight hard, since they were commanded by the toughest and most brutal N.C.O.s in any army. In other words, they had been metamorphosed into military automats, and no general could ask for more.

We find them appearing more and more often in the North African campaigns wherever the fighting was the most vicious. The nature of the war is seen in all French despatches of the time: no prisoners were taken; or, if they were, they were first interrogated and then shot. If the Kabyles revolted, which they did repeatedly, a battalion of the Legion was sent on a *razzia* against their villages. Other foreign battalions were given the job of holding the advance forts in the mountains and desert, and they were often besieged in these strong places, sometimes for weeks at a time. This aspect of the Legion's history is the one the outside world is most familiar with, for there is no more splendid setting for a Hollywood epic than a Foreign Legion fort with its crenellated walls, its central courtyard, its great gates leading out into the empty desert, the tricolour flying at the mast, the legionnaires at their post, the enraptured audience waiting for the relief column to get through.

If film producers are still interested in Foreign Legion epics, and are looking for locations, the Fezzan in Libya is certainly the place to go. Sebha, Murzuk, and Ubari have some splendid examples of desert forts. The fact that they were built by the Italians makes no particular difference. They still present the traditional 'image' from which the scenario can almost write itself: a massive gateway in the centre of crenellated walls; and inside the rectangular fort a courtyard with a well, barrack rooms, stone stairs leading up to the redoubts, and embrasures for cannon and machine-guns. These desert forts, in fact, have a wonderful historic aura of the Roman *castra*, the medieval castle, and the eighteenth-century colonial fortress. The military architecture of all three periods is combined into the one strongpoint, and antiquarians should begin to think about preserving these edifices, along with the ancient monuments.

I recall my arrival at such a fort in Murzuk after a long ride across a desert of black stones. To the student of Saharan history, Murzuk, as we have seen, is a milestone on his journey. One approaches it with nostalgic memories for those gallant and now-forgotten explorers who passed through here on their way south to 'the interior parts of Africa'. In the old days the traveller reported in at the Turkish fort, which still stands in a state of almost complete dilapidation. Concerning the Turkish guards of the time, the guide-books say:

> At every step one meets soldiers in rags and tatters, *mais d'allure très martiale*. Those tourists who have omitted to obtain the necessary travel documents should lull to sleep the vigilance of the guards with the help of a gratuity. The same means should be employed to put an end to the nonsense of the custom officers.

The Turks have, of course, gone. So have the Italians who built the fort, and the French who occupied it for a brief period. Nowadays one is courteously welcomed by the Libyan police who use the immense structure as a barracks. This was the place I approached on a winter's evening to wait in the shadow of the great gates to pay my respects to the chief of police. It was still vaguely a Hollywood scene what with the two World War I cannon pointing their rusty muzzles towards a passing camel caravan. But suddenly the mood changed from nostalgic to comic, as the commander of the fort emerged from his quarters and slowly approached across the courtyard. His stately progress, I observed, was due to the need to button up his flies before he greeted and interrogated me. He was a dignified man; and when his uniform was adjusted could have passed for an elderly major in the British Army, *cap à pied*. He welcomed me graciously and saw to it that I had a room in the fort for the night. And there I slept amid the remnants of the Italian plumbing and electric wiring—with lots of time to dream on what life must have been like in such a fort in the palmy days of the Foreign Legion.

We know, of course, what it was like in the Hollywood epics. We have seen the spectacle many times; and standing on the walls of the Murzuk fort at sunrise, looking out over the desert, I could have sworn I saw the swarms of white-robed tribesmen galloping across the dunes. Was I—were the gallant defenders—in danger? No. For the difference between the fiction and fact was that an organized unit of European fighting men armed with the latest weapons and positioned behind thick stone walls were in very little danger from the tribesmen outside armed with ancient muskets, spears, daggers, and the like. The danger came from another source, as this report of what it was really like inside the Foreign Legion outpost at Miliana in 1841 shows:

> In the month of July the oppressive and overpowering heat caused an outbreak of fever and dysentery of fearful proportions. Out of 1,200 men, Lieutenant-Colonel d'Illens was unable to assemble 150 capable of active service. Soldiers on sentry duty had to be led to their posts, and they were permitted to sit down. . . . Sentries often died at their posts. . . .
>
> When the relief column finally got through to Miliana, 800 of the 1,200 were dead. Nearly all the survivors were taken to the hospital at Blida.

This is not, of course, what war *à la* Foreign Legion is supposed to be like, since of the 800 who died not more than half a dozen died a hero's death. The rest died of dysentery, which is not a romantic disease and hence seldom written into film scripts.

Still, with the incredibly fierce resistance of the Berber tribesmen spurred on by the patriot and fanatic Abd-el-Kader, the Legion had plenty of fighting to do from 1840 to the end of the century when the natives of these regions were finally crushed, partly by a system of peonage introduced by the colonists. But in the early days the foreign battalions were kept busy, mainly because the enemy would never surrender. The fact that he was shot if he was taken a prisoner of war had something to do with it, no doubt; but there was also a desperate fear of the legionnaires, the men who made the *razzias* on the Kabyle villages. We are not surprised at the report that a party of Arabs who were burying a dead sheik threw the body over a cliff and themselves after it on the appearance of a party of legionnaires. Elsewhere, in another official report, we read:

> The walls of the fortified village having been breached, the inhabitants pursued by the grenadiers and riflemen, threw themselves down the sides of the cliffs in order to escape certain death.

The inhabitants in this case were, of course, the women and children. The general of the troops who drove them over the cliffs 'congratulated the men who had taken part in this victory'.

When they were not on active duty the legionnaires were employed as navvies in building roads, forts, barracks, and such projects as the 'public garden' at Sidi-Bel-Abès. 'They brought to Africa their culture and enlightened the native barbarians.' The natives who fought them seem to have had other ideas; and, unluckily for the French, they never forgot them.

But what of the 'public garden' at Sidi-Bel-Abès? In a way this small park, with its long associations, symbolizes the Foreign Legion from its arrival in this village south of Oran in 1843. Here the Legion band played on Sunday mornings while the townsfolk paraded in the manner of a French provincial city; and here, during later years, came the occasional American and British soldier of fortune attracted by the 'romance' of this celebrated unit.

One of them who came, in 1915, was an American who, as he tells us, 'wanted to do something in this great struggle' and so volunteered for the Red Cross in France, Russia, and Serbia. When all his attempts failed—the countries he applied to naturally and automatically supposed that he was a spy—he decided to join the Foreign Legion; and for this purpose made his way in March 1916 to Tunis. His name was Maurice Magnus, and he later published a book called *Memoirs of the Foreign Legion*, with

a long introduction by D. H. Lawrence. It is, in its way, one of
the most revealing books on the subject ever written. The fact
that it was written by a grandson of the German Kaiser Frederick
Wilhelm by his illegitimate daughter and that Magnus himself
was, in Lawrence's view, a scoundrel does not detract from the
authenticity of his account.

I was but a few days in the Legion before I realized I had
come to the wrong place. . . . The typical legionnaire existed
as he had existed ever since the foundation of the Legion: the
murderer, thief, cut-throat, deserter, adventurer, embezzler,
forger, gaol-bird, and fugitive from justice. . . . Seventy per
cent of the Legion were Germans, and it was German food,
German manners, German discipline, German militarism,
German arrogance, German insolence, and German arbitrari-
ness. The severity of the punishments were decidedly German.
It was a German regiment of the lowest type transplanted to
Africa. They retained all their German habits of excessive
drinking, excessive smoking, swearing, and blaspheming.

There was not a man in the Legion who could be trusted
either as to his word or honesty. There were no morals—not
even the morals of the *Apache*, who at least protects his associate in crime. It was a crowd of men nowhere else to be seen.
Genuine feeling was unknown in the Legion. To rob openly,
to steal secretly, to murder when lust prompted, were all one
to the legionnaire. There was no friendship, no self-respect, no
respect for others, nothing was sacred. Any attempt to retain
self-respect was impossible and the last ray of decency was
extinguished. He was made a beast of so often that he himself
became a beast like the others. . . .

And so on. Magnus is not, obviously, condemning the legionnaires on purely ethical grounds; he hated them because they
were unhuman. At the initiation party he gave them, for instance:

There was no *esprit*, no jokes, not even vulgar ones, no one
became talkative or sociable—it was like a herd of beasts whose

business it was to get drunk. All my attempts at hilarity fell flat. But it was what they wanted: all the wine they could drink and all the cigarettes and cigars they could smoke; the rest did not interest them.

The long, dull, and largely pointless routine of the day Magnus was prepared to accept: it was the regime or the *règlement*, the same senseless procedures as form the basis of barracks life in all professional armies, with the difference, which Magnus emphasizes over and over again, that everything was based on German discipline and militaristic ruthlessness. What this amounted to was an unnecessarily brutalized form of soldering for men who had neither family nor country nor even any friends or comrades: they were simply automata in human form. Could it surprise anyone that they were used like machines and expended like the more easily replaced animals? The outside world, knowing nothing of the regime Maurice Magnus describes, associates the Legion only with the heroic defence of desert outposts against hordes of savages. The fact is the legionnaires were the savages.

This, according to Maurice Magnus, was what the Legion was really like:

The horror of the sleepless nights, the stench of the room, the vile language of my companions, their thieving—which was so much the order of the day that it was a surprise if anything stealable wasn't stolen—their continual attempts to embroil me in their lies and discredit me, their evil-mindedness, which attributed every action to the lowest motives, their physical filth, and finally their drunkenness and habits, revolted and disgusted me to such an extent that life became an unbearable burden.

The most fiendish medieval torture chamber could not have been devised more cleverly than the methods employed for systematically breaking the spirit; first, until there was no resistance left to struggle against anyone, not even against one's own self; and then commenced the breaking up of the body until it became degenerated and befouled; and when there was nothing left worth the name of human man, he was thrown down, trampled on, like dirt under foot of vermin, and life crushed out or thrown to the cannons for fodder. . . .

FIFTEEN

'Onward Christian soldiers, marching as to war . . .'

I

IN CONTRAST with the life and work of the Foreign Legion in the Sahara and its confines was the approach of another great and powerful European force bent on the conversion of this region for its own particular purposes and by its own particular methods.

This second 'army' was the Church, which regarded the desert and its inhabitants as a new world to conquer. The 'soldiers' employed by the Church were in their lives and characters the antitheses of the foreign legionnaires; but they were soldiers, none the less, and before their work was far advanced they had to live and sometimes fight like soldiers. Their general, in fact, Cardinal Charles-Martial Allemand-Lavigerie, Archbishop of Algiers, papal delegate to the Sahara and the Sudan, primate of Africa, was, in his way, as great an empire-builder as Lord Kitchener or Cecil Rhodes. His principal troops were the White Fathers, or Missionaries of our Lady of Africa of Algeria.

Cardinal Lavigerie and his missionaries are, in a sense, the last chapter in the nineteenth-century story of the conquest of the Sahara Desert which began with the explorations of the first British travellers in the early 1800s. After 1900, or certainly after the mid-twentieth century, the Sahara, like Africa itself, begins to divorce itself, as it were, from Europe and Europeans and begins a new phase in its history. But before this was to happen the soldiers of the Church, in their white robes and sun-helmets, mounted on camels, a big cross on their breasts and a rifle slung across their backs, tried to make their mark on the desert. It is difficult without the eye of faith to see how far they succeeded.

Their leader, the founder of the society, never doubted for a moment that his work of converting Arab Moslems and negro pagans would be crowned with success. Cardinal Lavigerie had the advantage of never compromising about either the need or the benefits of conversion. His official biographer writing under the imprint of the Church tells us that young Charles-Martial at the age of ten began catching and forcefully baptizing all the little Jews of his own age in the streets of Bayonne:

> If they refused he grabbed them, pummelled them, shoved them towards the stream or a fountain, and sprinkled them copiously whether they liked it or not, afterwards throwing them a few sous to stop them crying.

The gift of the few sous to the 'baptized' Jews may show what a kind-hearted lad Charles-Martial was at heart; or it may have shown some apprehensions about the correctness of his methods. But if the future cardinal had doubts in his nonage he had none as a full-fledged prince of the Church; hence his announcement that he intended to convert the whole of Africa to his particular way of thinking—namely, to the orthodox tenets of Roman Catholicism. What the Africans thought of this is not recorded. It is recorded that many of his own countrymen, particularly the generals who had to keep the natives in order by *razzias* and the colonists who had to keep them in serfdom to work the land, were seriously alarmed. Africa, they felt, was no place for Christianity; or certainly not for the actual practice of the theory.

Charles Lavigerie had no patience with this sort of nonsense. As his official biographer, the rector of the Catholic faculty at Lille, tells us, 'his nature was authoritarian, uncompromising, dominating, and imperious to the point of despotism'. When, as a little boy, he decided he was a priest, he demanded that every member of his family, including his old granny, addressed him accordingly. '*Il faut que sa grand'mère elle-même la lui réponde révérencieusement, il le veut.*' The servants had to come and confess to him, and on their knees. Obviously Charles Lavigerie wasn't going to brook any interference in later life: the Moslems and pagans were going to be Christianized whether they liked it or not. Useless

for the civil and military government of Algeria to cut off the
prelate's funds. He appealed directly to the Pope—in fact
threatened this rather bewildered and browbeaten old man, and
so was given the authority and funds to continue his holy work.

For some, God's hand was discernible in the process, since in
1867, the year before Archbishop Lavigerie took up his North
African post, first an epidemic of cholera, then a tremendous
famine had, as it were, prepared the field for the salvation of
souls. At least 60,000 natives had died of cholera when the
locusts arrived. These pests arrived in such numbers that the sun
itself was hidden as though by thick black clouds. They settled
on the ground as far as the horizon in a writhing, heaving mass
several inches thick. They even stopped the trains in certain
places. And when they had passed on, there was not a leaf or a
blade of grass left in almost the whole of Algeria.

That wasn't all. A two-year drought had parched the land and
not a drop of rain had fallen in the province throughout 1867
until November, when it rained like the Flood—torrents of rain
which carried away the soil and destroyed every vestige of agricultural development. In the mountains and in the mountain
valleys snowdrifts finished the work the drought, the locusts, and
the rains had begun. There was nothing left to eat except the
dead, animal and human. It was as Allah or God willed. By this
time one-fifth of the entire Moslem population was dead of
starvation.

We have a picture of what it was like by an eyewitness:

One met at each step these walking skeletons: women
carrying dead babies on their dried-up breasts; children left
to die by their parents; and everything veiled in the grim
silence that Islamism throws over suffering and death. Finally,
in addition to these extremes of misery, extremes of cruelty
and crime: crimes without precedence in the history of civilization—fathers and mothers butchering and eating their
children; brothers killed by brothers; and all human feelings
stifled beneath a kind of savagery which lit up men's eyes with
a sinister and menacing light.

In addition, the rich, who had taken the precaution of preparing for the catastrophe, shot at sight the poor who asked for
something to eat.

To the new Archbishop of Algiers, however, all this was a
challenge; and there can be no doubt that he was the man for the
job. He began by succouring the orphans who now wandered
the countryside and the city streets living on grass and roots. A
member of the Archbishop's retinue describes these children
who arrived in convoys from the Arab villages sent to the
Lavigerie orphanage by the priests both Christian and Moslem.

Every day the army waggons stopped outside the archbishop's country house with their loads of children. They were
emaciated to an extent not thought possible in a human being,
their legs and arms like those of skeletons, their bellies swollen
by the grass which was all they could find to eat, and their
bodies, covered with sores, exhaling the stinking odour of
typhus. . . . Sometimes among the children in the carts, one
saw a small bent body, the head fallen back, the eyes wide open,
and the arms extended. This was a child who had died on the
journey of hunger, cold, or disease.

This was the beginning of Cardinal Lavigerie's work in Africa
—first the care of the starving children; next the establishment
of missions and schools; and finally the formation of a spiritual
army, the White Fathers, which was to go out and conquer
Africa. The Sahara Desert was, as it had been to all conquerors
and explorers before, the great obstacle to this endeavour; and,
as before, it was not so much the vast wasteland that stopped and
sometimes killed the Europeans, but the people who inhabited
it. A report of the White Fathers states:

The natives [of the Sahara], whether Tuaregs, Arabs, or
negroes, are all Mohammedans; consequently very few conversions take place, and all individuals who have the courage
to embrace Christianity have been compelled to leave the
country.

For some observers the final words in this report have cast some doubt on the justification of Christian evangelization, since an inhabitant of the Sahara, uprooted from his village and tribe, has nowhere to go.

But all was not discouraging. The missionaries were to find that they had a triumphant success among the negro pagans even if they had little among the Moslem Arabs. The Moslem population of Algeria, for instance, numbered some 4,000,000 in 1927, fifty years after Cardinal Lavigerie began his work of conversion. The total number of Christians was around a thousand. In Negroland there were thousands of conversions every year, and the number of black men calling themselves Christians in Central Africa ran into hundreds of thousands. Evidently the negroes took to Christianity like ducks to water, as the Apostolic Vicar of Nyassa, Monseigneur Dupont, present at an examination of the candidates some years ago, was delighted to discover. For all the postulants knew the catechism by heart, which meant that they were ready to come into the fold.

That morning two old grannies presented themselves for examination [states the report]. One of them, Mshawa by name, is something of a witch and is supposed to obtain her occult knowledge by studying the entrails of fowls. By way of ornament she has a large button hanging on to her upper lip and an old pencil-case dangling from the lower one. Father Burdet began examining her. . . . The old woman interrupted him. 'Look here, Bwana, you are doing all the talking. Suppose you let me talk instead.' So saying, she put out her tongue slightly, winked her eye, and gave Father Burdet a malicious look. Then she proceeded to expound the catechism quite well enough to deserve the honour of receiving the cross. We advised her to give up her evil practices, and she assured us that she had done so long ago.

The various hand-outs from the mission no doubt also aided the old granny with the button in her lip to profess her Christian faith when the occasion demanded.

II

Archbishop Lavigerie's first missions, however, had no such easy success. The first of them were planted in the Kabylia, in those Atlas Mountain villages which the Foreign Legion had periodically burnt to the ground. As a result, the Kabyles were inclined to be wary of Christians; but they were never so violently anti-Christian as other Moslem groups, and they had no objection to being helped by the White Fathers since times were bad. Gradually a few schools and hospitals were built in the Kabyle country which had remained the only region of North Africa and the desert where Christianity was tacitly tolerated.

But the Archbishop was determined to go farther afield than Algeria, and in 1872 the first Saharan mission was sent in the person of Father Charmetant, who left for Laghout, the farthest south that French rule had so far reached. Possibly to his surprise, the White Father was not only welcomed by the Moslem chieftains of the area but practically killed with kindness. 'O marabout!' cried the Sheik Si Lalla, 'my tent will be yours, and so will my camels. Go where you like. Nobody will touch you.' The fact of the matter is the old sheik appears to have thought that the Catholic priest, on account of his Arab costume and fez, had become a convert to Islam. Things had got a bit confused. Neither side quite understood what on earth (or in heaven) the other side was talking about. Thus, a Father reports from the desert:

> Too often their diseases are the result of their vices. When we scold them for this, they reply, 'O marabout! God himself inspires you with wisdom, but the sons of Adam are weak and sinful. May God have mercy on us.' Then we reply with our Saviour, 'Peace be with you. Go and sin no more.'

In brief, relations were most amiable between the White Fathers and their potential flock until Archbishop Lavigerie decided in 1876 to send off the first trans-Saharan mission, with disastrous results. This was only seven years after the murder of Mlle Alexandrine Tinne in the desert and five before the wiping out of the Flatters column. Manifestly the Sahara was still extremely hostile, even to those who came offering, they said, the most precious gifts of all—the Cross and the Bible.

The first to attempt to conquer the desert on behalf of the Church—or, in ecclesiastical language, 'for love of the Cross'—were three White Fathers who were missionaries on the frontiers of the Sahara in 1875. All three were Frenchmen, as the Society of Missionaries of our Lady of Africa was not yet the international organization it was later to become. They were Father Palmier, Father Menoret, and Father Bouchaud; and when they declared their intention of crossing the Sahara from the oasis of Ghardaia in southern Algeria to Timbuktu in the Sudan, the tribesmen among whom they had lived and worked for a couple of years were not only alarmed, but afraid in case they should be held responsible. The local sheik, in fact, demanded that they sign a statement exonerating him from all blame in the event that they were killed by the Tuaregs. The missionaries signed and set off, accompanied by one guide. It was perhaps the most ill-prepared and foolhardy expedition that had ever attempted to cross the Sahara. 'Chanting the *Te Deum* as one, they were soon lost in the immensity of the desert,' says their Father Superior, who was present to see them go. 'The caravan disappeared before my eyes.'

After three months the first news of the whereabouts of the White Fathers came through via the wandering tribesmen and the northbound caravans: they had got as far as the oasis of In Salah in the country of the Hoggar Tuareg. But that seems to have been the end of their journey, less than halfway to their far destination: they were massacred soon after by the Veiled Men. What was officially described as 'a glorious end' concealed the fact that they had been decapitated as they knelt on the sand while their guide had been transfixed many times with a lance. There was no doubt that this was the work of the Tuaregs who still preferred the sword and lance for finishing off their victims. Evidently the guide had fought for his life; the unarmed priests could do nothing but sacrifice theirs. The Tuaregs, as in the case of

Major Laing, were not content to kill their enemy; they tried to wipe out what they stood for, their spirit itself, by burning all their possessions—their holy ornaments and books and few belongings and the severed heads which symbolized the alien faith.

The loss of his first mission to Central Africa was a serious shock to Archbishop Lavigerie, comparable with the loss of the Flatters mission to the French military, and there was a great deal of soul-searching both in Algiers, headquarters of the White Fathers, and in Rome where the Vatican was strongly supporting its African prelate in defiance of Paris and the French politicians and army. We are told that when Archbishop Lavigerie received the telegram confirming the death of the three missionaries, he went pale and refused to say a word—either from grief, rage, or disappointment. The old Spanish bishop who happened to be visiting the Archbishop resolved this awkward and embarrassing moment by joining his hands in prayer, casting up his eyes to heaven, and shouting at the top of his voice *Te Deum laudamus*. After a time, Lavigerie joined in and, regaining his old self-assurance, was able in due course 'to thank God for this kindness He has done to my children'. Soon he is able to write to the parents of the 'martyrs' the following letter:

You can finally rest assured of the happy though painful certainty that you longed for and, at the same time, dreaded: your sons have suffered death for God's cause! Your hearts, illuminated by faith, have thrilled with joy, I know—even while you have wept. . . . It is true that you won't see them again down here. You will never see again their gentle and strong eyes, their calm smile; you will hear no more their deep voices; you will not feel again the beating of their strong, pure hearts. But one day, which is near, you will again meet them triumphant, shining with an eternal light, belonging to a troop of angels, close to Stephen the first of our martyrs, and carrying in their hands the palms of victory.

In the meantime the Archbishop, though he had been instrumental in creating three new martyrs for the Church, had received a serious setback in his campaign for the conquest of Africa. The authorities, both in Paris and Algiers, were sick of these priests wandering about in the desert where travellers were being murdered every year, thus creating a serious problem on the level of international politics. For if a nation is not able to police its conquered territories, other nations are only too eager to take on the job for them; and what with the British, Germans, Belgians, and Spanish jockeying for position in North and Central Africa, the French were extremely nervous about the Sahara Desert, particularly as it didn't quite yet belong to them by international agreement.

In short, the Central Government now warned Archbishop Lavigerie that his so-called missions to Timbuktu and Central Africa were rash and unjustifiable; that they had disapproved of them from the outset; and that, while the prelate was about it, he had better withdraw his missionaries from the southern posts.

Was the apostolic road in Africa to be closed for all time? asks a contemporary observer.

No. French politicians at this time, memories of defeat by the Prussians still fresh in their minds, were in no position to fight anybody, let alone a man who, as a child, had forcefully baptized ten-year-old Jews and obliged his granny to address him 'reverently'. The African prelate went right ahead with his plans. Africa was to be Christianized. He reminded his critics that Jesus was an African, 'because He was made an African by His residence in Egypt . . . therefore He had a special liking for African children'.

It was a very difficult argument to refute.

There was an even more difficult problem for the politicians back in Paris to contend with: in the Church this was referred to as 'the Protestant menace'; in the Ministry of Foreign Affairs as 'Anglo-Saxon infringement of a French sphere of influence'. In other words, a sort of undeclared war of the missionaries was about to break out to decide which sect was to have the glory, honour, and monopoly of saving the Africans' souls. The governments of the various missionary societies involved in this pious work of evangelism were vitally interested in the southern infiltration of the White Fathers on the one hand; and in the northern advance of the Protestant missionaries on the other. There was a distinct odour of sulphur as well as of incense in many districts of Central Africa as the soldiers of the Cross sometimes met head on in some remote African village.

It was really hardly necessary, then, for Archbishop Lavigerie to argue at all for his great project to extend the empire of Christ as far and wide as possible in Africa, since the politicians were well aware that missionaries were not only the cheapest, but often the most effective, of empire-builders. They were certainly used throughout the African kingdoms as quasi-political agents, whether they liked it or not.[1] In many cases it was difficult to say who came first to conquer such kingdoms, the missionaries or the soldiers.

In many of the 'softer' parts of Africa the White Fathers arrived before the army, a cause of deep suspicion to the British in the case of the East African territories. Archbishop Lavigerie resented this attitude and now spoke openly of the 'Protestant peril', which, if it wasn't as grave as the 'yellow peril' and various similar 'perils' that afflict mankind, was the cause of grave concern to both Rome and Paris. He pointed out the great number of tradesmen and workmen who were disguised under the honorary and lucrative title of 'ministers' among the English missionaries. Moreover, these so-called preachers were going around telling the African chieftains that Catholic priests baptized cows and sheep and that Catholic missionaries engaged in the slave trade, witness the great number of children whom they bought and put in their orphanages.

So what with these Protestant lies and the difficulty of persuading the African monarchs to give up their harems in return for an eternity of harp-playing in heaven, the archbishop's problems were manifold at this time. But he pushed on with his programme, the most important item of which was the establishment of a mission in Timbuktu, centre of the slave trade. It was thither that the unfortunate mission of 1876 had been bound.

1. See the illuminating incident reported in Monseigneur Baunard's biography of Cardinal Lavigerie, Vol. II, pp. 315 ff.

Now, only five years later, three more Fathers, burning with zeal 'to face the enemy's fire', were given permission to cross the desert for Timbuktu. The missionaries didn't get even as far as their predecessors. Leaving Ghadames on December 9th, they were dead less than two weeks later, only thirteen miles from their starting place, murdered apparently in their sleep. The crime was blamed, significantly, on 'the enemies of France'—in this case the Italians in league with the Turks. It was all very distressing and discouraging to Archbishop Lavigerie who announced the incident at a meeting of the Society in Carthage, 'his voice full of sobs'. After he had paused for long enough to get possession of himself, he continued: 'Right, my children. Let us now thank our Lord all the more for doing us the honour of giving our Society some more martyrs.' After which he launched into the *Te Deum*, which, as we have seen, was in frequent use at this period, ten Fathers having been 'martyred' in so many years.

The army now felt it was about time it stepped in to make the work of saving African souls easier for the missionaries—provided, of course, these soldiers of the Cross were Frenchmen. In short, it was decided to see what a little shot and shell would do to soften up Timbuktu for the coming of Christianity.

III

The taking of Timbuktu in 1894 was a typical operation of a colonial army of the period, in that the arrogance and stupidity of the white officers were responsible for far more deaths than any enemy, human or inanimate. The military expedition was big enough to conquer most of the Niger territory if it had wanted to, whereas Timbuktu was completely defenceless and ready to surrender to anybody who came along. In fact, throughout its history it had always surrendered to whatever army threatened it. In 1894 it was dominated by the Tuaregs and various other local gangs, belonging, as far as ownership was concerned, to everybody and nobody. The French were able to walk in. Having occupied the city without firing a shot, they next marched out into the desert and allowed a whole column to be massacred in the night by the Tuaregs. The eleven French officers, including Colonel Bonnier, their commander, were said to be playing cards in their tents at the time, and their Senegalese lackeys were probably too intimidated to warn them that the Tuaregs were skulking about in the area. When a real soldier came along in the person of Major Jouffre, as Joffre, the future commander-in-chief of the French Army was then known, the Tuaregs ceased to be a threat. Major Jouffre was able to kill them off like flies for the loss of one native trooper.

In a very few months Timbuktu was safe for its first Christian mission, a fact of which the British Protestants were well aware. And though Cardinal Lavigerie was now dead, his policy for the spiritual-cum-territorial conquest of Africa was still in force. By 1895, less than a year after it had been subjugated, the White Fathers were established in Timbuktu. Among them was Father Auguste Dupuis, who remembered how Cardinal Lavigerie had once used his head as a lectern during a discourse to the novices under the palm trees of Maison Carrée. Dupuis had been kneeling in front of the great prelate at the time and was too pious to rise while the Cardinal was speaking. The thumps on the top of the young novice's head had been merely to emphasize some spiritual truth to his audience. Father Dupuis, who was to become famous as Father Yakouba, 'the White Monk of Timbuktu', remembered the incident forty years later when he was still living in Timbuktu with his wife, the negress Salama, and a large family.[1]

After the occupation of Timbuktu by the French Army the Tuareg tribesmen who had ruled the Sahara from time immemorial were, in the larger sense, finished as a nation and finished as the last obstacle to the exploration, conquest, and pacification of the desert. The reason was partly that Timbuktu and its caravans, particularly those coming from Morocco and Libya, were the source of the Tuareg wealth and strength, or sometimes both, the caravans crawling across the Tanezrouft and the Hoggar from oasis to oasis; and for hundreds of years they had raided and looted Timbuktu itself. All this was about to stop with the stationing of French troops in the city and the numerous

1. See Chapter Nine.

forts flying the tricolour along the Niger River. And this curbing of the Tuaregs by cutting off their livelihood (that is, thieving, looting, and plundering in general) made the work of Laperrine and his tiny camel corps which came on to the scene a few years later much easier. The Tuareg tribesmen, in other words—these feared and hated Veiled Men of the Desert—were no longer an obstacle to even the Christian penetration of an area which was one of the most fanatically Moslem regions in the world.

The White Fathers, then, were soon able to come and go pretty much as they pleased. Their missions, clinics, schools, and monasteries appeared in many parts of the desert. The Moslems accepted them with a sort of weary resignation. After all, the true Prophet had said that it was right and justifiable to convert men with the aid of the sword. Well, the Christians had sharper swords; or, more to the point, quicker-firing rifles. They also had efficacious medicines. All these things were most acceptable. The nonsense talked by their priests about Jesus being the Son of God (how could God stoop to have sexual congress with a woman?) could be, and was, ignored.

A great expert in the desert, E-F. Gautier, says:

> The two religions, Christian and Moslem, seem to be divided by an impassable wall. There has perhaps never been a Moslem who allowed himself to become a Christian in good faith.

It would seem that the Catholic White Fathers, in contrast with the Protestant missionaries, were well aware of this fact, perhaps because they were dealing with tribesmen like the Tuaregs, not with African negroes. This was certainly the case with the greatest of the desert priests, Charles Eugène de Foucauld, who was murdered in his monastery in the middle of the Sahara one night in December 1916. Father de Foucauld never claimed to have converted a single Moslem; in fact, he never even baptized his negro altar boy who officiated with him at Mass. All the same, in his character, life, and work this aristocratic priest personifies the most, and perhaps the best, that an evangelist can do in a region of the world as bitterly hostile to Christians as

Christians are to Islam; or, for that matter, as Christian denominations are to each other.

Perhaps the reason for Father de Foucauld's peculiar achievement is that he belonged by temperament to the early Christian community of stylites, hermits, cave-dwellers, and ascetics in general—a type of religious practitioner that has always appealed to desert people. Indeed, Father de Foucauld's later *régimen* when he had built his monastery in the heart of the Hoggar Mountains —1,250 miles from his father-superior whom he was obliged to visit once every two years for confession and absolution—this *régimen* was very comparable to the practices of the fourth-century ascetics whose 'mortifications' often pass belief, except that the evidence for them is overwhelming and, for that matter, reaffirmed in the endurance tests of the modern Indian fakirs.

Palladius tells us of a hermit who dwelt for twenty-five years in a cave on top of a mountain and never once faced west during that whole period—a difficult feat to accomplish, if you think about it, and one requiring enormous control and discipline. St. Gregory of Nazianzus assures us that he personally saw a solitary who stood upright for many years, absorbed in contemplation, without ever lying down. It is possible, of course, that this holy man had become mummified in the process; but whether alive or dead, he was greatly revered in St. Gregory's time. More comfortable, one supposes, was the hermit who passed ten years in a tub suspended in mid-air between two poles; while those stylites like St. Simeon who sat, or those like St. Alypius who *stood*, on the top of columns at least had the advantages of fresh air and a good view of the surrounding scene. But the endurance and tremendous asceticism required for these privations were what distinguished the stylites from other men, for who else but a saint like Alypius, whose pillar was erected near Adrianople in Paphlagonia, could have stood upright for fifty-three years on his perch and then, when his feet began to ache, could have lain down on his side to spend the remaining fourteen years of his life in that position?

The privations which Father de Foucauld willingly and, indeed, joyously endured were, in the ascetic sense, of this kind.

There can be no other explanation of his way of life, for a man born a viscount, educated in an aristocratic military academy like Saint-Cyr, and breveted into the army as a hussar, does not become a hermit unless that is what his whole nature longs for. That this is the case became evident very quickly in Lieutenant le Vicomte Charles-Eugène de Foucauld's career; because six months after he was posted to the Oran military zone as an army officer, he asked for his discharge and received it. He was no doubt able to escape army life that easily first by reason of his family connections; and secondly in view of his proposed expedition into Morocco, on which the French were for ever casting covetous eyes. Very few explorers, particularly French explorers, had really penetrated into the mountainous regions of this fiercely Mohammedan and independent state, for the Moroccans had no love at all for the French. The usual practice, then, was for Frenchmen to disguise themselves as Turks, Egyptians, Syrians, etc., as René Caillié, the first of them, had successfully (but dangerously) succeeded in doing sixty years before. Ex-Lieutenant de Foucauld, however, conceived the extraordinary idea of travelling throughout Morocco disguised as a Jew—the most despised folk in Moslem Africa. Those who knew the missionary assert, with reason, that he chose this course deliberately, in order to suffer the humiliation which his less fortunate brother-men were exposed to. It was his first atonement for the wrongs of the world.

Once his mind had been made up, the way seemed clear to him; and though the Church neither encouraged nor commended extreme forms of asceticism, it recognized the need of such as Father de Foucauld to practise his Christianity in his own way. His request to live as a 'missionary hermit' among the remotest tribes of the Sahara Desert was granted, and in 1905 he arrived at Tamanrasset in the Hoggar Mountains.

IV

He arrived on foot, for this was how he always travelled in the desert, carrying two pairs of sandals, one pair on his feet to be

replaced when they were worn out by the spares. He used to
walk ahead of the main caravan with the guides so as not to be
distracted in his meditations and orisons. The hour of the day
was struck by a timekeeper mounted on a camel, banging on a
tin can. The priest, well ahead of the column, would then turn
round and bow his thanks. He celebrated Mass in his tent at night.
In this manner he arrived at the oasis of Tamanrasset which he
describes as 'a village of twenty homes, right in the mountains
in the heart of the Hoggar, far from all important centres. I don't
think there is ever likely to be a garrison, telegraph station, or a
European here: I choose this abandoned place, and here I stick.'[1]

He began, in true hermit style, by building himself a rush
cabin in which he lived while erecting his chapel, a primitive
building twenty feet long by six feet wide. His nearest neighbours
were a few wretched farmers who lived in rush huts like his own
and grew a little barley, carrots, and red peppers in the stony
ground along the dry river bed, the inevitable Saharan wadi. The
only other human beings he was to meet were the caravaners
travelling south to Timbuktu, or north to Ghadames. In other
words, he was in the middle of the country of the Tuaregs, called
'masters of the desert' by some; and 'thieves, bandits, and
murderers' by most. To Father de Foucauld they were brothers
—actually the only companions he wanted near to his hermitage,
and not too near at that. Otherwise he was 425 desert miles from the
nearest 'civilized' centre at In Salah with which he was in contact
by means of a monthly courier. His 'flock' consisted, therefore, of
a few wretched barley-growers, a few shepherds, passing caravaners, suspicious Tuareg warriors, and their negro slaves.

How did he propose to convert these Moslems without the
usual aids with which missionaries were able at least to gain the
interest of the natives? He tells us:

> To do my utmost for the salvation of the infidel peoples by
> the total forgetfulness of self. Every year to make a round of

---

1. Father de Foucauld was mistaken: Tamanrasset today is a main stopping
place on the Hoggar route from Algiers to Kano. It has all the items he lists,
plus an airfield and hotel for tourists.

the settled colonies in the Hoggar; to accept invitations to journeys in the Sahara, if they are useful; and if possible, to spend a few days every year in the tents of the Tuaregs. To translate extracts from the Holy Scriptures into Tuareg.

But because he was a completely dedicated ascetic, that doesn't mean he was impractical, for we find him requesting a supply of sewing-needles from headquarters to attract the Tuareg women to his 'mission'. Moreover, when these women discovered that the French marabout was handing out needles, they came for miles riding on donkeys to beg for one, since most of them had never sewn with anything but a thorn before. In the meantime, the good Father taught himself how to knit so that he could pass on this skill to the Tuareg housewives 'who work so little and talk so much'.

While the women were appreciative of such an 'invention' as the needle, the Tuareg men continued to regard all foreigners as 'pagans' and 'savages'; they were not in the least impressed by European culture, medicine, religion, or machinery. The aeroplane for them was merely a 'tent that flies'; the wireless, the utilization of the wind; the motor-car, an iron box in which white men had imprisoned the genii of fire. The proof was the drubbing which had to be given the incarcerated spirits (cranking the motor) to force them to work. But the most difficult argument the priest had to contend with was the Moslem assertion that Christians had the earth for their profit and pleasure, but Mohammedans would have Paradise.

The fact is that after a time, 'happy and peaceful at the feet of the Well-Beloved', Father de Foucauld gave up any thought of mass conversion of the Tuaregs amongst whom he was to spend the rest of his life. He had, instead, found the secret of living with them as a spiritual *influence* rather than a religious dictator. He became more like them without really expecting them to become like a Frenchman. He reveals this rather charmingly in his advice to a doctor in the French Colonial Service sent to tend the Tuaregs.

You must be simple, affable, and good to the Tuaregs. Love them and make them feel they are loved, so as to be loved by them. . . . Be human, charitable, *and always gay*. You must always laugh even in saying the simplest things. As you see, I am always laughing—showing very ugly teeth. Laughing puts the person who is talking to you in a good humour; it sometimes brightens up a gloomy character; it is a charity. When you are among the Tuaregs, you must always laugh.

And he adds that if one of them asks the doctor to attend on a goat he should not be annoyed.

In a land where constant physical mortification is a fact of life, the true ascetic is king, perhaps because he justifies privation and suffering by spiritual redemption. Be that as it may, desert people have always admired hermits, cave-dwellers, and the more ascetic of holy men, just as Western observers have always tended to despise them. Father de Foucauld, then, was lord of the desert in the eyes of the Tuaregs; whereas he would have merely seemed an unwashed eccentric in civilized Europe. He had identified himself with the former, and it is not surprising that when he was bitten by a horned viper, whose bite is nearly always fatal, he was treated according to the medical practices of the country, almost exactly as they were described by travellers like Captain Lyon:[1] in other words, the wound was burnt with hot irons, which were then applied to the soles of the feet until great blisters formed. The priest survived both the snake-bite and the cure, though he never walked strongly again.

On December 1st, 1916, Father de Foucauld was murdered.

Perhaps the most curious and tragic aspect of his assassination is that some of 'his own people' were involved in the plot to wipe him out. It was almost as though his years of sacrifice and physical suffering on behalf of the Tuaregs were in vain. For it was a Tuareg who murdered him, without any compunction at all. At the moment of his death Father de Foucauld was not, in the eyes of his enemies, a holy man at all; he was an infidel, an enemy, and a spy. According to the laws of war of any country, his captors were entitled to shoot him. And this is exactly what happened.

1. See pages 154–5.

To the French, and to the Church whom he served so well, Father de Foucauld was, of course, a martyr who died in an ambush by the dastardly hands of traitors and barbarians. It is an interesting historical and philosophical question—and typical of the controversies which divide mankind. For whereas Father de Foucauld was, in his life and teaching, a devout Christian meriting, indeed, beatification by the Holy Roman Church, he was to his enemies—the equally devout Moslems of the Senussi persuasion—a representative not of a religious faith but of an imperialistic power whose kingdoms were very much of this world, not of the next. It was the Senussi tribesmen, incidentally, who were collaborators of the Allies in World War II against the Italians, as they were the allies of the Germans in World War I against the French. A study of even fifty years' history is, of course, confusing in this respect, since enemies became allies, allies enemies, within the space of one generation. But from the point of view of the Senussi, ardent Moslems comparable to the more rigorous Christian sects, there could be no compromise for the sake of political advantage: the Senussi remained faithful to their creed which was, in its simplest form, the expulsion of the infidels from Africa and the restoration of the glories of Islam. If, therefore, the Senussi wrote the history of Father de Foucauld, they would say:

(a) the priest was living in a French fort which was supplied with rifles and munitions, contrary to the accepted laws of warfare (true);

(b) the priest was supplying military information to their enemies in the form of daily reports to the nearby French fort (true); and,

(c) the priest was upholding the enemy's cause beyond the limits and requirements of his religious affiliation (true).

In other words, Father de Foucauld's immense sacrifices were, to some extent, in vain; for while he was mourned by some as a martyr to his faith and by others as a great patriot, the people who meant most to him the Tuaregs themselves, killed him in good conscience, as they would have killed any other Frenchman who had taken up arms against them. In short, the priest had become a soldier. It is notable that even in the official French accounts of Father de Foucauld's murder, those who proclaim their grief loudest were those who held their position of authority by virtue of French arms. The rest keep silent.

If there is one thing that stands out quite clearly in the life and career of Father Charles de Foucauld, it is that he was first and foremost a Frenchman of France; and when the time came to choose between a religion based on the principle of loving one's enemies and a militant patriotism based on their destruction, the potential saint chose the latter. The evidence speaks for itself. In February 1912, writing about the proposal for a Trans-Saharan Railway, he states: 'Let them hasten to build a railway! It is a necessity for the preservation of our African empire, *but also for bringing all our forces, in case of need, to the Rhine.*' He was evidently anticipating, better than the military, the events of 1914. In December of the same year, 1912, we find him writing to the Duke of Fitz-James:

> We French have two essential duties to fulfil in Africa: the first is the administration and civilization of our North-West African Empire. Algeria, Morocco, Tunis, the Sahara, and the Sudan form an immense and magnificent empire in one lump, having this unity for the first time. . . . How are we to attach this empire to us?

This doesn't sound like a man of God so much as a professional politician; and though it is followed by pious references to 'morality', evangelization, and the like is still typical of nineteenth-century imperialism. The 'piety', in fact, reminds one of the comment of Bismarck who, after hearing Gladstone refer to 'the will of God', said of the British statesman, 'If the ace of hearts dropped out of his sleeve during a card game, he would undoubtedly bless God for the miracle.'

So, from the point of view of an enemy in wartime when, in any case, both sides claim the protection and blessing of God—the holy man's commitment to supply the French High Command with almost daily military intelligence from the war zone in Africa—the kind of information that only a super-spy could supply—was reason enough to silence him. For *every* letter that Father de Foucauld sent to General Laperrine from December 1914 to November 1916 was, in the words of his official biographer, 'quite military'.

They tell all he knows of the friendly and hostile tribes and their movements, of intrigues entered into by the Senussi, who were closely linked with the Turks of Tripoli and with the Germans; of sudden attacks and the whole news of the desert. . . .

It is not surprising, therefore, that the enemies of France— who included the entire population of North Africa with the exception of the bought men—regarded the Christian marabout (despite his odour of sanctity and his good works in distributing needles and safety-pins) as a 'military objective' of the first importance, particularly as his headquarters was a fortified place in the heart of the battle zone. Thus it was that on that night in December there was a knock at the door of the priest's fortress; Father de Foucauld, without opening the door, put out his hand to receive what he thought was the mail from the nearby Fort Motylinski, with whom he was in daily contact; had his hand seized; was pulled outside; bound as a prisoner; and subsequently shot in a typical night fight in which both sides were trigger-happy and killed without rhyme or reason as troops fighting at night are inclined to do.

Thus died Father Charles de Foucauld at the hands of the people he had come to 'save'. The French Army captain who was on the spot at Fort Motylinski at the time makes this surprisingly frank report of the incident:

Nothing up to the present makes us think that a single Tuareg noble of the Kudia region favoured the murderer's plan. Nevertheless, the event is still quite recent, and a wise prudence bids us leave time to do its work of making things plain before being affirmative on this point.

And he adds this significant comment:

From the general point of view, it may be said that at the time of Father de Foucauld's assassination all hearts in the Hoggar had been won over to the cause of our enemies and that their dearest wish was for our speedy and final disappearance from the region.

(Signed) Captain Depommier

The enemies of France, despite the efforts of Father de Foucauld, the White Fathers, their leader Cardinal Lavigerie, the Roman Catholic Church, and the French Army, were, of course, to triumph in the long run. For the second time in a thousand years Islam was to evict Christianity from Ifriqah and the Sahara Desert.

SIXTEEN

'Across the Sahara by motor-car'

I

THE murder of Father de Foucauld in the Hoggar Mountains marks the end of a period in Saharan history—what might be called the era of the explorers of whom Dr. Barth was the exemplar; the soldiers ideally represented by General Laperrine; and a few saintly men personified by the French priest who chose the desert as his earthly habitation. And just as World War I brought the Victorian age to its close in Europe, so it ushered in a new era even in this vast and still unconquered region of the world which had scarcely changed in 5,000 years. The catalytic agent in this process was, of course, the machine—two machines, to be precise, which emerged out of the chaos of the Great War—the aeroplane and the tank.

First, the crossing of the whole length of the desert in 1920 by Major Vuillemin in his primitive biplane foreshadowed the disappearance of the old desert of the camel caravans and the beginning of the modern era of travel and communications. And Vuillemin's flight was followed two years later by a second achievement, a similarly 'historic' event and another triumph of machine-man over nature. The second achievement was the traverse of the Sahara, from the Mediterranean coast to Timbuktu, by automobile. Though both of these triumphs of planning and performance have been forgotten, they are still landmarks in the conquest of the desert, and their effects are still being felt and will be felt for many years to come.

In 1922, then, M. André Citroën, the engineer who had built up a huge factory and fortune during the war, planned and organized what the French called a 'raid' across the Sahara, the practical object of the exercise being to test his newly designed 'caterpillar' cars which were an adaptation of the British tank. Being an engineer and business man, M. Citroën didn't expect any help or encouragement from his government, but went ahead and made his plans at his own expense and with his own resources. He tells us that the idea of crossing the Sahara by car came to him during the war when the resources of Equatorial Africa were so desperately needed by France—not only the oil of Senegal and the rubber of the Congo, but even more, the vast supplies of manpower which were needed at the rate of ten thousand men a day, to feed the guns on the Western Front. Moreover, the old French dream of linking their Niger River colonies with their Mediterranean territories, and of so making a solid *bloc africain-français*, was still never far from the thoughts of patriotic Frenchmen: the phantasmagoria of a trans-Saharan railway still flickered, as it were, in the back of their minds. And M. Citroën refers to such a reverie in his account of the genesis of his 'raid'. A railway, he readily agrees, is the solution to the problem and the hope of the future; but in the meantime the automobile would offer an immediate and practical means of linking Tunis with Timbuktu.

Accordingly, from 1921 to 1922, the Citroën works under the personal direction of their founder himself built and experimented with a 10 h.p. tractor car, derived from the tank, which could travel over almost any terrain. By December 1922 six cars were ready to make the crossing. Almost exactly a month later, on January 4th, 1923, all six drove into Timbuktu. A journey which took Major Laing fifteen months and which the fast camel caravans needed at least six months to complete had been successfully and easily accomplished in thirty days.

The Citroën expedition ranks, therefore, as one of the most important events in the history of the Sahara, for its effect on the actual life of the desert was to be greater than that of any previous penetration by Europeans. For that matter, even the animals were affected. Their chances of survival in the camel era were fair; it is obvious from what goes on in the desert today that, thanks to four-wheel-drive vehicles, gazelles, antelopes, desert hares, and moufflon will soon only survive in zoos.

But M. Citroën was certainly not to blame for the massacre of the desert fauna, for he had very different ends in view, and those ends had been, in part, attained. This is clear from the report of the leaders of the expedition, Georges Marie Haardt and Louis Audouin-Dubreuil. Here is a summary of their conclusions:

> We reckon the waterless country at about 250 miles, a life-less strip which the boldest caravans never tackle without anxiety. We, full of confidence in our caterpillar cars, and dis-posing of the element of *speed* which logically reduces all risks to a minimum, tackle the quintessence of the desert with a light heart, though it is the last word in aridity and desolation.

The 'lifeless' strip Haardt and Audouin-Dubreuil were referring to is the crossing over the Hoggar Mountains in which General Laperrine's aeroplane crashed and where he died. It is a route which nobody takes any longer, or not by car, though there is a 'piste' marked on the maps, running south-westwards from Tamanrasset to Kidal, and so, via the Tanezrouft route, to Bourem, Timbuktu, and Gao. For the camel caravans, as the earlier travellers trying to reach Timbuktu discovered, it was the most terrible part of the desert, known as the Land of Fear and Thirst. To them it is 'a desert within a desert'. It is the desolation of a graveyard. No life, either animal or vegetable, can survive there. Yet it must be crossed at some point in order to reach the Sudan. The nomads have crossed the Tanezrouft for centuries; but they dread it more than any other part of their journeying. It means a twelve days' march in intolerable heat with no chance of replenishing their water supplies. Camels and men have died by the thousands crossing the Tanezrouft. Henri Lhote describes such a crossing like this:

> We have the impression of being in hell. . . . At the end of three days, we seem to be living a horrible nightmare, and yet we have only just begun our journey. Crouching over our

saddles, we proceed, completely annihilated by the heat, insensible after a while to our pain, because this has surpassed what the imagination can conceive. We are stunned, hallucinated as we advance, driven on by the mad obsession that we shall soon be able to quench our thirst, roll about in water, and rest in some green corner of a wood; and because of these dreams, we manage to survive, cost what it may, even to the extent of doubling the normal stages to escape from this hell.

This, however, was the region which the French cars scurried across in just over two days with the minimum of danger and of suffering, since they had no problems of water and supplies. In fact, they carried enough water in their convoy for twenty days! Their main trouble was that they couldn't eat during the day because of the simoon, or perpetual sand-storm, which blows all day and every day, and only stops at night. The camel-men never try to eat at all during the day. The French automobilists did, and found it impossible. As soon as they opened a tin of food it was smothered in sand. They only succeeded in munching some bits of dry bread by squeezing against the body of the cars on the lee side.

But apart from hunger and fatigue, this first crossing of the Tanezrouft, forty years ago, was relatively as easy as the run from London to Brighton today, the average speed being about the same, i.e. around fifteen miles an hour. Now cars and trucks pass regularly down the two main north-south tracks across the western Sahara; and André Citroën's claim that his 'caterpillar cars' would be the greatest forward step towards the conquest of the desert since the introduction of the camel proved true. It was only logical that with the unqualified success of the mission, Citroën should predict the development of '*le grand tourisme*', thanks, he says, to 'the might of French industry and the valour of our countrymen'. In fact, the French now felt, for the first time in a hundred years, that they had truly conquered the desert which, by right of conquest, had become, and should remain, a wholly French reserve. This is subtly implied in the 'solemn pilgrimage' the Citroën car drivers made to the house of René Caillié in Timbuktu. Unlike many other French travellers who never mention Major Laing at all, Messieurs Haardt and Audouin-Dubreuil make a cursory reference to the British explorer; only they make sure not to give him the credit he was due.

Externally, the house where René Caillié lived from April 20 to May 4, 1828 does not differ from its neighbours. Inside it is better lighted owing to a small loophole looking out on a side street which the explorer is said to have cut with his knife . . . [the 'which' must refer to the 'loophole'. The ambiguity is due to the translation made by M. Fournier d'Albe from the French into the English]. He probably did this as a precaution, in order to be able to write his notes far from prying eyes. The mere fact of not writing from right to left, or in Arabic characters, might have revealed his identity. Then it would have been the end of him, and he would have suffered the tragic death of Gordon Laing, the British explorer, *who was killed in the same street a few years later*.

That the two Frenchmen made this mistake inadvertently is unlikely, since Caillié himself describes, in a moving passage in his *Travels*, how he visited the grave of his predecessor far from Timbuktu on the road to Araouan. In addition, it was another Frenchman who had written a definitive account of the Englishman's death only ten years before the Haardt-Audouin-Dubreuil visit. All Saharan travellers of the period must have known of Bonnel de Mezières's book *Le Major Laing*, so we can only conclude that the French, now that they had conquered the Sahara at the cost of so much effort—of which the Citroën expedition was, at the time, the culmination—were unwilling to allow any other nationality to share in the victory, particularly the British, their greatest rivals in Africa.

André Citroën, himself an ardent nationalist, was especially conscious after the successful crossing of the desert by his auto-cars of the great opportunity to make of this vast region of Africa a veritable holiday resort, shrewdly calculating that nothing pacifies a country as quickly as tourism. Sales prospects for his caterpillar cars were also taken into account. He therefore set about drawing up a grandiose scheme for building hotels across the Sahara, fitted out with all modern comforts, including bathrooms, running water, radios, and air-conditioned bars. The Citroën project was, in fact, well advanced, with millions of francs poured into the building of rest houses along the proposed route from Algiers to Timbuktu and millions more into the manufacture of the tractor cars, when the French Government vetoed the scheme on the grounds that a crossing of the desert was placing too heavy a responsibility on the Army owing to the unsettled state of the tribes. That was the end of '*le grand tourisme saharien*'. André Citroën was fifty years ahead of his times.

The fact was that the French Army in Africa, together with the 'mystics' (of whom Father de Foucauld was the archetype), were loath to give up their desert, to see it swarmed over by hordes of tourists in stinking caterpillar cars. To these 'Saharans' of the old school, the vast wasteland meant more than mere territory, and even more than a potential source of wealth: it meant a *mystique* conceived and systematized by a few inspired and heroic men who somehow symbolized the finest aspects of French culture and aspirations. Henri Lhote, himself a great Saharan and a great 'mystic', sums it up thus:

Above all, let us remember that the Sahara has been for our country a crucible of inspiration in which French genius has found the opportunity to prove and to ennoble itself.

Let it be noted, however, that the French are not the only nation to have their *mystique*. All highly civilized countries have 'some corner of a foreign field' over which their bravest and often most colourful explorers, soldiers, or saints have had, as it were, spiritual, as well as a physical, monopoly. Religious mysticism having become outmoded since the Middle Ages, some other form of asceticism has taken its place. Such was the *mystique* of the Sahara.

What Lhote calls 'French genius', however, was manifested in a more practical form by some of the colonial administrators, including the young army officers and intellectuals who became *engagés* with the desert. Many of these expatriates had been trying for twenty years or more sincerely to help the natives of the regions they administered—to teach them the rudiments of agriculture; to encourage them to settle on the land and farm it instead of despoiling it with their omnivorous flocks and herds; and to live according to decent community principles. But unfortunately for the well-meaning officials both the population and the tide of history itself were against them. That ominous report made by a young French officer in 1916 as a result of his investigations into the murder of Father de Foucauld was still true twenty years later—and another twenty years later still: 'One is obliged to conclude that they do not want us.'

In 1958 a French Saharan was writing:

> The Tunisians want us out of Bizerta; the Moroccans out of the Desert. The Front du Libération Nationale has penetrated as far as the Central Sahara, and their terrorists are sabotaging our public utilities. The nomads who were most loyal to us and enabled us to conquer the Desert are going over to the rebels; the Tuaregs are listening again to the religious fanatics sent out by the Senussi. The Americans pretend to support us in the United Nations. But what do they want in return? The Sahara?

Such was the situation after one hundred years of expenditure of French lives, money, and aspirations; and such was the situation at a moment when the Saharan territories were suddenly known to be among the richest areas in the world. One can appreciate the feelings of the 'mystics', even more than those of the French politicians and industrialists. The Sahara Desert, their spiritual home, was about to be lost to them.

II

By this time it was the same all over Africa, of course. The day of the Europeans was ended, with a few die-hard exceptions. A comparison of the map of the African continent today with the maps drawn in 1800 and 1900 is a study of the historical process in its very essence. As we have seen, in 1800, the whole of Central Africa was *terra incognita*, its cartography about on a par with that of the moon. By 1900, or shortly thereafter, it was parcelled out in huge blocks between the major European powers. Scarcely an acre of it was independent. Today there are, at the last count, thirty-two independent African states—some of which the average Westerner may never have heard of. Where is the republic of Upper Volta? What is the capital of the Islamic republic of Mauretania? Who is the president of the republic of Chad? And so on. . . . In all fairness to the non-specialist it is devilishly difficult to keep up with developments in an area of the world larger than the United States, Europe, India, Japan, and New Zealand combined.

The visitor to these new countries since their independence will find that very little has changed on the surface. The differences are all underneath, and there has not yet been time for them to manifest themselves. The big cities of the Mediterranean coast and the larger towns of the interior look pretty much the same as they did when the occupying powers were in control. They are, that is, semi-Europeanized and give the impression of pseudo-modern, jerry-built communities set down amid the casbahs and medinas of the old Arab-Turkish settlements. As for the desert itself, its oases and its inhabitants, there is no radical change from what life was like 2,000 years or more ago.

Still, the independence of the Saharan states is a very definite fact of international life—a fact that has an increasingly significant effect on the manœuvrings of high-level diplomacy. For while these new nations are no threat in terms of the old military politics—for none of them has an army worth considering within the framework of modern nuclear warfare—they have two relatively potent weapons: a vote in the United Nations; and, in the case of the Saharan states, untold and untapped oil and mineral resources. To this extent, Western (and by the same token, Soviet) politics and diplomacy are determined by these otherwise impotent nations.

This quite intangible factor—the influence of Africa on the great powers—is made subtly obvious to the Western observer. Sometimes it is not so subtle, as when one of these states plays off the West against the East. Then there is the perennial talk of 'colonization', which will undoubtedly be with us for decades to come, like the talk of the wrongs done by the British to Auld Ireland. To the visitor sitting in Cathedral Square in Tripoli, for instance, a Libyan might remark that when the Italians were in control, Libyans weren't even allowed to walk on those particular streets. The observation is not without an implied menace. It is then that the Westerner realizes that his white skin, his powerful army and navy, and his multiplicity of machines are no longer guarantees of his inviolability in Africa. He has to change his attitude and manner, whatever he may think within the privacy of his own mind.

Some indication of what light-skinned as well as negroid Africans are thinking and now saying was made clear to me in many 'tea sessions' in the huts and tents of the actual desert where international politics in their more grandiose aspects are as remote as who is to get first to the moon. One sits on the floor while the host brews the thick sweet tea of the desert. It is made with two little enamel teapots, one of which packed with green tea leaves is boiled on a little fire of palm wood. When the concoction of tea and sugar has reached the right degree of viscosity by repeated pourings of the brew back and forth between the two pots, a small glass is handed first to the guest, and the ceremony begins. And how often on these occasions the Africans of all colours and degrees returned to the topic of racial discrimination so that it soon became clear their attitude towards the West was dominated by their indignation that white men considered themselves superior to black men on the strength of the colour of their skin. There were many references at this point to God

Himself, meaning, of course, the Moslem God who would be in the normal anthropomorphic process more pigmented than the nordic deity. All such talk is, of course, 'ancient history', but it is history that has much more significance when it is discussed in a continent of several hundred million 'coloured' people who are masters in their own house. It is then that one realizes the doctrine of white supremacy can well become a myth, like the legends of the Greek gods.

On the other hand, a hundred years of white supremacy—especially the indisputable evidence of the monuments—can't easily be forgotten or overlooked by the Africans; and hence it is that the white man, despite the stigma of racism that attaches to him, is not only tolerated, but accepted. There is no corner of the Sahara that he can't visit and where he won't be treated with respect and courtesy. Nor is he, for a single moment, in any danger, except from the normal hazards of desert travel. In fact, one could almost say that he was in greater danger when European armies were in control of areas now policed by native gendarmes.

The principal reason for the North Africans' toleration of the white man is that, apart from the prolonged struggle over Algiers, and the Belgian Congo, the Europeans evacuated their colonies with the minimum of bloodshed and ill will. The British for their part had learnt the lesson of India, and to them goes the premium for having withdrawn in good time and good order. Britain's two former Saharan colonies, the Sudan and Nigeria, are consequently kindly disposed towards the old colonial power. For that matter, there are many citizens of these states who would not be averse to seeing their countries administered by British officials, though this is a matter of internal politics which can't be discussed here. The same can't be said of the former French and Italian territories, though the French in the ultimate years of their dominion made every effort to bind these enormous areas to metropolitan France by cultural and economic ties. In the southern Saharan states they certainly succeeded, for the plain fact is that these new countries could not survive without French subsidies and French technicians. The former Italian colonies of

Libya and Ethiopia, on the other hand, have broken all ties with the conquerors.

The colonial powers, then, withdrew in the nick of historic time, and would have withdrawn without any particular regrets from the 3,000,000 square miles of the Sahara had it not been for the discovery, during the final years of occupation, of unprecedented wealth in the sterile sands of the Great Desert itself. This, of course, was the main reason for the 'agony' of France in having to abandon Algeria: the discovery of immense oil deposits throughout the province south of the Atlas Mountains. Tunisia, Morocco, Mauretania, and Mali, on the other hand, where no comparable wells have yet been found, were granted independence much more expeditiously. Algeria was desperately clung to up to the very last moment.

III

Within a very few years of leaving the Saharan countries as masters and owners, the Europeans were back in the role of agents and employees. The fact of the matter was the new governments couldn't run their countries without them. Politically, perhaps yes; economically and technically, definitely no. For while politics is a random art practised by schemers, the operation of an electric generator is a precise skill based on science. The Moslem world has a plethora of politicians and a chronic lack of engineers.

But there was another and more pressing reason for the return in force of Westerners. For after over two thousand years of a desperate and seemingly fruitless struggle against the African desert, they had finally found a reward for all their efforts and all their expense: they had found wealth on a scale sufficient to justify the exploitation of the immense wasteland. The Sahara had finally become an ally after centuries of enmity.

The Romans, as we have seen, considered Africa a good enough investment to stay there for 500 years and to pour into its development the full resources of an empire. They got in return enough grain and oil to feed the poor and enough ivory and gold to satisfy the rich. In comparison with this, the modern colonial nations got little.

But the difference between the Roman occupation of Africa Proconsularis and the European occupation of the Sahara was more profound than a disparity of rewards. The Romans, materialists though they were, were not unmindful of their mission to civilize, as well as to exploit. They were even prepared, as in the case of Britain, to give more than they got. They got some tin, silver, hides, oysters, and hunting dogs from Britain; in return they gave the country law and order, farms and roads, and the beginnings of art and science. It could be argued that the imperial policy of Rome was based on the One World concept which was the pagan version of the brotherhood of man. To this extent, the methods and results of Roman colonization were more successful and conceivably more humanitarian than those of the Christian colonists a thousand years and more later.

The Romans were also less hampered by purely economic considerations. For instance, it is reasonable to argue on the evidence of their activity elsewhere that if a Caesar had decided to build a trans-Saharan road from Tunis to Timbuktu, the legions would undoubtedly have built one no matter the cost; and, according to Pliny, they did have a paved road across the Fezzan which explorers have been hearing about ever since. But even if this particular road has not yet been discovered, there are enough Roman monuments in Africa—temples, theatres, libraries, and schools—to show that the Latin conquerors were interested not only in commerce, but also in incorporating their colony into the framework of the *civitas romana*.

The European colonialists have unquestionably been more concerned with the economics of occupation. The basic principle was simple: a guaranteed return for a capital investment. 'Development', therefore, was largely determined by private enterprise, whence the poorer the region, the less was done for it. Consequently, outside the exploitation of the fertile plains of the Mediterranean littoral, there was no valid economic reason for investing anything other than the bare minimum in the Great

Desert itself. This, the Country of Fear, was left to the mystics and adventurers. Father de Foucauld handing out needles to the Tuareg women, other missionaries distributing bibles and medicines, army officers presiding at tribal disputes, and an occasional doctor tackling the impossible job of combating disease constituted about the sum total of aid inside the actual desert.

Then suddenly this policy of economic quiescence changed. In 1955 a well producing natural gas was tapped in the desert. In 1956 seven oil wells were brought in. The basic requirement for economic exploitation had been met. Now that there was 'gold' in the Sahara the attitude of the politicians and business men changed: a new and fervent interest in the desert was noticeable in the official pronouncements.

> The people are hungry for these subterranean foods [says a French statesman. One of the foods he lists is uranium.] The roads leading towards gold have created cities even in the icy deserts of Alaska. The skill of man during the second half of the twentieth century and the powerful forces that science has put into his hands will give him the victory over the Sahara, the country parched with thirst, solitude, and death.

It is by no means certain that it was 'the people's hunger' which marked the turning point in this long battle with the desert. It seems more likely that the international oil companies who now moved in with all the resources of modern science and technology had something to do with it. Certainly what the colonial governments had not been able to achieve in a hundred years of occupation the oil companies completed within a year or two: that is, the conquest of the desert in terms of surveys, travel, communications, light and heavy machinery, airfields, and camps.

All this was made possible, of course, by the expenditure of vast sums of hard cash, in significant contrast to the attitude of the national governments who sent off the first explorers without sufficient funds to buy their food along the road. Thus, in the first two years of drilling in the Sahara, the oil companies spent

£10,000,000 without a single find. In the next year, 1956, they invested £15,000,000 to sink twenty-two new wells. Seven of these brought in oil. The international financiers were satisfied, as they had good reason to be. In one zone in southern Algeria alone, one of the world's ten largest fields had been discovered, a reserve of over 450,000,000 tons of oil.

The search continues non-stop in almost every corner of the desert. As you fly over the vast and empty sand seas, wondering how men survived in their crossings of these dunes and salt lakes, you see the arrow-straight geodetic lines of the oil exploration teams running due north and south over mountains and plains. And somewhere tucked away in the lee of an escarpment, or even in the open desert itself, you can spot the camp of the geophysicists—two tents and three barrels, as they say. A plane will land here once a week with mail and supplies, and because of the camaraderie of the desert, you will often be welcome to go along for the ride. It is an unusual experience in an age of quasi-automated jet aviation. For the pilots—American, British, Belgian, French—fly planes twenty years or more old, an essential factor being that the two landing-wheels should be forward for a safe descent in soft sand. The job of these pilots is to find a dot somewhere in the desert, and the navigation involved has no resemblance to that of the transatlantic airliners. One watches for a black mountain, or a red wadi, or an elliptical salt lake; and every oasis and well along the route is known—or had better be known. 'If an engine goes out, I could get back to such and such a place,' says the pilot. 'There's some sort of airfield there. If they both go out, I'm always watching for a flat stretch where I could put the plane down. We carry plenty of water. . . .' It is all very free-and-easy, and if the pilot gets lost, he heads back to the Mediterranean coast and, fuel permitting, starts south again looking for his landmarks in the hope that he will find his camp before dark.

There are two types of oil camp in the desert: the temporary and the permanent. The former is manned by riggers and drillers who are sinking an exploratory well which may, or may not, yield. These are outposts in the petroleum empire, and conditions are rough and primitive for those who live there. The permanent camps, on the other hand, are prime examples of how the desert can be conquered with modern machines and skills. Such a camp, deep in the Sahara, will consist of rows of boxlike houses, each with its air-conditioning unit, toilet, shower, bed, armchair, and desk. European food is provided in the mess hall; European newspapers and magazines are flown in by the company's planes; European music is heard on the radio sets. The only luxuries missing are European women and television. A week off once a month takes care of that. The oil men are flown back to the Mediterranean cities by private plane and set down in a limousine outside the luxurious hotel which caters almost exclusively for them. Such hotels, costing more than their counterparts in New York, London, or Paris, see to it that these Texans in from the desert have the attractions on which to spend some of their enormous earnings—enormous bars, lounges, dining-rooms, barber shops, night clubs, and an army of servitors.

The discovery of oil in the Sahara, then, has changed the whole aspect of the desert. It has released tremendous new forces, political and social, as well as economic. The most obvious effect at the moment is the flow of money both into and out of the oil-producing countries. Some of these states literally have an embarrassment of riches. How are they to spend these millions of dollars annually derived from oil royalties? What can they spend so much money on? The glib answer is education, agriculture, roads, modernization, and all the refinements of life which Western nations have acquired slowly, over several hundred years of hard work and endeavour. This is the formula proposed by those who have never visited a true desert community and so know nothing of the conditions and problems of Saharan life. People who plough a few square yards of sand with a camel and a wooden ploughshare have no use for a diesel tractor; and splendid metalled roads criss-crossing the sand seas would only lead from nowhere to nowhere. All proposals to modernize overnight a people who are still living in the early Middle Ages are completely unrealistic.

All the same, oil will eventually change the lives of the desert-dwellers, whether they want the change or not. The very existence of those miniature modern cities amid the sand-dunes, the continual flight of aeroplanes and the regular passage of the convoys across the desert, the need for manpower and machine-minders, the higher wages paid by the oil companies—all these are everyday occurrences which will ultimately modify the old ways and the old convictions. It is a truism of history that the house will always displace the tent, as the tent displaced the cave. And with the house come the necessities of a settled life—a tap with running water, a toilet, a bath-tub, and so on until the apogee of modern man's desires is reached—a television set with a choice between a 'Western' and a domestic comedy. The people of the Sahara Desert are no different from the rest of us in wanting these amenities once they are aware of them. And they are beginning to be aware that they not only exist, but are attainable.

The effect, then, of Western standards have already been felt by the inhabitants of the most remote oasis and even by the Tuaregs who hitherto have always associated fixed abodes with serfdom. From time immemorial they have left agriculture to their *harratines*, or negro slaves, captured in their raids along the Niger River. In order to cultivate the few miserable acres of barley, tomatoes, and peppers, the serfs had to live permanently in the oases, near a well, or on the banks of a wadi. They built themselves cabins of clay and rushes—and these shacks were the only type of house to be found in the desert, with the exception of the mud or thatched huts of permanent commercial centres like Ghadames in the north and Timbuktu in the south. The Tuareg nobles preferred to live in tents which were symbolic of their status and their aristocratic freedom from all forms of drudgery.

Yet all this way of life, where the men are warriors and hunters and slaves provide the necessities of existence, will have to go as soon as Western civilization with its roads, machines, and—above all—comfortable homes introduces a new concept of living into the desert. As Father de Foucauld found, once a Tuareg woman had sewn with a needle she never wanted to go back to sewing with a thorn. Once the tribal women have seen the interior of an oil company's house they are going to be conscious of the squalor of their own tents; once the young men have worked for the rich foreigner they are going to become disillusioned with the drudgery of the oasis routine. Already tribesmen who ten years ago were convoying camel caravans from village to village are driving petrol tankers or the Land Rovers of the oil exploration teams; and farmers who tended half a dozen date palms are digging ditches along which the pipe-lines to the Mediterranean ports are being laid.

The second factor which will ultimately change the Sahara of history and romance is the *malaise* of the average 'white' man in the desert. Life in even an air-conditioned oil company camp is infinitely tedious, especially for employees with families back home. The only Europeans who have surrendered unconditionally to the desert are those who have been willing to renounce their Western heritage and to 'go native'. Such a man was Father de Foucauld, who went completely 'Tuareg': there was no basic difference between his day-to-day existence and theirs. And such were the French officers in command of companies of *méharistes* who, while maintaining certain symbolic differences in their role as conquerors, actually lived the life of the oases. They were not 'fixed abode men'. And elsewhere throughout the desert one could find Europeans serving in one capacity or another gradually sloughing off their European prejudices as most of them put off their European clothes.

But this sort of psychological metamorphosis can't be expected of engineers, mechanics, clerks, administrators, and executives who are interested in earning their living and not in the *mystique* of the desert. These men are not living in hot countries from religious or patriotic motives. Isolated within their air-conditioned hut, awaiting the company plane with its fresh supplies of orange-juice and canned beer, they have no more feeling for the desert around them than the submariner has for the ocean outside the hull of his craft. Why should they? The desert is vast, arid, uncomfortable, and boring. Anybody who doesn't think so should visit an oil camp in the Libyan Desert.

The white men, then, are temporary residents, though they

will have to come and go until the nationals of the oil-producing countries can operate the machines themselves. It will be a long time before they can do any such thing, that much is certain. But that time will surely come. And when it does there will be still another change in Africa, affecting the remotest village in the sand seas. The change is already apparent: the old life of the Sahara is becoming archaic; and the new breed of politicians are already claiming the resources of their land as their own.

EPILOGUE

I

WITH the granting of complete independence in 1962 to Algeria, another epoch of Saharan history was ended as definitely as the Roman conquest ended the prehistoric era, the Arab invasion the Roman era, and the French occupation, in its turn, the Arab era. The entire desert is now autonomous from the Atlantic to the Red Sea and from the Mediterranean to the Niger River, with the exception of two enclaves boxed in along the Atlantic coast— namely the Spanish colonies of Ifni and Rio de Oro. On that day in April 1962 when the French peoples voted for the independence of Algeria the age of colonialism was, to all intents and purposes, ended. Africa is no longer a dependency of Europe; Africans are no longer a subject people. What they do and how they develop in the future is their own affair.

What, then, will be the next phase in Saharan history?

To the observer who can look at the signs without prejudice or emotion, the pattern is becoming evident; the broad outlines, at least, are beginning to emerge. The first conclusion he is bound to draw is that the new states are undeveloped, badly governed, ill-organized, and usually autocratic. Most of them have no concept of nationhood whatsoever. The village is their state and the tribe their government. If you try and discover what it is that holds them together within the theoretical confines of a 'country' you are forced to conclude that it is the self-aggrandizement of the local politicians (backed by the army) plus a strong undercurrent of xenophobia. An African politician has only to mouth the words 'colonialism' or 'imperialistic exploiter' and the people respond with cries of indignation and their vote, if they have one.

326

To this suspicion of the foreigners (meaning white men) there need only be added the *mystique* of a national flag, and something resembling a nation emerges. Regarding the *mystique*, it is standard that in every city and in the remotest village of the Saharan states the flag flutters from every building that can afford to attach a pole to roof or wall.

These two constituents of nationhood, then—xenophobia and flag symbolism—hold together millions of people in one politically homogeneous group for purposes of internal policy. They also simplify the new nations' role in external affairs. All that the African statesmen have to do is to be neutral on the grounds that the democratic powers wronged them in the past and communist powers might wrong them in the future. It is a useful diplomatic argument with a built-in threat to both sides, which hitherto has paid handsome dividends. And in point of fact, it is a legitimate argument since the new states have had no experience of either European political system—democracy or communism—so they are in no position to advocate either. All we can say is that today some African states lean towards the West, others to the East; but this is no indication of how they will align themselves tomorrow.

The great powers are well aware of this vacillation and their spokesmen are careful to present themselves as friends and allies, with no ulterior motives towards the emergent nations. Thus we find President Eisenhower demanding at the General Assembly of the United Nations in 1960 that all member nations pledge themselves 'to respect the African peoples' right to choose their own way of life and to determine for themselves the course they choose to follow; to refrain from intervening in these new nations' internal affairs . . . by subversion, force, propaganda, or other means'. Such altruism obviously has no meaning in practical politics, since the United States must, by the very nature of the power struggle, intervene in the affairs of all foreign states, and particularly those that are not committed. The problem is how to do so without getting tagged with the old labels of colonialism and imperialism. Bribery in one economic form or another is usually the solution.

At the same time the United States has always been put at an unfair disadvantage in the tricky game of winning the African nations' goodwill. One of their official spokesmen points this out in frank terms for a change:

> We needed friends in both Europe and Africa, and whatever we did to please one angered the other. . . . The view that we need not worry about our western allies because 'they had no place else to go' was fundamentally wrong in its implication that a great leader can hold his followers by kicking them in the teeth. The argument that we should have done what was 'right' instead of trying to please our friends was of little value to government officials. . . . For these reasons the United States continued to sit on the fence.

Not surprisingly, the Soviet Union's public pronouncements regarding the new African nations is almost identical with those of the United States. The communist spokesmen, however, have an added 'attraction': they can truthfully argue that Russia was the only large European power that had no tradition of colonialism in Africa and that no square foot of that continent was ever subjugated by Russian soldiers.

The Soviet Union, therefore, had nothing to lose and everything to gain in supporting—without the dilemma which faced the United States—the aspirations of the Africans for independence. Nikita Khrushchev was thus able to state Soviet policy at the fifteenth session of the U.N. General Assembly in these words:

> All colonial countries, trustee and other non-self-governing territories must without fail be granted complete independence and freedom in building up their own national states in accordance with their own freely expressed will and the desires of their peoples. All forms of the colonial regime and colonial administration must be completely abolished so that the people of these territories may have the opportunity to decide their own fate as well as the form of government they wish to follow.

An official Soviet spokesman gives us a useful commentary on this policy:

> The Soviet Union [writes Mr. Vladimir Kudriavtsev] is giving all those African states which have gained independence every assistance and repelling the attempts of the colonial powers to subjugate them once again under one guise or another. . . . The Soviet Union's position with regard to Africa accords not only with the interests of the African peoples themselves but with the vital interests of all nations who are determined to prevent a small group of colonial enslavers from sacrificing the peace of the world for their own selfish ends.

In contrast to the self-righteous pronouncements of the Americans and Russians, the French and British were obliged to take a more deprecating tone. With the loss of Indo-China and India still fresh in their memories, they recognized that the tide of nationalism was flowing far too strongly to be stemmed by rhetoric; that the old concepts of empire and the old methods of maintaining it were being swept away by forces over which they no longer had any control. The French and British view was that they had better save what they could—whence the organization of the *communauté française-africaine* on the one hand; and the offer of Commonwealth status to Britain's former African colonies on the other. The two types of alliance are temporary expedients. The indications are that all of Africa will, in due course, sever those ties with Europe which smack of any implication of servitude. The continent will develop in its way and in its own time. There will eventually emerge an entity characteristically 'African', which will equal, and possibly surpass in vitality and force, the contemporary white civilizations.

II

What form will the culture of a new and independent Africa take? At present there is, of course, no common racial heritage and no common historical experience: the continent and its peoples, in any case, are divided into two by the Equator. Those to the north of this line are preponderantly Moslem; those to the south, pagans. Religion is one of the strongest divisive forces in human relations, and Africa has more than its share of religions. But despite the multiplicity of people and creeds the whole vast region has certain natural affinities, just as other continents have.

The first of these which the traveller notes is the desire to modernize and to slough off many of the aboriginal customs and modes of life which are not 'progressive'. As we have seen, the Tuareg culture, to take one example, is almost finished. Once the new generation of tribesmen have glimpsed what life is like today outside the desert, they are not content to sit in tents listening to the sagas of the old days. Similarly, native handicrafts, folk-lore, music, and 'art' tend to survive principally as tourist attractions. It is quite obvious that the bronze figurines and wooden masks which the Sudanese tribes were making in the sixteenth century will never be made again, not merely because the crafts-men have lost their skill, but because Africans no longer see the world in this way. Their artists—sculptors, painters, and writers —have evolved—*évolués*, as the French say. For one thing, these new men no longer regard themselves as the creators of wooden masks, drums, camel saddles, and the kind of knick-knacks which were popular in European gift 'shoppes' in the twenties when civilized people were discovering African primitivism. They are much more concerned with expressing an entirely new concept of their world, a concept which transcends the multiple boun-daries of the African states and appeals to Africans in every region of the continent. It is, in fact, the nucleus of an idea, or even a philosophy, on which a common culture may be built.

The distinctive feature of this idea is the glorification of colour, the best word for which is the French *la négritude*. Strong pigmen-tation of the skin, of course—strong in comparison with the conventional prototype of the European or North American— is the one characteristic which all Africans have in common, despite the popular idea that such ethnic groups as the Berbers and Tuaregs are white-skinned. Nordic blondness is practically unknown anywhere in Africa, though the pure negroid type is

found only in certain areas. But the intermingling of semitic and
negroid is so widespread that it is pointless to make distinction
on purely ethnological grounds. More to the point, the African,
including the North African, has to make a choice of allegiance—
to the white skins on the one hand; the coloured skins on the other.
He has made his choice, and for obvious reasons. The white skins
symbolize the exploiters; the coloured ones the exploited.

The more articulate and fervent exponents of this new creed
of *négritude* express the idea in unmistakable terms:

> Woman nude, woman black,
>   Clad in your colour, which is life—
> Your beauty strikes me to the heart
>   As lightning strikes the eagle.

and,

> Our God is black,
> Black of eternal blackness,
> With large, voluptuous lips,
> Matted hair, and brown liquid eyes . . .
>   For in his image are we made.
> Our God is black.

'The manifestation of the black soul,' says Sartre. But only one
face of it; for there is an obverse which completes the picture.

> The white man killed my father.
> My father was proud.
> The white man seduced my mother.
> My mother was beautiful.
>   The white man burnt my brother
>   Beneath the noonday sun.
> My brother was strong,
> His hands red with black blood.
> The white man turned to me
> And in the Conqueror's voice said,
> 'Hey, boy! A chair, a napkin, a drink.'

If anyone wishes to know, then, what young and articulate Africans are thinking, these poems will give him a clue. *La Négritude*, in other words, is the fountainhead of the new culture.

III

Admittedly this obsession with the colour of the skin is an emotional undercurrent in the main stream of African life. On the surface other forces are observable. It has already been pointed out that the continent is split by the Equator. To the north lie all the Saharan states which are Berber-Arab-Negro; and these states form, or may form, a single block whose cohesive force will be Islam. Egypt, Libya, Tunisia, Algeria, Morocco, and the Moslem nations of the south Sahara think in terms of pan-Arabism, and President Nasser of Egypt is their popular hero. The central and lower African states, on the other hand, think in terms of pan-Africanism, and their spiritual leader varies with the winds of political fortune. It is not certain that the two blocks will ever cohese into one inseparable unit. If they do, the emergence of Africa as a world power will be that much quicker. We have no way of knowing at present, since each single state is too busy consolidating its newly won independence.

What we do know is that this process of consolidation entails the setting-up of European-type democratic systems with all the paraphernalia of the ballot-box, parliaments, and constitutions. With this goes lip-homage to the rights of citizens, a free Press, and a fair judicial system. In point of fact, nearly every new African nation has some form of dictatorship, either political or military. The actual practice of democracy is almost unknown. Any form of opposition to the man in power and his henchman is ruthlessly crushed.

And this denial of criticism of the ruling clique will also shape the future of Africa, for it can only mean one thing in the long run: all really fervent opponents of the regime (they include nearly all the intellectuals) will eventually have to form a united front with the outlawed communist party, for the simple reason that that party, by going underground, is the only one to survive.

It follows that communism is another force to be reckoned with in the shaping of the Africa of the future.

That future, of course, cannot be included even in the first chapter of the history that has yet to be written. For the present, and for a long time to come, the great continent, and the Great Desert within it, remain almost as they were when the first historian Herodotus came to see Africa for himself nearly two and a half thousand years ago. The girls are still drawing water at the oasis wells; the boys are still climbing the date palms to gather in the harvest; the donkeys are still carrying the loads and being beaten; the flocks of goats are still nibbling among the black stones; and a flight of gazelles can sometimes be seen disappearing into the dunes at sunset. All the rest—the squabbling politicians, the platitudinous statesmen, the desert oil rigs—seem, for the moment, as unreal as tomorrow's dream.

NOTES

INTRODUCTION. There are, in general, two kinds of books on the Sahara: the standard texts of the historians, ancient and modern; and the personal accounts of travellers. The total literature of the desert, then, is enormous. R. Capot-Rey in his *Le Sahara Français* (1953) lists 800 'standard' titles—a bibliography which doesn't take into account the thousands of non-academic books and the tens of thousands of articles in the non-scientific periodicals.

The student of the subject need not be too alarmed by this plethora of reading matter, however, since he will quickly discover that his main sources of worthwhile information are clearly defined. They are: the classical historians and geographers themselves; the works of a few reliable Arab annalists; the books of the first 'African Travellers'—the Europeans who actually explored the Sahara in the nineteenth century; and the histories of modern scholars who have combined erudition with a first-hand knowledge of their subject.

The bibliography given in this book is based on these four sources. And though there are many interesting and entertaining 'adventure story' accounts of Saharan sights and sounds by recent travellers, it has not been possible to include them here.

Detailed references to sources will be listed chapter by chapter.

CHAPTER ONE. The literature of the Saharan rock engravings and paintings is still strictly limited: first, by the fewness of specialists with the training, time, and money to undertake expeditions to inaccessible regions of the desert; and second, by the cost of reproducing the pictures in commercial book form. For the specialist, two valuable reports are available: Yolande Tschudi's *Les Peintures Rupestres du Tassili-N-Ajjer* (1956); and the Abbé Breuil's *Les Roches Peintes du Tassili-N-Ajjer* (1954). A popular account of the Tassili paintings will be found in Henri Lhote's *The Search for the Tassili Frescoes* (1959).

For the prehistoric Sahara there is the first volume of Stephane Gsell's massive work of scholarship *Histoire Ancienne de l'Afrique du*

Nord (1913); R. Capot-Rey's *Le Sahara Français* (1953); and Maurice Reygasse's *Monuments Funéraires Préislamique de l'Afrique du Nord* (1950). These books list long bibliographies which include special articles in scientific and scholarly journals.

CHAPTER TWO. The authorities consulted in this chapter are chiefly the classical historians and geographers themselves, as well as the standard histories of Carthage and Africa Proconsularis.

Very little has yet been discovered, let alone published, about the Garamantes, whose capital is now being excavated by Dr. M. S. Ayoub, Controller of Antiquities for the Fezzan. Much of the material used in this chapter is based on my talks and field work with this archaeologist.

CHAPTER THREE. For the cities of Roman Africa, see the classical dictionaries and atlases, notably Gsell's *Atlas Archéologique* (1902–11) for Algeria and Tunisia; and D. E. L. Haynes's *An Archaeological Guide* (1956) for Tripolitania. For Roman roads I have consulted Pierre Salama's *Les Voies Romaines* (1951) and R. G. Goodchild, *The Roman Roads* (1948).

The indispensable work for the history of the Third Augusta Legion is R. L. Cagnat's *L'Armeé Romaine de l'Afrique du Nord* (1892). The soldier's letter to his mother quoted on p. 80 is taken from a papyrus found in Egypt and now kept in the archives of the Royal Museum, Berlin.

CHAPTER FOUR. The new concept and understanding of the Roman occupation of the desert south of the official *limes*, or frontier, are largely due to the achievement of Colonel Jean Baradez of the French Air Force. Colonel Baradez's aerial photographs, together with his scholarly interpretation of his three years' findings in the south Algerian desert, are published in his *Fossatum Africae* (1949). While French archaeologists, aided by their armed services, were redefining the Algerian and Tunisian frontiers of Africa Proconsularis, British scholars were working along much the same lines (also with the help of the military) in Tripolitania and Cyrenaica. In 1949 R. G. Goodchild and J. B. Ward-Perkins published their first report on the *Limes Tripolitanus* in the *Journal of Roman Studies*, vols. xxxix and xl, 'The Limes Tripolitanus in the Light of Recent Discoveries'. Since that time, a great deal of work has been done every year by resident and visiting archaeologists on the nature and extent of the Roman frontier system. The difficulty is that the colonists and frontiersmen stay, as it were, one jump ahead of us. We are still not sure how far down in the desert the Romans pushed their outposts. Ksar Mara, described in the Introduction, may be an example. So, perhaps, is the 'lost' kingdom of Zuila, about which we know hardly anything, despite the presence of its massive fort and watch towers (see Chapter Seven). Some indication of what is being found appears in the scholarly journals and papers read at archaeological conferences. The older books on the subject, including Gsell and Cagnat, are now out of date in this respect, though a useful treatise on the subject of desert irrigation and agriculture is still P. R. M. H. de la Blanchère's *L'Aménagement de l'Eau dans l'Afrique Ancienne* (1871). It is de la Blanchère who points out that the climate in Roman times was no different from what it is today, so that the fertility of the land had nothing to do with meteorology, but was 'the prize of hard work'.

CHAPTER FIVE. Alban Butler's *The Lives of the Saints* (1956) and *The Catholic Encyclopaedia* have been consulted for the large field of African hagiology; for Donatism and its long history of conflict and controversy, Auguste Audollent, *Carthage Romaine* (1901); J. Mesnage, *L'Afrique Chretiénne* (1912); and Paul Monçeaux, *Histoire Littéraire* (1924). The late Christian and Byzantine period is also described in *L'Afrique Romaine* (1951) by Eugène Albertini.

The bulk of material concerning Roman frontier forts and farms still remains to be collated and published in easily accessible form. Up to the present, individual archaeologists, many of them intelligent amateurs who did some digging while serving in the French and Italian armies, have excavated frontier posts here and there all along the fringes of the Sahara, sometimes publishing their findings in pamphlets which are exceedingly difficult to come by, even in the archives of the North African governments. Yet some of these *ephemera* contain extremely unusual data. Here is a rather typical extract from one of these reports entitled *Recherches Archéologiques aux Ouled-Djellal, 1949–1950* (Constantine, Grande Imprimerie Damremont, 1959):

> The architect of the Commune Mixte de Biskra had notified us of the existence of an inscription on the walls of one of these wells, with letters and numbers.

In order to check this statement, we decided to explore the wells at the beginning of June, 1950.

The deepest was located at several yards east of the fort. It had been cut through the living rock. After setting up a trestle and pulley, we descended half way down the well-shaft, not without difficulty. A well-digger who was sent down was overcome by giddiness as he approached the water and had to be quickly brought up again. This well is not less than 120 feet deep, with rounded niches cut into the walls. No inscription was found, but it must be added that the investigation was not completed, due to the lack of adequate material and helpers.

The last phrase sums up in a few words the problems of Saharan archaeology.

CHAPTER SIX. An excellent bibliography of early Arabic writings on North Africa and the desert will be found in Brown and Playfair's *A Bibliography of Morocco* (1892). Phillip K. Hitti's *History of the Arabs* (1942) has been consulted for the rise of Islam. The *Travels* of the Spanish Moor Leo Africanus is still the best account we have of Central African history and geography prior to the classic work of Dr. Henry Barth whose book *Travels and Discoveries in North and Central Africa* has been out of print since its publication in 1890—an offence to one of the greatest explorers of all time and a grievous lacuna in African studies.

There is no one authoritative book on the Saharan slave trade, since the Arabs who organized and ran the system left no records of the traffic. But all the *human* material a researcher requires will be found in the eyewitness accounts of the nineteenth-century travellers, most of whom actually journeyed with slave caravans. The first of these was Frederick Hornemann, whose *Journal of Travels* was published posthumously in the African Society's *Proceedings* in 1802. A fuller and livelier account of conditions on the road is given by Captain G. F. Lyon, R.N., whose *Travels* appeared in 1821. He was followed in 1826 by Oudney, Clapperton, and Denham whose findings were published under the title *A Narrative of Travels* (see Notes, Chapter Seven). The greatest work of all, however, is still Dr. Henry Barth's *Travels and Discoveries*, for this scholarly explorer, historian, and anthropologist saw the slave trade at its source—in the petty African kingdoms around Lake Chad and along the Niger River.

A very lively account of the trade as it was within living memory is given in Hanns Vischer's *Across the Sahara* (1910), still one of the best travel books of its kind and full of useful information. References to many other Saharan travellers who comment on the slave trade as they saw it in practice will be found in later chapters.

Several very early books touching on African slavery are important if the historian is to get the institution in its right perspective. A book like the *Istorica Descrizione di Tre Regni del Congo* by Pietro Cavazzi, published in Bologna in 1687, establishes the fact that slavery on an unprecedented scale was established throughout Central Africa long before the Arabs and white men arrived to exploit it. Another aspect of slavery—almost a separate department of the subject—is the Moslem capture and treatment of white Christians throughout the Crusades and long after—a practice which created tremendous indignation throughout Europe and, later, in the United States. A useful source book as regards the Algiers and Tunis slave marts is the curious *Histoire de Barbarie et Ses Corsairs* (1637) by the sixteenth-century priest Father Dan, representative of the Redemptionist Order of our Lady of Mercy, founded in 1218 for the ransoming of Christians captured and enslaved by the Infidel. Among other books consulted: P. H. Grierson, *The Silent Trade* (1903); Sir F. D. Lugard, *The Dual Mandate* (1923); E. W. Bovill, *Caravans of the Old Sahara* (1933); Sir Godfrey Fisher, *Barbary Legend* (1957); Benjamin E. Thomas, *Trade Routes* (1957); and P. Ceulemans, *La Question Arabe* (1959).

There are several books of high scholarship on the subject of the Tuaregs and their culture: the classic *Les Tuareg du Nord* (1864), and other works by Henri Duveyrier; *People of the Veil* (1926) by F. Rennell Rodd; and the monographs of Father Charles de Foucauld who devoted his life to the welfare and study of the Hoggar Tuareg. The bibliographies should be consulted for the hundreds of monographs by French anthropologists and army officers on various aspects of the Tuareg culture. Most of the popular books on the subject, in contrast, tend to be misleading and invariably treat the Tuareg as romantic 'knights of the desert' when even a superficial knowledge of their history shows that they were basically thugs and bandits, as incidents in the subsequent chapters of this book will amply show.

CHAPTER SEVEN. For the beginnings of the exploration of the Sahara, the 'Proceedings' of the African Association are indispensable. The First Report, issued in 1790, contains a notice of the Ledyard-Lucas mission. The Report of 1802 includes Frederick Hornemann's *Journal of Travels from Cairo to Murzuk*, together with the comments of Sir William Young and William Marsden.

The *Travels* of Mungo Park, an African explorer whose name (unlike that of most of the others) has never been entirely forgotten, are still available in fairly recent editions and even in the larger public libraries. On the other hand, nearly all the other *Travels* mentioned in this and subsequent chapters can only be found in national and specialized libraries. Such a book is Captain G. F. Lyon's *A Narrative of Travels in Northern Africa in the Years 1818, 1819, 1820*, printed in London in 1821 and out of print ever since; similarly, the *Narrative of Travels and Discoveries* of Oudney, Clapperton, and Dixon Denham, published in 1826. These two books, together with all the African Travellers' narratives published in the first half of the nineteenth century, are beautifully illustrated, printed, and bound: and like the majority of books written about the Sahara before the popularization of the subject, are as fascinatingly fresh and original today as when they were written.

CHAPTER EIGHT. The accounts of the Ritchie-Lyon and Oudney-Clapperton-Denham expeditions (see above) have been extensively drawn on for this phase of Saharan exploration. *The Travels of Richard and John Lander*, edited by Robert Huish (1836), and the *History and Description of African Exploration* by Dr. Robert Brown (1896) have also been consulted.

CHAPTER NINE. The Arabic chronicles, some of them translated into French, some into English, are the source books of the history of Timbuktu and the Niger River kingdoms: they include the following books available in the Publications of the École des Langues Orientales Vivantes: *Tarikh es Sedan* of Es Sadi (1900); *Tedzkiret en Nisian el Akhbar Moulouk es-Sudan* (1901); and *Tarikh el Fettach* of Mahmoud Kati (1913). Arabic writers available in English include the Hakluyt Society's editions of Leo Africanus, done into English by John Pory (1896); and Ibn Mohammed Abd Allah Batuta's *Travels in Asia and Africa, 1325–1354* (1929). The *Account of Timbuktoo and Hausa*, written by El Hadj Abd Salam Shabeeny, was edited by J. Jackson and published in 1820.

The first authentic European description of the city was René Caillié's, whose *Travels Through Central Africa to Timbuktoo* was published in London in 1830; the first scholarly report, Barth's *Travels*, followed by Oskar Lenz's *Timbuktu: Reise durch Marokko die Sahara und den Sudan in den Jahren 1879, 1880* (1884).

Soon after the French occupied Timbuktu, modern histories and descriptions began to appear fairly regularly—until the once fabulous city started to lose its aura of mystery. The first was Felix Dubois's *Tomboctou, Ville Mystérieuse* (1896). From a score of recent publications, the following have been selected as most useful to the student: 'Histoire de Tomboctou de sa fondation à l'occupation française (xi siècle—1893)' in the *Bulletin du Comité d'Études Historiques et Scientifiques de L'Afrique Occidentale Française*, vol. xxii, pp. 81–93; *Timbuctoo* (1927) by Leland Hall; *The White Monk of Timbuctoo* (1927) by William Seabrook (1934); and Horace Miner's *The Primitive City of Timbuctoo*—this last an excellent study by an American anthropologist, with a valuable bibliography.

For the life and travels of Major Laing, reference is made to his own book *Travels in the Timanee, Kooranko, and Soolima Countries* (1825); *A Biographical Memoir of Major Alexander Gordon Laing* (1830) by Thomas Nelson; *The Quarterly Review*, vol xxxviii, pp. 100 ff., 1828; and A. Bonnel de Mezières's *Le Major A. Gordon Laing* (1912).

The curious story of Robert Adams can be traced from the following sources (provided the researcher has access to a national library): *The Narrative of Robert Adams, a sailor, who was wrecked on the western coast of Africa in the year 1810, was detained three years in slavery by the Arabs of the Great Desert, and resided several months in the city of Tombuctoo. With a map, notes, and an appendix* (1816); *The North American Review*, May 1817, July 1817, and January 1826; the *Antologia* (Florence), January 1828; and Playfair and Brown's *A Bibliography of Morocco* (1892). The Adams controversy, which was exceedingly bitter between the British and Americans, involving, at one time, all the scholars of Europe, has never been resolved to the complete satisfaction of the supporters of the American mulatto's claims.

René Caillié's *Travels Through Central Africa to Timbuktoo*, first published in England in 1830, remains the greatest classic of Saharan adventure stories; but it is, of course, unobtainable in any but the largest libraries.

CHAPTER TEN. The account of Dr. John Davidson's travels is taken from *Notes Taken During Travels in Africa*, a privately printed book issued in London, 1839. Additional biographical and bibliographical data concerning Davidson and other African travellers will be found in the *Dictionary of National Bibliography*, which is particularly valuable for the more obscure nineteenth-century personages. The quotation on p. 193 is from William Lemprière's *A Tour from Gibraltar Through the Dominions of the Emperor of Morocco*, third ed. (1813), pp. 310–11.

The nineteenth-century German explorers form a separate group whose reports on Africa are more thorough and scholarly than those of the first English travellers. The narratives of these Germans— Barth, Lenz, Nachtigal, and Rohlfs—have, like their British counterparts, been long out of print, and are only available in the national and special libraries. Major M. A. J. Tilho's *Documents Scientifiques* (1906–10) and Conrad Kilian's *Au Hoggar* (1925) have been consulted in connection with the Tibesti and Hoggar.

Henri Duveyrier's works have already been listed in the Notes to Chapter Six. The quotations used in this chapter are from his *Journal du Route* (1903), published posthumously. The best biography of Alexandrine Tinne will be found in the article under her name in Larousse's *Grand Dictionnaire Universel du XIX Siècle* (1876).

CHAPTER ELEVEN. The archives in the Castello of Tripoli are still the best source of unpublished material on the subject of Mediterranean piracy, particularly in regard to the diplomacy involved. An old, but still excellent, book is S. Lane Poole's *The Barbary Corsairs* (1890); a more up-to-date study, Sir Godfrey Fisher's *The Barbary Legend* (1957). Both books have useful bibliographies. Nevill Barbour's *A Survey of Northwest Africa* (1959) and Allan Houghton Brodrick's *Parts of Barbary* (1944) have also been consulted.

The French conquest and punitive wars in Algeria are best studied in the contemporary accounts, notably Louis de Baudicour's *Histoire de la Conquête de l'Algérie* (1860) and *La Guerre et le Gouvernement de l'Algérie* (1853) from which the quotation on p. 226 is taken. The descriptions of the French officers' experiences in the desert are from C. Trumelet, *Les Français Dans Le Désert* (1863); E-F. Gautier's several books on the Sahara; and André Berthelot's *L'Afrique Saharienne* (1927).

CHAPTER TWELVE. The quotation on p. 241 is from Conrad Kilian's *Au Hoggar* (1925), p. 127. The literature of the now-forgotten *transsaharien* is voluminous and highly polemical. The following key books have been consulted: Henri Brosselard, *Voyage de la Mission Flatters* (1883); Adolphe Duponchel, *Le Chemin de Fer Transsaharien* (1878);

Eugène Hennebert, *De Paris à Timbouctou en Huit Jours* (1889); C. Longobardi, *L'Agonie d'une Mission* (1938); Charles Philebert, *La France en Algérie* (1890); and *Documents Relatifs à la Mission Dirigée au Sud de l'Algérie par le Lieutenant-Colonel Flatters*, issued by the Ministère des Travaux Publiques, 1884. For a discussion of Colonel Flatters himself, see E-F. Gautier, *La Conquête du Sahara* (1910), in which Gautier quotes one of the Colonel's fellow officers as saying: 'Of a nervous and irritable temperament, on the verge of a breakdown, he had passed the age for this kind of enterprise for which he had neither the coolness nor the real strength of character.' The quotation on p. 254 is also from Gautier's book *La Conquête*.

CHAPTER THIRTEEN. R. Capot-Rey, *Le Sahara Français* and E-F. Gautier, *La Conquête du Sahara* (1910) have been consulted for nineteenth-century French policy in her North African and Sudanese colonies. The quotation on p. 263 is from E. Perret, *Recits Algériens* (1905), vol. 2, p. 419. General Laperrine's life and achievements are described in José Germain and S. Faye, *Le Général Laperrine, Grand Saharien* (1936) and E-F. Gautier, *Figures de Conquêtes Coloniales* (1931). The story of the first trans-Saharan flight and the death of Laperrine is given in Appendix I of the Germain-Faye biography as the 'Journal de Marche du Commandant Vuillemin, pilote'.

CHAPTER FOURTEEN. For a generalized account of the origin and early exploits of the French Foreign Legion, Larousse's *Grand Dictionnaire Universel* is available. The following books have also been consulted: Comte P. de Choulot, *L'Histoire du Premier Régiment de la Légion Étrangère* (1864); Emile Mayer, *La Légion Étrangère* (1909); P. Lambert, *La Légion Étrangrèe* (1923); Mariel Bigeard, *Aucune Bête* (1959); and an 'anniversary' history of a hundred years of the Legion, *Le Livre D'Or de la Légion Étrangère* (1931). There are numerous personal accounts of the Legion, both biographical and fictional, which treat the subject in romantic fashion, and the interested reader is referred to G. Marrington, *A Soldier of the Legion* (1907) as an example of the type of book which promulgated a legend. The realistic view will be found in Maurice Magnus, *Memoirs of the Foreign Legion* (1924), extensively quoted here. This book has the advantage of a fascinating preface by D. H. Lawrence. *La Question?* (1958), H. Alleg's terrible account of his tortures at the hands of legionnaires and 'paras' during the Algerian war, completes the picture of a brutalized form of soldiering which has been constantly misrepresented in popular fiction and films.

CHAPTER FIFTEEN. The definitive biography of Cardinal Lavigerie is by Monseigneur Louis Baunard from whose book the incidents and quotations in this chapter have been taken. Also consulted, the periodical *The African Missions of the White Fathers*, published at Bishop's Waltham, Hants, notably Nos. 1 and 3. Stylites and hermits are extensively discussed in the *Catholic Encyclopaedia* and *Analecta Bollandiana* (1909). The standard biography of Father de Foucauld is René Bazin, *Charles de Foucauld* (1921). The priest's own monographs on the Tuaregs have also been consulted. For those interested in the written language of this tribe, T'ifinagh, it is interesting to note that de Foucauld was able to complete his dictionary before he was murdered, a memorial to his scholarship and devotion to the people for whom he gave, in a sense, his life. What literature we have of the Tuaregs was also recorded by the French priest.

CHAPTER SIXTEEN. Consulted: Charles-André Rocherand, *L'Histoire d'André Citroën* (1937); Georges Marie Haardt and Louis Audouin-Dubrueil, *Across the Sahara by Motor Car* (1924); Henri Lhote, *Le Sahara, Désert Mystérieux* (1937); Jean Larteguy, *Sahara An I* (1958); Daniel Strasser, *Le Sahara* (1958); and Jean Gabus, *Au Sahara* (1958).

EPILOGUE. The quotations concerning American-Russian policy *vis-à-vis* Africa are from *Africa, a Handbook to the Continent*, edited by Colin Legum (1961). Also consulted: Nevill Barbour (editor), *A Survey of North West Africa* (1959) and J. Padmore, *Pan-Africanism or Communism* (1956). The poems quoted on p. 331 are from *An Anthology of West African Verse*, edited by Oumbe Bassir (1956).

INDEX

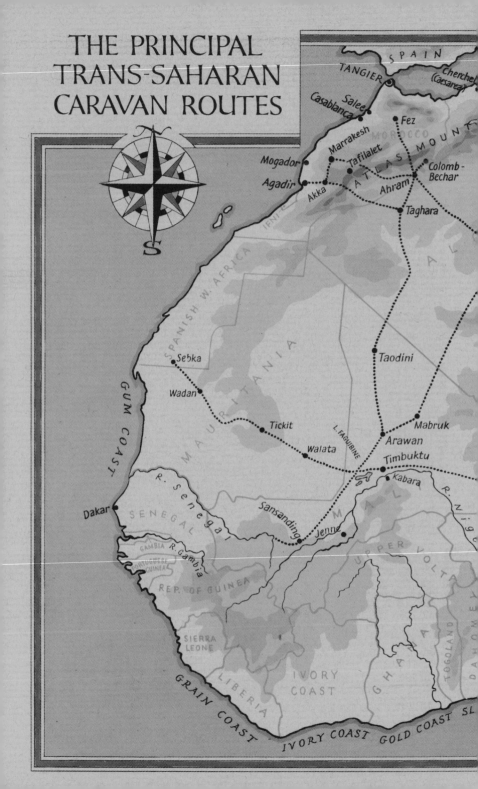

THE PRINCIPAL
TRANS-SAHARAN
CARAVAN ROUTES